On the Back Road to Mandalay

Robert Gustave Johnson, D.D.

FOUNDATIONS OF GRACE PUBLISHING
HARRISBURG, OHIO

Published by
Foundations of Grace Publishing
P.O. Box 261
Harrisburg, Ohio 43126
www.FoundationsOfGrace.org

Library of Congress Number: 2022921879
ISBN: 978-1-7343499-3-1

For questions or more information, email us at
FoundationsOfGracePub@gmail.com

TABLE OF CONTENTS

PUBLISHER'S FOREWORD

The family of the author, Robert G. Johnson, is well-known among the Chin people for his many years of selfless dedication and service to the advancement of the Christian faith. As Arthur and Laura Carson are known as the first missionaries to the Chin, Bob (Robert) and Betty Lue Johnson are known as the last. The Chin are one of the many distinct ethnic groups in Burma, now also called Myanmar. By the grace of God through the arduous work of these and several other missionary couples, ninety percent of the Chin people consider themselves Christians.

Officials forced the Johnsons to leave Burma in 1966 four years after a brutal military junta took over the country. It was nearly fifty years before Burma finally opened up to foreigners again. This came after democratic elections and the addition of religious liberty to their constitution. Since then, many new missionary efforts have been launched in the country, revealing what God had been doing among the converts who were isolated from the rest of the world.

Sadly, Burma has returned to a state much like it was before under harsh military rule. At least 70,000 Chin people now live in the United States as many fled Burma in search of religious freedom and economic opportunities. In September of 2020, the Chin Heritage Foundation was formed as a 501(c)(3) non-profit organization. One of its major missions is to build a museum in Columbus Junction, Iowa dedicated to telling the story of the evangelization of the Chin people. The Chin living in the United States have formed about one hundred churches and have sought to rediscover their Christian story.

This ongoing story began with the famed Adoniram Judson's arrival in Burma in 1813 and came to where it was in 1966 through the work of the Johnson family. Part of the legacy of the Johnson family is this book, *On the Back Road to Mandalay*, as well as Johnson's magnum opus, *History of the American Baptist Chin Mission*, which details the history and story of the Christianization of the Chin People. This 1,300-page two-volume work has also been acquired by Foundations of Grace Publishing and is being made available to the public for research online and in hard copy.

Mission To Myanmar President and Foundation Church Pastor Mark A. Robinette, Rev. Hai Vung Lian (Pastor of Emmanuel Chin Baptist Church of Columbus, Ohio), and Rev. Benjamin Sang Bawi (President of the Mid-American Chin Christian Fellowship and Pastor of the Carson Chin Baptist Church of Columbus Junction, Iowa) agreed to form the Chin Heritage Foundation together as an organization for the mutual benefit and encouragement of the Chin people.

The organization's purpose is to build up the body of Christ among the Chin through education, printed and online materials, and conferences that teach Chin people about their history as Chin and as Christians.

The organization is publishing new and out-of-print books and scanning out-of-print books to make available for research as well as building the museum in Columbus Junction, Iowa to house historical artifacts. This museum will also serve as an education and research center for the many tribes of the Chin here in America and abroad. With these resources and much more, the organization hopes to inspire Chin people to raise their children in the nurture and admonition of the Lord, helping them establish families that represent the work of Christ.

The Chin Heritage Foundation is also working with descendants of Arthur and Laura Carson, descendants of Dr. Erik Hjalmar East (the first medical missionary to the Chin and the one who baptized the first Chin convert), and the still-living children of Rev. Robert G. Johnson. Rev. Johnson's son Richard and his daughter Ruth have given us permission to republish this book and his book, *History of the American Baptist Chin Mission*.

We are working on publishing the full story of Dr. Erik H. East from his memoirs and hope to publish a more extensive book about Arthur and Laura Carson to supplement Laura's account in *Pioneer Trails, Trials and Triumphs*. We have also acquired a small collection of original photographs from the early years of the first Chin mission, and we are in discussions with museums and historical societies about obtaining material for display in the Columbus Junction education and historical center.

This book as well as several out-of-print books on the beautiful history of this missionary endeavor and new books we have planned for the future will continue to inform others of God's masterwork among the Chin people.

M. A. Robinette
Foundations of Grace Publishing

FOREWORD

Once upon a time, in the far distant past, when God made the Earth, great continental plates collided with titanic energy, casting up the mighty Himalaya Mountains and the ranges north and south which now form the boundary between India and Burma.

In one of these convulsions, a mighty escarpment rose, facing the eastern sun. We locate it at 93 degrees 32 minutes east longitude and 22 degrees 42 minutes north latitude in western Burma, not far from the India border.

This escarpment rises a thousand feet, sheer cliffs, and is the home of bees and wild goats. The morning sun strikes first at this sheer cliff, and so the local people call it Zing Hmuh Tlang, which means Morning Seeing Mountain. I call it Dawn Mountain.

The inhabitants of these mountain ranges, which rise to 9 and 10 thousand feet, are called Chins by the Burmese. They are part of the Zo tribes inhabiting parts of eastern India and western Burma. They do not look like the Indians of India. Rather, they seem to have just stepped out of Tibet, where probably they originated. My wife Betty Lue and I lived among them for twenty years following World War II and grew to love and respect them. Our three children grew up in their midst and consider their childhood in the Chin Hills as a precious part of their lives.

At the time we arrived, there was only one short road, which was merely a widened mule path. Not one inch of it was paved. In the rainy season it could be used only by four-wheel drive jeeps and drivers willing to slog through the mud. In the dry season some old army trucks, also four-wheel drive, could navigate the steep and dangerous road. From the end of the jeepable road a dirt mule path led fifty miles to a large village called Haka, which became our home. The road leads along the base of Dawn Mountain to this village at an elevation of 6,000 feet—which means the place was cool in the summertime and could be bitterly cold in the winter, even though we were actually in the tropics.

In the early days of the 20th century the pioneer missionaries, Arthur and Laura Carson, built a small bungalow at Haka, and a few years later Hjalmar East, a doctor, built a larger two-story house which became our home. In this mountain village, out in the boondocks, far removed from the ebb and flow of Western and even Burmese culture, we lived and worked to advance the Chin people in hygiene, education, citizenship, agriculture, and the Christian faith.

We worked on what are the back roads of Burma. Foot paths and mule paths connected the Chin villages to each other and to the larger roads on the Burma plain leading to the cities—Mandalay and Rangoon. This inspired the title of our book, On the Back Road to Mandalay. Rudyard Kipling is the poet who made "On the Road to Mandalay" famous, and in a real sense my wife and I for twenty years traveled on those back roads of Burma which are on the road to Mandalay.

PREFACE

The country of Burma, now called Myanmar, is so little known to the Western world, and the various tribes even less known, that a few facts about the land, the people, and the mission may be helpful.

1. The Chin Hills, now the Chin State, has an area of 13,902 miles in western Burma and a population of 438,000 (1994 estimate). Think of the Chin Hills as 45 to 90 miles broad, east to west, and 250 miles long, north to south—all of it steep mountain ranges reaching 9,000 to 10,000 feet high. Travel is mostly on foot, and a day's journey or a "stage" is ten miles.

2. The Chin people originated probably in Tibet and migrated southward centuries ago. Their languages are classified as in the Kuki-Chin branch of the Tibeto-Burman language family.

3. Religious affiliations in Burma in the year 2000 were: Buddhist 72.7%, Christian 8.3%, "traditional" 12.6%, Muslim 2.3%, Hindu 2.0%, Others 2% (*Encyclopedia Britannica 2005 Yearbook*}. During our time in Burma the Christian percentage was lower.

4. Christian work among the Chins (technically the Northern Chins) began in 1899 in Haka. A second mission station was established in Tiddim, one hundred miles north, in

1910. Seven missionary couples served in this area. We, the Johnsons, were the last couple. Foreign missionaries have not been permitted in Burma since 1966.

5. Mrs. Johnson and I spent twenty years in the Chin Hills of Burma in a remote village called Haka. These years were from 1946 to 1966.

6. Our mission was the American Baptist Foreign Mission Society located in New York, later moved to Valley Forge, Pennsylvania. This organization began work in Burma in 1813 and in the Chin Hills in 1899. In Burma the mission headquarters were in Rangoon, the capital city.

7. Our twenty years in Burma were divided into three terms of service, with two furloughs in the United States. These were First Term, 1946 to 1951, Second Term 1953 to 1959, Third Term 1960 to 1966.

8. Burma has renamed itself Myanmar after its ancient name, and has changed many other names of cities, towns, rivers, etc. I have chosen to retain the names commonly used for decades and known to Western peoples.

MAP OF BURMA

INDIA

CHINA

•Tiddim

Falam

•Haka

CHIN HILLS

•Mandalay

BURMA

LAOS

•Chiangmai

THAILAND

Ran-
goon

```
0      50    100   150
└──────┴──────┴──────┘
        MILES
```

Chapter 1

TO BURMA'S BACK DOOR

~~~

Commissioned as Missionaries

The missionary journey of Robert and Betty Lue Johnson began in New York City in April, 1941, in the offices of the mission society. We were there to meet the Board, to appear before the chief people and be examined as to our fitness for arduous missionary service abroad. I warned Betty ahead of time to study up a bit on Baptist history, and so for much of the train trip from Illinois to New York she did study a book. It turned out to be unnecessary study, for the Board did not ask a single question on this matter.

Dr. Randolph Howard came out of the closed session and announced to us that all was well, our answers were okay, and that we were accepted and commissioned as missionaries of the American Baptist Foreign Mission Society (ABFMS) and designated for Burma, specifically to Thayetmyo, a town on the main river of Burma, the Irrawaddy. The work there is among Chin people, he said. He said that we would go on salary a month before sailing, and that we would have an outfit allowance.

I left my little church in New Jersey and Betty and I prepared to sail for Burma later that summer. We did not go that year. World War II came, with the Japanese forces invading many parts of the Pacific area and Asia, including Burma.

We start the journey

I served as a Navy chaplain during the war, and upon discharge from service in December, 1945, we were free at last to begin our missionary service. By then we had one son, Richard, a healthy boy ten months old when our ship sailed from San Francisco on March 23, 1946, bound for Calcutta, India. It was a troop transport sent out to fetch American soldiers in India and return them to the States. It was a safe trip made memorable by passengers being separated, women on one side of the ship and men on the other, and 18 in each cabin—not a cruise ship certainly. Our ship docked in Calcutta on the day before Easter, and we worshiped on Easter Sunday in a church just recently restored after being desecrated and burned by a Hindu mob. We realized that we no longer were in a country with Christian values.

To Assam

There was no chance to get passage on a ship to Burma, so the mission sent us up to Assam to await an opportunity to get into Burma by a different route, by land, not by sea. Assam is the "tea garden" state of India farthest to the northeast. We went by train to Gauhati, the capital of Assam, and then by river boat on the Brahmaputra River to the town of Jorhat, where there were a mission hospital and high school. We were asked to teach in the high school and set out to do so while we waited for the summer monsoon rains to be over and a way might open to Burma.

We learned then that the war had changed things so much in Burma that our assignment was changed, and we would go to the Chin Hills, not to Thayetmo. We would be in the mountains, not on a riverside town on the plains. The assignment sounded exciting to us. Both Betty and I were from Illinois, and I never saw a mountain until I visited Colorado during college days and saw snow-covered peaks. Yes, I would like the work in the Hills.

Franklin Nelson

The persons who knew first-hand about the Chin Hills were Franklin and Phileda Nelson who were preparing to return to Burma

18

and were not too far away. They were visiting in the little mission station of Kangpokpi in Manipur State. I decided to make a quick trip there to get acquainted, as they were to be our "senior missionaries." I went alone and found them poised for leaving. I arrived just in time. Overnight Franklin told me that he would get his wife and two children settled in Burma and then would come for us "if there is time before the rains break."

As Frank explained it to me, the roads are passable if dry, but rains turn roads into deep mud and flood creeks and wash out bridges. "If the rains hold off, maybe I can get you through to Burma," he said.

In Jorhat

I returned to Jorhat and told Betty that there was a very slight chance of getting into Burma this year, but that we must begin our teaching jobs. Betty was a professional teacher, having taught school five years in Illinois. I was well educated but had no experience in high school teaching, but I could teach religion classes and the like. So we hired a cook to prepare meals, and we were just thinking of hiring a nanny to watch over little Richard, who was now walking, when our plans suddenly changed. One afternoon, late in the month of May, the quiet of the mission compound was broken by the sound of an olive drab jeep coming in a cloud of dust to our mission compound. The driver was Frank Nelson and he had with him a slim young Chin man named Lian Khen, his cook. They arrived dusty and tired after a quick journey in one long day on the road.

The Unexpected

"Bob, I'm here to get you and the family into Burma," he said. "When can you go?"

The unexpected arrival, and his invitation to go at last to Burma, bowled me over. I was speechless for joy. I brought Frank and Lian Khen in to the house and they met Betty and our son for the first time. Around the table we talked over the proposed trip and especially his desire to go at once. "Tomorrow, if possible," Frank said. We pointed out that for us tomorrow was impossible, but we could try for the day after tomorrow.

"Bob and Betty," he said, "Phileda and I can put you up in the church in Tiddim which was not destroyed in the war, and you can eat meals with us until you can get a cook and get settled, but you have to know that it will be tough, and things in Burma are shattered and broken down, and food is scarce; you'll have to haul in on my trailer your baggage and enough food to last you about five months."

Our excitement mounted as Frank described the devastation to the mission property, to their town of Tiddim, to the Chin Hills, and to Burma in general. We knew that life there would not be easy. But we felt God's call to service no matter the problems, and we wanted to go. I was 29 years of age and Betty 28, young enough and strong.

We Decide to Enter Burma

I asked Frank his age. "I was born in 1909 so I am 37 now and Phil is 29," he said. (Frank often referred to his wife Phileda as "Phil") Frank was 6 years my senior and was indeed the senior missionary, but I felt a warmth right away for him, and over the years we found ourselves working heart and mind in tune.

Betty and I went to bed that night with minds whirling with thoughts of things to do on the morrow: get funds, buy food for 5 months and have it packed up, pack up our own suitcases and boxes, pack up baby things, don't forget to get milk for Richard, say a sad farewell to the local missionaries and to the teachers and principal of the school, etc...

I forgot to mention that Betty and I made this trip a matter of prayer. We prayed for divine guidance, and we felt clearly that the trip in with Frank was indeed God's will for us, and we felt confident that the Lord would guide and protect us.

Quick Preparation

We figured that the jeep and trailer could carry 1,000 pounds besides the four adults and child and the necessary gasoline. We allotted 450 pounds for our family's food, as almost nothing was available in Tiddim. One important item was evaporated milk for our son, and we managed to buy 200 pounds of that. We also took 40 pounds of rice, 50 pounds of flour, 30 pounds of sugar, and 15 pounds of salt, 12 gallons of kerosene, 10 pounds of tinned butter,

10 cans of compressed oatmeal, 7 pounds of cheese, 7 pounds of marmalade, and 7 pounds of peanut butter. I was surprised at the need for rice and asked Frank about it. "Bob," he said, "It's hard to believe this, but the Chin people are almost starving, and we can't go there and deplete the little they have."

On Saturday we got under way—Franklin, Betty, Dick, and I on the front seats, Lian Khen in the back with baggage, and the trailer loaded down with supplies. We made the trip easily to Dimapur, at the head of the Manipur Road. Here a sign informed us that we were 11,599 miles from New York and 8,316 miles from London. We felt a bond of sympathy for the American GI who had also noted that it was 13,309 miles from Wichita Falls, Kansas. We stopped for a few days at the mission in Kangpokpi, where John and Elaine Anderson made us welcome. Frank and I had business to do in Imphal, capital of Manipur, where we checked in with police and government officials and bought gasoline.

Approaching Burma by Road

Thursday, May 30, 1946, was a red letter day for us—a day for entering Burma, but by a back door. Most visitors enter Burma via Rangoon. We were to enter by a back road on the border of India, at a place called Tamu. We would make it by travel first on the Manipur plains, then over low mountains to Moreh, a hamlet on the India side of the border, then on to Tamu. We rose early, had breakfast, and took off on a nice sunny day.

We ate lunch somewhere along the road in India, and cut the birthday cake that Elaine had baked special for our son, for it was Richard's first birthday. He loved the chocolate cake .We moved along well. Frank said that our whole trip to Tiddim was 235 miles and we could not tarry to look at the scenery. We did not realize at the time that we were traveling over roads that were bitterly fought over by the Japanese versus the British and Indian troops in 1944.

Our anticipation mounted as we neared the Burma border. We reached the little village on the India side, Moreh. Now we left asphalted roads and were on a dirt road. As we approached Tamu, we wondered if we would have problems at the border with immigration and inspections. Of course we had visas and other papers

21

on hand, but one never knows what to expect at a remote border crossing on a seldom traveled road.

Through the Tamu Gate

We Americans had remembered that May 30th is Memorial Day, a day for flying the flag. Just before leaving India Frank fastened a small American flag to the front of his jeep. "It's a patriotic thing to fly the flag," he said. It might help us at the border and also deter bandits who infest the Tamu-Kalemyo road in Burma.

We approached the border guard. This was out in a forested area, a jungly place, with no village nearby, just a thatched roof bamboo shed for protection from the sun. In front was the familiar pole across the road, weighted by stones on one end.

As we slowly approached the barrier, a soldier rushed out and lifted the pole and waved us through without stopping.

We waved gaily at the guard and drove on, now inside Burma. I could hardly believe our good luck. Was it the flag? Did the guard think that we were American military? We'll never know.

After our easy entry into Burma, we drove on a distance and stopped to eat in the early afternoon. We finished the lunches given us by Elaine and then finished the chocolate cake. Dick greatly enjoyed his birthday cake, and we found a small stream nearby to wash him up. Then we had a special time of thanks to our Heavenly Father for the good trip so far and asked His continued blessings as we traveled.

We were on a "back road," one seldom traveled, one built during the war and heavily used then, but now almost empty. We were really On the Back Road to Mandalay.

Ahead lay 53 miles of bad road to the town of Kalemyo. A left turn there leads on to Mandalay. A right turn at Kalemyo leads to the Chin Hills, our destination.

At any rate, we were on a road to Mandalay.

Chapter 2

ENTRY INTO THE CHIN HILLS

On the Tamu-Kalemyo Road

As we rattled along in the jeep on the Tamu-Kalemyo road, Frank explained to Betty Lue and me more about this portion of a back road to Mandalay. "It's level and fairly straight, and parts are paved with metal plates used for air landing strips, now bent up," he said, "but there are bridges that can get washed out in the rains. That's why we have to move fast to get your things in before the road is closed down." He continued, "We are in the Kabaw Valley and this road was just a jungle path in 1944 when the British and Indians and civilians walked out to India on this road with great suffering and loss of life. They went up to Tamu and then into India and safety. They were bombed and shot at, and also the place was full of malaria."

"In my case," Frank said, "Phil and Lois walked out of Burma through the Chin Hills, following the Manipur River, and so got to India. Some other Baptist missionaries were with them. Later on I also walked out of Burma following the Manipur River."

Betty and I thought about the plight of those people fleeing from the Japanese during the recent war. Now it was so peaceful along the road. There were almost no marks of warfare. There was only one village along the road and it had a teashop, a typical shack of bamboo and mats. I cannot remember seeing another motor vehicle on the road the whole time we traveled those 63 miles.

Our son Dick was a happy traveler. He slept some in Betty's arms or mine, ate a good lunch, enjoyed his birthday cake, and ate well again when we stopped for supper in a shady spot at the base of the Chin Hills, just before starting the long climb up to Tiddim. We had reached Kalemyo, turned right through little Chin villages, and traveled for five miles along groves of lovely, majestic teak trees. Teak is a marvelous wood, very resistant to water damage and hence much used on ship decks, and here we saw what was one of the principal export products of Burma.

The Mountain Road to Tiddim

Franklin had prepared us for this 44 mile stretch of mountain road. "It is steep, narrow, all dirt and stones, really a widened mule path. It is dangerous. There are sharp switchbacks, but it is cool and even cold when we get high," he said. Frank was healthy, in the prime of life, always an optimist, and we trusted him.

The road turned out to be all that Frank said. Worst of all were the switchbacks. The hills were so steep that gentle turns were impossible. The corners were so sharp that our jeep had to turn as hard as possible, then back up, and thus get around. For a jeep alone the turns were hard, but with the heavily loaded trailer the turns were seemingly impossible. But Frank was used to these dangerous turns and we continued on and up, passing near only one village, until we reached a hamlet called Fort White. This once was a stronghold of the British in their takeover of the Chin Hills in the 1880s, but now it was just a small cemetery and one government "dak bungalow." Here we turned right, to the road leading still upward until we were close to 8,000 feet elevation. It was cold now. We wrapped our son in a blanket and we wore all the cold-weather clothing we had.

At one point in the mountain trip, perhaps at about 6,000 feet elevation, we were startled by a leopard jumping across the road from left to right not more than 50 feet ahead of us. It was a beautiful animal and graceful in its leap. "That's the first leopard I have seen in the Hills," Frank exclaimed, "and you see one on your very first day in the Hills!" Dick was sleeping and did not see the leopard. We knew that there were tigers also in the Chin Hills, and once I did see a tiger on the same road, many years later.

24

The Arrival

The road to Tiddim led along the side of Mount Kennedy, 8,600 feet elevation, then descended slowly on a fairly level road to the town of Tiddim, about 5,200 feet elevation. We came to Tiddim by night, of course, and could see nothing, for there are no lights in a Chin village. Thus at 11 p.m. Franklin pulled up to his home, which was a 12 foot addition on the side of the Baptist Church which had survived the war. The Nelson home consisted of a tiny sitting room and two tiny bedrooms attached to the church. Very temporary. It was built with green lumber which dried and shrank, leaving countless holes and cracks which, over time, Frank filled up. He also added some screen doors.

Phileda had no idea, of course, when her husband would return. The two girls, Lois and Karen, were sleeping. Lian Khen, the cook, was quick to make a fire and prepare some coffee for the weary travelers. Betty Lue met Phileda for the first time and it was a joyous time as we talked together in this lonely and remote mission station. There was no room for my family in the Nelson home. We just moved into the church and got settled down in our sleeping bags with Dick beside his mother on the floor.

We thanked the Lord for the adventures of the day and the safe trip into the Chin Hills, and we fell asleep.

Chapter 3

GETTING SETTLED IN TIDDIM

~~~

First Night

We arrived in Tiddim in the dark midnight hours and saw nothing of the town. We went to sleep on the floor of the small wooden church, behind the pulpit. Little Richard was sound asleep when we carried him in and put him to bed on the floor beside us. We awoke to a bright sunny day. Our first glimpses of Tiddim town were from windows facing to the east, toward the rising sun. We saw a single spigot where townspeople could draw water. Beyond that was a dirt road, the main road lined with broken-down shops and houses, and off in the distance a mountain range. Beyond that lay the plains of Burma.

Then we looked over the little church with simple wooden benches. The church had survived the war, but the Nelsons' lovely pre-war bungalow was gone, burned down. So the family of four lived in three tiny rooms built on the verandah of the church, much like a shack added to the side of the church. For lack of lumber, this addition was all the local Christians were able to do to prepare for the missionaries' return.

The Children

It was here that our son Dick met Lois, 4 years, and Karen, 16 months old. As Dick and Karen were so close in age and Lois only

27

a few years older, the children quickly bonded together and enjoyed life in this far backwoods place. They were the only white children in all of the Chin Hills and the only children speaking English. All three children quickly learned the local Chin language, and I often wished that I had the ability of a child to learn to pronounce words correctly.

Meals with the Nelsons

We had breakfast with the Nelsons that morning. Lian Khen cooked on iron bars over an open fire in the corrugated iron shack that was the cookhouse. He was a single man, and devoted to the service of Frank and Phil. In fact, he was their pre-war cook and had buried their good china and other cooking items in the earth to hide them from the Japanese.

The addition to the church that was the home of the Nelson family was just large enough to allow Betty, Dick, and me to sit at their dining table. We ate with the Nelsons until a cook came from Haka in late July to work for us. Sitting at their table regularly, we had ample opportunity to talk, discuss problems, and dream of the future. They were giving us good orientation to work in the Chin Hills. Thus I believe that our orientation to mission work in Burma was probably superior to that of most missionaries who enter by Rangoon, the usual door, and who are not thrown into seven months of close contact with the senior missionaries, as we were.

Tiddim Town

Tiddim was considered a "town" because it had government buildings, a post office, a school, police, a jail, and a bazaar line of little shops. I suppose that it had perhaps 300 or 350 houses. When we arrived in 1946, we saw everywhere the marks of war's destruction, for it had been fought over twice by the Japanese against the British and Indian forces. Rebuilding was going on very slowly due to poverty and lack of dry wood, nails and bolts, cement, roofing, and a lack of carpenters. Franklin was right: the shops had almost nothing to sell and we had to depend on our supply of food brought in from India.

Frank and Phileda had been able to get a fair supply of tinned foods in India and hauled it in to Tiddim before we arrived. We ourselves had brought in rice, sugar, flour, dahl (yellow split peas), salt, and milk sufficient for the five months, we thought, but we had nothing in the way of meat or vegetables. So the Nelsons gave us generously of their supplies. We cannot thank them enough for their kindness, for they too were limited, but they were willing to share in order that we, the new missionaries, could get to Burma and make a start.

A Place for the Johnsons

After the war the government had taken over the private house of U Pau Cin for use as a dak (mail) bungalow. We were able to rent this house for our own use during the rainy season—a generous concession from the local British official. This house was down the hill from the mission compound about 200 yards from the Nelsons. It was not far from the one water spigot operating in the town. Early in June we were able to move to this place.

Our Rented Bungalow

It was a rather dismal prospect. The bungalow itself was sturdy, being made of brick and whitewashed inside and out, and the corrugated-iron roof did not leak. But it was cold and damp. It had a living room, two tiny bedrooms, with shed-like appendages for the bathroom and storeroom. There were some tiny windows and they did have glass. There was a smoky fireplace in the living room. Outside was a 12 by 12 cookhouse connected to the house by a walk made of steel treads of an army tank.

There was no furniture of any kind, shape, or description. There were no screens and the house was full of flies. However, the Nelsons loaned us two camp cots, a small chest of drawers, two small rugs, a chair, and a table from the church. A church deacon loaned us another chair and a small table. So things began to look up. Later Frank gave me some nylon screening and I made screens for the windows and doors. Everything was primitive indeed, including bathroom facilities, but we thanked the Lord that we had a roof over our heads.

Quick Trip to India for Supplies

Both the Nelsons and we were very concerned about our limited food supply and our inability to buy anything locally. Even the government was concerned about getting rice up from the plains to feed their workers, as pack mules were ill and dying of disease. The rains were holding off, so Frank made a quick decision to return to India for supplies. Betty and Dick stayed in the church and continued meals with Phileda and the girls, and Frank and I took off just five days after our arrival in Tiddim.

We drove to Jorhat in three days, picked up the baggage I had left behind, got supplies of food, kerosene, needed office and household supplies, and returned safely to Tiddim in a trip of seven days. The cooking pots, enameled iron commode, tea kettle, pails; and washbasins I brought in made life much easier. I also brought in a kerosene wick lantern made in China. It leaked.

Later on, down-country missionaries criticized the Nelsons for bringing us into the primitive living conditions in Tiddim in 1946 during the monsoon, saying that "it would be a sure way to lose the Johnsons." Actually nothing of the sort happened. Never did we really get downhearted, and never did we feel like quitting and returning to the States.

Close Missionary Relationships

The bond between the Nelsons and us grew very strong. For one thing, Franklin Oliver Nelson, born in 1909, was six years older than I, just right to be our "senior missionary" as he often jokingly reminded us. He was very proud of his Swedish heritage, for he had been named after the famous pioneer Baptist minister in Sweden, Rev. F. O. Nelson, who was persecuted for preaching the Gospel. Phileda was also of Swedish heritage, as I am. So we had this bond. Also, and more importantly, we thought very much alike on religious and theological matters.

The first weeks in Tiddim, therefore, were days of getting acquainted with our colleagues and also with the people of the land.

The Tiddim area people speak Kamhau, one of the many Chin languages. The Baptist mission station in Tiddim was opened in 1910 by Dr. J. Herbert Cope who gave 30 years of service in both Tiddim and the more southern station of Haka. During Cope's time, growth in numbers of believers and churches was slow; after World War II the growth in numbers was spectacular. Betty and I did not know it then, but we came at the beginning of a tremendous spurt in worldwide evangelism and church growth.

In our first week we had our first worship service among the Chins. I cannot say that I enjoyed it, not understanding a word of Kamhau, but I appreciated it for I could see joy on the faces of the people. At the church service on Sunday we were introduced to the congregation and learned how to say "thank you" in Kamhau.

Chapter 4

GETTING STARTED

B etty and I were now in the mission station of Tiddim, about 100 miles as the road winds, north of the large village of Haka, our future home. It was nice to be so near the Nelsons, eating with them every meal. But we were stuck in Tiddim for the rainy season. There was no possible way to move south to Haka because the two mission buildings there were occupied by the government, one as a hospital and one as an officer's residence.

Busy Months in Tiddim

The months in Tiddim were not wasted, however. First was the need to learn the Haka Chin language, which is not used in the Tiddim area. We needed a language teacher. Frank therefore, soon after our arrival, wrote a letter to the Haka Chin Christians asking them to send us three persons: a language teacher, a cook, and a girl to be a nanny or ayah for our son. The letter went by mail coolie. Before the war, there had been a telegraph line between Tiddim and Haka. It was gone, stolen, and the wire doubtless was holding up laundry in many villages. We faced a long wait until these three helpers could arrive.

Hau Go Helps

A well-educated Tiddim Chin young man named Hau Go was employed by the mission as an assistant to the Nelsons. Hau Go spoke excellent English and became our first language teacher. However, he spoke Kamhau, not Haka, so he enlisted the help of a Haka Chin young man named Vai Kulh, who knew no English. For almost two months we struggled to learn some Haka Chin in a roundabout fashion.

It worked like this: I wanted to know the word for a plate. I asked Hau Go in English; he asked Vai Kulh in either Burmese or Kamhau and got the answer. Then Hau Go told me in English, "The word for plate is pakan, p-a-k-a-n." I wrote it down in the dictionary we made. We did this for hundreds of words. Of course, words for things are quite easy. It is much more difficult to get verbs, pronouns, prepositions, and adjectives. But we kept at it and began to learn a vocabulary and to get an idea of grammar.

We had no such helps as a dictionary or grammar book. The ones done by Mrs. Carson and Chester Strait had not been published. If those missionaries left any language helps, they were lost in the war. We had to start from scratch and laboriously learn on our own.

On July 29, almost two months after our arrival, three very welcome travelers arrived at our door. They had been en route eleven days walking to Tiddim. They were Saya Lal Hnin, Ram Hlun, and Pente.

Rev. Lal Hnin

Lal Hnin was 30 years old and a preacher from the Haka area who had taught school during the war. He had studied one year in the Cherrapunji (India) theological school and spoke English fairly well. With him as our language teacher we began to make rapid progress. In later years he became for some years the pastor of the Haka church, and all through our twenty years in the Chin Hills we continued to have close contact with him.

Ram Hlun

Ram Hlun, 26 years old, had been the cook for the previous missionaries, Rev. and Mrs. Strait. He was married and had three children. From the name of his oldest son, Van Awi, he took his name with us, Van Awi Pa (father of Van Awi), and he was a delightful man, full of wry humor. He had one bad eye and did not have a good sense of perspective; hence when he poured a cup of tea, he invariably poured a fraction of an inch from the rim. Chins love skits, and in later years we would kid Ram Hlun by demonstrating how he couldn't pour anything into the middle of a cup or pot. In return, he would convulse audiences by demonstrating the peculiar customs of the white people, such as how an American will kiss his wife good-bye before setting out on a trip. Indeed, our lives were to be entwined with Ram Hlun and his family. He remained with us as cook for twenty years, ever faithful in his work, and long after leaving the Hills we sent money to help put his children through school.

Pente

Pente was a 14 year-old girl, a relative of Ram Hlun and an orphan. She could not speak a word of English and was quite uneducated. She became Dick's ayah and she too became a long and fast friend of our family. Eventually she married Chia Ling, a man who became our houseboy and second cook and who served us for 19 years. Pente served as ayah for our children until she had children of her own, eventually twelve. The oldest girl was named Mary, or Meri as the Chins spelled it, and we still speak of Pente affectionately as Meri Nu (Mary's mother).

When Pente came to us, she knew little about how to care for a child. But Betty taught her everything she needed to know and she proved an intelligent and teachable girl. Of course, our son picked up the Haka Chin language from her and Ram Hlun and soon excelled us in the ability to pronounce words correctly.

Meal Arrangements

As I mentioned earlier, until our cook arrived we ate most of our meals with the Nelsons. When Ram Hlun came, we were able to make our own meals for breakfast and lunch, and we organized it so Lian Khen cooked dinner at the Nelsons on Monday, Wednesday, and Friday, and Ram Hlun cooked at the Nelsons on Tuesday, Thursday, and Saturday each week, and we all ate dinner together. This gave us much needed fellowship and chances to talk.

Cooking was quite primitive. Our stove at the dak bungalow consisted of two bars of iron, each 24 inches long, resting on 13 bricks—I counted the bricks out of curiosity. This "stove" was on the dirt floor of the cookhouse, and the cook squatted on his heels to work. This is nothing unusual for the Chins, however, as they love to squat on their heels and it evidently is not tiring to them.

Ram Hlun wished to do some baking for us; so Lal Hnin and I made an oven from a little 5 gallon steel drum. We cut out and hinged one end, fixed a piece of tin on top to hold coals, and fortunately this thing worked. Ram Hlun was able to make cakes, pies, and bread in this little oven.

Language Study Begins

As soon as our Haka language teacher, Lal Hnin, arrived, we began to make good progress. Our little dictionaries grew larger and more accurate, and we began to understand how sentences were put together. Certain sounds were very difficult for us to master, and we envied our little son learning so easily and quickly from Pente how to speak correctly.

I won't say that we could really speak Haka Chin by the end of the rainy season, but we could talk about simple things like potatoes, onions, cooking, sleeping, asking simple questions. We could not yet discuss family affairs, illnesses, and certainly not religious matters. That was to come much later. One thing in our favor was that the Chin languages are written in roman script like English, not in the Burmese alphabet.

Colonel Tommy West

In July Col. Thomas West, a veteran of the battles in and around Tiddim, arrived in Tiddim to take up his post as Assistant Superintendent of the area. He was single, a disappointment to our wives who had hoped a British woman might come to town. He seemed to me to be the epitome of the British soldier. Tall and thin, he was a pleasant man, but his Scottish accent was so heavy that often we did not know what he was talking about. Nevertheless, it was nice to have another English speaker in town. We became friends, and called him "Tommy" behind his back. Tommy was a magistrate, a judge, a friend and advocate of the Chins. In my experience, these British officers were genuinely liked because they doled out impartial justice and did not take bribes.

We did not know then, as we ate meals together with Col. West that the time of the British in post-war Burma was to be short. They had only about 18 months; they were gone by the end of 1947.

Chapter 5

WE MEET REV. SANG LING

~~~

As Frank Nelson drove Betty and me into Burma, he had time to tell us something about the large village of Haka where we would go after the rainy season was over, and something about the remarkable pastor of the Haka church. "You will like Sang Ling," he said, "for he is a gentle and lovable old man." Frank told us that he was an early convert from a chief's clan and was baptized by the first missionary, Rev. Carson. "He endured hardships and some persecution as a Christian and evangelist, but now he is revered as a leader of the churches," he continued.

A Pioneer Preacher

We looked forward to meeting this pastor, whose views carried so much weight when decisions had to be made.

We had been in Tiddim about three months when Rev. Sang Ling arrived at the mission house. He was on his way to Rangoon for some important meetings of Baptist leaders from all over Burma in late September, and had made a side trip to meet us in Tiddim. That meant five extra days of walking. He planned to go to Rangoon in the company of our language teacher Lal Hnin and three other local pastors.

Sang Ling proved to be a wiry little old man of 60 years with gray hair and a white turban always around his head in the Burmese fashion. He had a ready smile and was, as Frank said, a pleasant and lovable man, always cheerful and always supportive of us and of the Lord's work. We grew to love him and respect him dearly and he was helpful to us during our entire first term.

After Saya Sang Ling had been with us for four days it was time for the five pastors to start for Rangoon. Frank and I were to help by carrying them by jeep and trailer to Kalemyo at the foot of the hills.

On to Rangoon

We started out with the pastors and their kits, but only got as far as milestone 11 when we came upon a huge landslide. Hundreds of tons of dirt had slid down onto the road, perhaps enough to collapse the road itself. It was impossible to pass. The pastors had to take their gear and start walking the remaining 33 miles down to the plains. Frank and I turned around, struggled for two hours to get through a smaller slide at milestone 8, and finally got home to Tiddim at 2:30 in the afternoon. We had made a total of 22 miles in six and a half hours and had not succeeded fully in our mission, but at least we had helped these men eleven miles on their long hike.

Chapter 6

FRANK'S JEEP-DRIVEN WASHING MACHINE

~~~~~~

One of the very nice things that I found out about Franklin Nelson was that since we both came from Swedish parentage, we could call each other names such as dumbbell or numbskull and not get angry. We wouldn't relish outsiders, such as Danes or Norwegians, using such names! This is the story of how both us were numbskulls but it turned out all right.

The Problem

It all began in Tiddim when Frank and I got tired of helping with the weekly laundry. After we returned from India to get supplies in early June, we really needed to help our wives, because washing clothes on a washboard was hard work, hard on the skin and knuckles, and we did not want to employ anyone to beat our clothes on a rock. India is full of dhobis (laundry men and women) who pound things on rocks, and clothing wears out too fast. Anyway, there were no Indian dhobis in Tiddim, and the Chins were not anxious to do this work.

After one or two weeks of helping with the wash, we men agreed that we needed to make a washing machine. We considered the possibilities: something that went up and down like a butter churn; something that flip-flopped back and forth; a barrel worked with a hand crank—we rejected all of these in favor of a washing machine that could be run by a Willys Jeep.

The Swing Idea

Frank's idea seemed very simple: a 50-gallon gasoline drum suspended horizontally by chains from an overhead beam, like a gigantic child's swing. A hole cut in the barrel's side, which became the top when hung horizontally, would allow us to put in water, soap, and clothing.

We decided to make it go by hitching the barrel in some way to the jacked-up rear wheel of the jeep. "We can do it," said Frank. "We'll attach a piece of steel water pipe about 12 or 15 feet long to the end of the barrel. Then we'll take off a rear wheel of the jeep and put on a spare wheel without any tire. We'll bolt a piece of wood, like a piece of 2 by 4, to this wheel and fasten the long water pipe to one end of the wood piece. When we jack up the rear end of the jeep, the engine will turn the wheel, and as the wheel slowly turns, it will push the barrel back and forth, like this." Frank showed me with his arm pumping back and forth, how the barrel would be agitated, sloshing the soapy water and clothes against both ends of the barrel.

The plan sounded good and we started the next day.

The Barrel Bomb

The first job was to prepare the barrel. Frank selected the least rusty one he could find, and we decided to cut a rectangular hole 8 by 12 inches in size in the side of the barrel.

Luckily, Frank had a hacksaw and two blades. We made fair progress for a while in places where the hacksaw frame could be used to hold the blade. But eventually we got to where the curvature of the barrel prevented using the whole saw. We then were forced to saw patiently with short lengths of broken blades. Progress was exasperatingly slow.

"Frank, it will take more than a day of work just to cut out this hole!" I finally said. "We need to speed it up."

"What do you suggest, Bob?" he asked.

I suggested that perhaps the solution would be to soften the steel a bit with a blowtorch so we could cut easier. Frank soon had a blowtorch working and played it on the spot to be cut.

Each of us sat on opposite sides of the barrel, waiting for the metal to soften.

Suddenly there was a thunderous roar—VRO-O-OOM!!!—as a blast of air and fire shot up right between us. At the same moment the two flat ends of the barrel instantaneously were rounded out by the force of the explosion.

We looked aghast at each other, our hands trembling with the thought of the powerful bomb we had unwittingly exploded. The remnants of gasoline in the barrel had formed an explosive mixture as powerful pound for pound as dynamite.

Frank was the first to speak. "Ah, what dumbskulls we are!" he said. "Thank God we're still alive."

Then he looked at the sun lowering over the mountain range to the west, grateful that he could see it, and said, "Bob, I think it's time for tea!" We went into the house and drank our afternoon tea that day holding our cups with both hands to quell the shaking.

Well, the explosion had effectively burned out all the gasoline fumes, so we had no more trouble cutting that hole, though it did take us 6 or 7 hours of work to cut, cutting inch by inch by the broken hacksaw blades.

The Test

Finally, one day the magnificent washing machine was ready. From the great overhead wooden beam, tire chains from a burned-out Japanese army truck held up the barrel. An iron pipe connected the barrel to the left rear wheel of the jeep, and the jeep was jacked up and blocked so it could not move. All was ready. We poured about 15 gallons of hot water into the barrel, added soap and some dirty clothes, and were ready for the test.

"What gear do you think is best, Bob?" Frank asked.

"Let's start with low," I said. "We don't want it to run too fast."

Frank agreed, put the far into low gear, and let out the clutch. The left rear wheel began to turn. Sixty horsepower began to shake that poor machine like a terrier with a rat. The barrel shot forward with a mighty surge. Hot water poured out the top like a geyser, and the jeep almost rolled backward off its moorings. A split second later, as the wheel began its backward thrust, the water pipe flexed and like a whip cracked the barrel sharply backward with a mighty thud. More water shot out the top. The barrel thrashed wildly and the jeep shuddered as Frank sat at the wheel, holding firmly on. A dozen Chins had come up to see the fun, and at the fiasco they burst into uproarious laughter.

Frank finally got the engine stopped, just in time to prevent the washing machine from completely disintegrating.

Low-Low is Best

So we learned the hard way that even low gear was much too fast. We then tried "low-low," the lowest of the jeep's six forward speeds, and that worked just fine. It suited the rhythm of the heavy barrel of water.

So it finally turned out that Franklin Nelson's washing machine operated successfully for several years until at last gasoline was unobtainable. In low-low gear it churned up scores of tubs full of clean clothing and was a never-ending source of amusement and wonderment to Chin villagers visiting the mission station. It became the star of Frank's movie on life in Burma, delighting many audiences in America.

Chapter 7

THE FINE ART OF SCROUNGING

When Betty Lue and I met Franklin Nelson in Jorhat, he was driving a wartime jeep and trailer and we learned how he acquired this treasure. It was a gift from the U.S. government, albeit quite indirectly. He was a pre-war missionary and had been able to get out to India in November, 1945. Mrs. Nelson and their children were still in the States, so Frank was free to prepare the way for his family. For about five months of the seven months Frank was in India before moving into Burma, he was able to move about Assam and engage in the fine art of scrounging. This is what we called it. It meant to go here and there and ask the military for surplus items which otherwise would be destroyed. Some things could be had free, and for others a modest payment might be asked, but essentially it was a way to prevent needless destruction of good things. There was nothing unethical about the practice. But scrounging requires some explanation.

Evidently when American food, clothing, vehicles, spare parts, and items of every kind used by an army began to arrive in India during World War II, the Indian government was afraid that such a flood of goods would overwhelm the local economy. So the U.S. government pledged that unused items would be destroyed. When the war ended, there were warehouses full of food, clothing, medicines, building supplies, spare parts, etc., all surplus. Officers were ordered to destroy all this fine stuff. But most good-thinking men hated to see clothing burned, medicines thrown out, food buried, or typewriters run over by bulldozers and tanks; so they simply arranged for some of this to go to dependable men and women who would use it for the good of the common people. Thus, our American Baptist Mission among others became the beneficiary of some of the surplus items.

Frank Nelson and John Anderson, Collectors

It happened that Franklin Nelson and a fellow missionary named John Anderson were in Assam at the right time. I, unfortunately, came five months too late to get in on the largess. Thus Mr. Nelson was given a jeep (put together from various parts by some helpful soldier friends) and later bought a trailer for the jeep. He also got a fairly large stock of food, which the Nelsons very graciously shared with us in Tiddim during our first rainy season in Burma, and which helped keep us alive. John Anderson was able to buy a weapons carrier truck, a 3/4 ton vehicle which was popularly known as a fifteen-hundred weight.

Franklin and John roamed around Assam scrounging things for the mission hospitals in Gauhati and Jorhat and for themselves and other mission families in India. Other missionaries were able to haul truckloads of material into Burma for schools and hospitals. One of the most successful of these was Bill Hackett who got hold of a 6-ton truck and managed to make several trips into Burma over the dirt roads. On one of these trips he hauled in an old army motorcycle which eventually was given to me.

Scrounging surplus military materials in Assam in late 1945 and early 1946 was just one of those never-never events that sometimes happen. Certainly it was a godsend to us trying to live in the war-devastated portions of Assam and Burma.

Chapter 8

THE ROMANCE OF MISSIONS

⮦

During our months in Burma, when Betty Lue, our little son Richard, and I lived with the Nelsons in Tiddim during the rainy season of 1946, Franklin and I sometimes made short excursions in his jeep to nearby villages. These were to attend meetings and do mission business when the conditions of the road permitted. But these trips used up our petrol supply and it was impossible to buy any more, either locally or in Kalemyo, 44 miles away at the base of the Hills. Only the government had gasoline.

Shortage of Rice

Now it happened that the government began to run out of rice to feed their employees in Tiddim. The government cooperative could not get any more rice because the pack mules were dying of a disease known as surra, and jeeps on the plains were broken down. Frank Nelson had the only jeep capable of hauling rice up to Tiddim.

So Col. Tommy West, the government Assistant Superintendent, a Britisher, and the only other Westerner in Tiddim, struck a deal with Rev. Nelson.

"Rev. Nelson," he said, "you have the only jeep and trailer operating, and we need provisions. If you will carry rice up for us, I'll give chits to get government petrol free of charge, 15 gallons for every 480 pounds of rice." As the round trip was only 88 miles, though the road was steep and muddy, Frank thought it fair.

Under this arrangement, Frank and I made numerous trips toward the end of the monsoon season to "help the starving government workers in Tiddim," as Frank expressed it. I know that this arrangement sounds rather crazy, but it was the only way we could get gasoline for the jeep so both families could make the trip back to India in November to get our freight.

Our First Trip for Rice

Our trip on September 2 was noteworthy as the first of these rice trips. Franklin and I left Tiddim at 9:30 a.m., chopped through three fallen trees and cleared one landslide on the way down to Singanau, a village near Kalemyo. Here we loaded the jeep and trailer, bought some rice and curry for lunch, and began the journey back.

The road was in dreadful shape with mud and fallen rocks, but we got along all right, though slowly, until about 6 p.m. when we were near Dimlo, about 8 miles from home. There was a certain steep downhill place which had had a mudslide. Frank was driving at the time. As we were carrying about a thousand pounds on the trailer, the weight of the overloaded trailer caused the jeep to jack-knife. We went out of control in the soft mud. We stopped with no injuries, but we were deeply mired in the mud.

The only way to get out was to unload the trailer, unhitch it, then extricate the jeep, hitch on the trailer, and reload.

Stuck in the Mud

Night had fallen by now, a light mist was blanketing the jungle, and there was no help. We were alone on the road, with no village nearby. With a sigh we spread a canvas on a solid place on the side of the road and proceeded to unload the heavy gunny bags of rice. During the day we had been talking together about people's perception of missionaries and their work—how interesting to be in the Orient, how fascinating to see the strange people and customs, how exciting to know other languages, how romantic to preach the gospel, how nice not to have to punch a time clock, etc.—all the perceptions and misperceptions of those who have not experienced such life themselves.

As we hoisted the 120-pound rice bags one after another from the trailer and struggled through the foot-deep mud over to the canvas, careful not to slip and fall down, I remarked to my colleague, "Ah, Frank, the romance of missions!" For some reason, this remark hit a responsive chord within him. We both began to laugh so hard that we could no longer work on the rice. We had to stop for a few minutes and just laugh at the absurdity of our situation. What we were doing was certainly not most people's idea of "missionary work."

We finally moved the last of the half-ton of rice, pulled the empty trailer to solid ground, managed to get the jeep aiming right again and out of the deep mud, hitched on the trailer, and hoisted the thousand pounds of rice back on again.

Thoughts on Earning Gasoline

Thus we reached home safely at 9:45 p.m., covered with mud. We had driven 88 miles in exactly 12 hours, and had earned 30 imperial gallons of gasoline. Frank figured that we had used 15 gallons on the trip and so had a profit of 15 gallons. This would be about 19 U.S. gallons. To earn this, we had spent the time of two men for a long day, used our own oil, and had certainly worn out the jeep and tires to some extent. The government got a good deal, but we were not angry about it; rather, we were thankful for the chance to earn the gasoline for our trip to India and to help the government rationing system in the process.

And some of the gasoline went to help run Frank's jeep-powered washing machine.

Chapter 9

MY FIRST TRIP TO RANGOON

W e heard that the first postwar missionary conference of our Baptist mission was to be held in Rangoon beginning October 14, 1946. Frank and I agreed that we should go and present the needs of the Chins. They were asking for a hospital and a high school. We felt that it was too tiresome a journey and too dangerous for our wives and children. But we had in Tiddim a very highly educated young man named Hau Go, a college graduate from India, a colleague supported by an American church. He spoke Burmese, of great importance on our trip. So we three men decided to go.

I tell this story as an indication of what travel in the Burmese rainy season was like in the postwar days.

Landslides

Franklin, Hau Go, and I planned to leave Tiddim on Friday, October 4. But on Thursday heavy rains caused landslides. When we heard about these, we gathered eight other men to help, drove out by jeep and trailer to mile 11 and spent several hours working on the slide. We returned home after dark, wet, tired, and hungry. A good chicken dinner and hot baths revived our low spirits.

On Friday it rained all day and we could not start.

On Saturday, although it rained most of the day, we decided we had to start. We hired some coolies to help us for the trip to the plains, and there were eleven people in the jeep and trailer. We had sufficient mattocks and axes for all, and a good thing, for it took us 11 hours to travel the 44 miles to Kalemyo. We cut through innumerable mud and rock slides, branches, and debris, including chopping through two fallen trees, each 2 feet in diameter. With sighs of victory over the elements, we finally reached the Chin village of Singunau near Kalemyo and put up for the night in a Christian home.

Floods on the Myittha

On Sunday we worshiped in the little church at Singunau. It rained again on that day and on Monday too, the fifth straight day of rain. The Myittha River, receiving water from the Chin Hills and from Manipur, had overflowed its banks and was a raging torrent, so boatmen dared not go down. On Wednesday the flood had subsided to within the banks, and Franklin, Hau Go, and I embarked on one of the "country boats," the long dugout canoes some 30 feet long and 4 feet wide. The boatmen, pleading the dangers of the river, demanded 150 rupees for the trip down to Kalewa. We paid it but recouped 41 rupees from some other passengers.

The river had fallen enough so the rapids were not too dangerous. We walked around the first rapids but shot the second one and arrived safely at 2 p.m. at Kalewa on the Chindwin River.

To Mandalay and Rangoon

On Thursday we started down river on a rice barge towed by a diesel tugboat, but reached only Mingin by dusk. We put up for the night in the dak bungalow, barring the doors to foil the ever-present robbers. On Friday we reached Monywa and stayed with Rev. Stanley Vincent, a Wesleyan missionary who later became the Burma Secretary for the British and Foreign Bible Society. On Saturday we took a series of post-office trucks across country to Mandalay.

Having come into the country by the "back door" and by back roads, the sights of Burma proper were new to me and sobering. Along the Chindwin we viewed the sunken wrecks of steamboats. Along the railway tracks we saw the wrecks of locomotives and cars strewn in the ditches. Bridges were out, notably the great Ava

Bridge between Sagaing and Mandalay. At Mandalay next to the railroad station there was an area a half mile wide and over a mile long completely leveled.

We went right to the depot, climbed aboard a box car, and the train took off at the leisurely pace of Burmese trains. The ride ended at 2:30 a.m. on Sunday at a town called Tatkon, north of Pyinmana. We were informed that some bridges were out. With much difficulty we got rides on two trucks to get the 100 miles to Toungoo, where we stayed the night on the verandah of a Karen school.

We caught the morning train on Monday at Toungoo and traveled somewhat better in second class to Rangoon, which we reached at 6:30 p.m. We went immediately to the mission quarters at 19 Sandwith Road for dinner and to meet the missionaries gathered for the first post-war conference. We thus finished the 750-mile trip in ten days, arriving a day late for the conference.

Chapter 10

STRANDED IN THE BURMA JUNGLE

~~~

In Rangoon

When Frank Nelson, Hau Go, and I reached Rangoon, on this my first visit to the capital city, we were immediately immersed in four days of fellowship and business with the other Baptist missionaries present, 24 in all. The Chin request for a hospital and high school was given a low priority because other needs were greater. Our mission had suffered war damage not only in Assam and Burma, but also in Japan, East China, and the Philippine Islands, and millions of dollars were needed to rebuild.

Although the mission was not able to promise the Chins' request, the executive council did allocate to me a motorcycle trucked over from India. I was delighted, visualizing myself saving time in village touring. I planned to take it up north in the truck Frank and I bought.

Purchase of a 15 Cwt. Truck

In some hours between sessions of the conference we visited the bazaar to buy things available only in the big city. We had no time for sightseeing. As Nelson and I planned to take a lot of equipment back to the Chin Hills, Frank bought a Dodge three-quarter ton "weapons carrier" from the American officer in charge of disposing of surplus military equipment. It was usually called a fifteen-hundred weight (15 cwt.) truck. This was a powerful machine, four-wheel drive, but simple and straightforward, fairly easy to repair. It had a winch on the front end, a most useful accessory when mired in mud or sand. There was also a trailer. These cost Rupees 2,500, about $600. We each paid half and later on, when we sold it, we recovered our investment.

Johnson Gets Malaria

It happened that on Sunday, soon after our conference ended, I came down with malaria, my first experience with the disease. I was laid up in bed for four days, unable to eat. It was during those days that Franklin bought the truck and trailer. I was too weak to help with packing the truck, so Frank and Hau Go did all the work. I was even too weak to try out the motorcycle. I supposed that it ought to start up and go okay, being an American built cycle, a Harley Davidson.

Return Journey: to Ye-U

By Friday I began to feel better, and the three of us, Franklin, Hau Go, and I, with the truck and trailer, left Rangoon on Monday, October 28. The road to Mandalay, running straight north from Rangoon, was reasonably smooth asphalt and we made Pyinmana without trouble. On the second day we reached Mandalay, staying with missionaries at both places. On Wednesday we went via Shwebo to Ye-U and put up for the night in a government rest house. We knew that the worst part of the journey lay ahead.

Thinking back now, I thank God that Hau Go was with us. Fluent in both English and Burmese, he was our interpreter, and without him we would have been as babies. He was our salvation in the days ahead.

Through Dry Rivers

We were not really prepared for the bad road conditions. From Ye-U the road runs northwesterly through desolate broken jungle country to a point on the Chindwin River seven miles downstream from Kalewa, following for the most part, and often crossing, a small river. Various armies using the road had made bridges, but now most of these were broken or had washed away, and the road was nothing but a track through the jungle.

Because the bridges were out, we had to go through dry river-beds, deep in sand, often using the winch to get us through. At 3 p.m. we got hopelessly stuck in a combination of sand and quick-sand. We broke the winch cable three times trying to get out. Finally we unloaded everything, almost one and a half tons of gear, and thus lightened were able to get out of the riverbed and to the road again. We had to camp for the night in the open, near the truck.

The next day, Friday, the engine refused to start and so the winch was unusable. We spent the entire morning pushing the truck up a gentle hill. Rolling downward the engine started and we reloaded the truck and trailer, which we had emptied, and continued joyfully toward the river.

Drive Shaft Snapped

At 3 p.m. we were again stuck in the deep sand of a dry riverbed, our 21st bridgeless crossing. This time Franklin determined to get through. He gave the engine full power and let out the clutch. There was a shudder, a snap, and we found that the main drive shaft had broken in two. The wheels were entirely without power and we were stranded in the river. But the winch worked, so we were able to winch ourselves out of the river and up onto the road. The truck could go no farther. We were stranded in the jungle, five miles from the nearest human being.

Stranded

We were 46 miles from Kalewa, the Burmese town at the confluence of the Myittha and Chindwin Rivers. We were on a deserted jungle road, and five miles from a small and squalid village called Pyingaing on the road back to Ye-U.

In spite of our predicament with the disabled Dodge truck , I felt some elation in having the motorcycle with us. On that Frank and I could ride the 39 miles to the Chindwin River, get back to Kalewa and eventually to Tiddim where we could search for a broken Dodge driveshaft from the wrecks in the jungle. We took the motorcycle out of the truck and found to our dismay that it would not start, no matter how hard we tried. I regretted having malaria and being too sick to try out the motorcycle before starting the trip. So we gave up and camped for the night, very thirsty. I recall opening cans of peas just to get the juice.

In the morning Hau Go and I hiked the five miles back to Pyingaing and Hau Go arranged for a drum of water to be carried out by ox cart. We rode back on the ox cart. As soon as these arrangements were made, Franklin and I left on foot to walk the 39 miles to Shwegin on the Chindwin River, leaving Hau Go to guard the vehicle. We traveled light, carrying only food, canteens, the broken truck part, mosquito nets, and a blanket apiece. We had no pistol or rifle, and we depended on keeping a fire going at night to keep wild animals away.

On to Kalewa and Tiddim

We left at 3 p.m. on Saturday and reached the Chindwin River hamlet at 9 a.m. on Monday, footsore and weary. We had camped overnight twice, once on the road and once on a river sandbank. When our canteens were empty, we had to boil water from puddles in the road, as the streams were dry. During our whole walk out we had passed but one village, and there we were able to buy some boiled rice. Aside from that, we saw no human beings until we reached Shwegin.

At Shwegin we hired a dugout canoe to take us the seven miles upriver to Kalewa. There we got rides on a truck going partway to Kalemyo. Then we had another 6-mile hike, making in all 55 miles on foot in three days without proper food, and so we reached the foot of the Chin Hills. Here at Singunau was Nelson's jeep. It was late on Monday, but we wanted desperately to get home, so we made the night trip up the dangerous mountain road and reached Tiddim safely at 1 a.m. on Tuesday. It was exactly one month to the day since leaving for Rangoon.

Our wives took pity on us and began to feed us properly, so we rebounded quickly from the grueling experience. Friends searched for a new truck driveshaft among the various wrecks in the jungle and found an exact replacement part. We rested on Tuesday and

Wednesday, and on Thursday started back to recover the stranded vehicle. We had worried about Hau Go, for we knew that dacoits (armed robbers) were very active in the Shwebo District in which we were stranded.

Chapter 11

HIT BY DACOITS

A mong the new words we learned in India and Burma was the word "dacoit" which usually means a band of robbers armed with knives and sometimes with guns. Probably our word "bandit" is nearest in meaning. Dacoits are often vicious and murderous, definitely not nice people.

Return to the Truck

After Frank Nelson and I got back home after the trip to the Rangoon conference and rested two days, we hastened to return to the broken-down truck with the spare driveshaft and recover the vehicle. We were worried also about Hau Go, left to guard the truck. When we got to Kalemyo, we heard that Hau Go had been robbed.

We reached Hau Go and the truck on a Friday night about 7:30 p.m. on a lorry we hired at Shwegin to take us to milestone 46. The lorry did well, as 40 coolies hired by the government had been working on the road for a few days to make it passable. It was a relief to find our Chin companion well and unharmed.

The Robbery

Here we got the full story of the robbery that had been reported to us. On Monday, the very day we finished the long hike out to civilization, Hau Go awakened on a chilly morning to see two Burmans warming themselves by a fire. He got up and they talked some, and suddenly he found himself looking in a pistol barrel. The other bandit threatened him with a two-foot-long dah (machete). They looked through the truck and finally made off with Hau Go's suitcase and mine. Frank's suitcase they left behind—it was lighter than the other two.

I lost most of my clothing, including a nice suit, about 200 rupees, and worst of all, my study Bible on which I had spent scores of hours putting in notes, etc. Without doubt these Burmans threw my valuable Bible into the jungle. Hau Go lost clothing and 400 rupees. We were just glad that this robbery had not happened on a good highway where the dacoits might have appeared with a truck and taken off the thousands of rupees of supplies we had with us. So we thanked the Lord it wasn't worse than it was and that no bodily harm had come to any of us.

The Journey Home

On Saturday morning Frank, who was getting to be quite an expert mechanic, put the driveshaft into the Dodge and we made the 39 miles to Shwegin without incident. The coolies had repaired the bridges enough for trucks to get through. Shwegin is a very small village on the bank of the wide Chindwin River and a place to find food and lodging. We reported the robbery to a policeman there, but the dacoits were never found and our property was gone forever.

The next day we found a ferry boat large enough to take the truck and we proceeded the seven miles upriver to Kalewa and then by our truck to Kalemyo. This town near the base of the Chin Hills was later to get an airport and become a port of entry to the Chin Hills. Near there, in a Chin village, we stored my motorcycle for future repair.

On Monday, November 11th, we drove the truck to Tiddim, for the road had dried enough for this 15 cwt. truck. Thus after 38 days of traveling and many vicissitudes we safely returned from the conference. On that one trip we spent 10 days reaching Rangoon, 13 days in Rangoon, and 15 days for the trip home via the back roads!

Meanwhile at Home

While we men were having these adventures, our wives and children back in Tiddim were carrying on the important work of teaching and learning, running the household, and language study. Lois, the older Nelson girl, began her first grade work, taught by her mother. Karen Nelson and Dick Johnson were only one and one half but their care was important. Then Phileda and Betty began to teach English to two Chin girls in preparation for their hoped-for entrance into the Tiddim Bible School which was to start in June, 1947.

Chapter 12

PREPARING FOR THE BIG MOVE

As the rainy monsoon season of 1946 came to an end, there were yet months of preparation for making the "big move" as we called it, the move to our permanent home in Haka and our permanent work alone, without the support of the Nelsons.

Trip to India

Both families needed to make a quick trip to India. The mission had shipped our freight to Calcutta and we had to go there personally to retrieve it. The roads were drying and travel was easier, so we went in our two vehicles, Frank and family in his jeep and I driving Betty and Dick in the Dodge 15 cwt. truck. It was a rather scary trip. The truck had no doors and the passenger seat where Betty sat had no protection, no restraint, from the rider sliding out and to the ground. When our son was awake or asleep, she had to hold him in her arms, very tiring to her.

We proceeded up the rutted road to the India border at Tamu, which we reached at 7:30 p.m. My lights were flickering on and off, but I followed Frank's jeep through the mountains to the gate at Palel. We reached this place, the entry into India, at 11 p.m. Here at the police and customs officers' gate Betty and I stopped for the night, exhausted. Frank and Phileda left us and headed on for the Kangpokpi mission station. Betty, Richard, and I spent the night sleeping in the truck parked near the gate. In the morning, some villagers came around and told us in English that we were lucky to be safe, for tigers roamed in that area.

To Gauhati and Calcutta

When we two families reached Jorhat, the town where Betty and I thought we would be teaching for the rainy season, we proceeded on by train to Gauhati. The American Baptist missionaries in Assam (the Assam Mission) were gathered for their annual conference at the time. Here we left Betty and the three children with the other missionaries, and Frank, Phileda, and I went by train to Calcutta and reclaimed our freight, shipped almost one year earlier. Some of my boxes had been rifled, but as far as I could determine I lost only two sugar bowls. A very strange theft!

Frank and I rented a boxcar, bought a very strong padlock, and managed with great effort to shepherd our freight to the railhead at Dimapur, then by lorry to Kangpokpi. When finally our families were together again, we had a merry Christmas with John and Elaine Anderson at the Kangpoki mission station. It was not a very merry Christmas for Frank who was suffering with malaria chills and fever, and along with that he was trying to recover from amoebic dysentery. We prevailed upon him to go to the mission hospital in Assam to recuperate.

A Truck Load of Freight to Burma

Because Frank was ill and in the Jorhat hospital, I decided to make a quick trip alone to Tiddim using the Dodge weapons carrier (the fifteen-hundred weight vehicle) and trailer to carry in a load of my freight and some foodstuffs and then return for my family. I marvel now that I dared to go on that dangerous road without a companion, but I did it. Just a task that needed to be done. I reached Fort White safely, the hamlet where the Haka road goes left and the Tiddim road goes right. I stored my boxes and sacks of food in the empty government dak bungalow and drove on to Tiddim where mail for our two families had accumulated for weeks.

Return to Kangpokpi; New Year's Eve

I had no car trouble on this trip for mechanics had repaired the truck in Jorhat, and so I returned to the Kangpokpi mission on the last day of the year 1946. It was on that day, December 31, that Betty opened mail which I had carried in from Tiddim, and found out that her father had died in October. The news took 65 days to reach her. She had not even known that her father was ill. Thus New Year's Eve for us was a time of sadness.

Back in Burma

On January 3 Betty Lue, Richard, and I packed the 15 cwt. truck with food and the remainder of our freight, leaving the trailer behind for Frank to use. We made the trip in three days, experiencing no trouble on the way and leaving some of our load at the Fort White bungalow. We then went on to Tiddim, where the Nelsons joined us in a few days, with Frank in much better health. But before our family left for Haka there were still two important errands to do.

Trip to Mandalay for Furniture

On my trip to Mandalay and Rangoon in October I purchased some teak furniture, knowing that the Haka bungalow was destitute of furnishings. Thankfully, Hau Go was available to go with me as companion and Burmese translator. I used the Dodge truck and we traveled the same road that we used when stranded in the jungle and where Hau Go was robbed by dacoits. But this was different. The road was dry; coolies had fixed bridges and cleared the road, so we drove without incident to Mandalay, loaded the furniture, and returned, again dropping our load at Fort White. With Hau Go on the journey, it was easy to get meals in teashops and Burmese restaurants, and to find lodging.

Shuttling Jeep and Trailer Loads to Lumbang

I have mentioned using the Dodge weapons-carrier truck to carry loads to Fort White. I stored them temporarily in the government dak bungalow. From Fort White the road toward Haka is too narrow for a truck, and even jeeps proceed with difficulty and often danger. The jeep-able road south from Fort White runs for the most part along the top of a mountain ridge, tolerably level. The rest bungalows are: Bamboo Camp, Pine Tree Camp, and Lumbang. Beyond Lumbang is the Manipur River valley (or gorge), then Falam, the government center.

Lumbang village has a strong Christian church, and the chief deacon, Kulh Ci, was a kindly man who allowed me to store freight under his house. I made five trips using Frank's jeep and trailer to move all my stuff from Fort White to Lumbang—32 miles.

My first trip was notable. I hired a young Chin man to ride with me and help move boxes, etc. We rounded a sharp right turn and came to a very narrow part of the road, so narrow I feared to cross the thirty feet of danger. I was unable to back up because of the sharp turn. There was no other road. I had to cross. I knew that my left tires would be almost over the crumbling edge of the road. Then we spied a tree uphill from this dangerous spot. I had a strong rope, so I tied the rope around my chest and the Chin lad tied the rope to the tree above. I figured that if the jeep and trailer went over the edge, I would be pulled out of danger by the rope.

With a prayer for wisdom—drive fast or take it slow?—I drove the jeep slowly over the danger spot. Safely through, I found a bunch of Chin men nearby and hired them to repair the road. The remaining four loads went well, and when all was finished, I returned to Tiddim.

We Reach Lumbang, End of the Motor Road, and Hire Chia Ling

When all was ready for the final leg of our long journey, Frank drove Betty Lue, Richard, and me the 50 miles to Lumbang and we put up in Saya Kulh Ci's house. He and his wife were gracious hosts to the three lonely Americans. We had services in the little church the two nights we were there.

A young man came up the hill to the home of Kulh Ci where we were staying. He was short, wiry, and strong.

"My name is Chia Ling," he said in Chin. "I would like to work for you."

Ram Hlun, whom we had hired months before as a cook, helped us understand about this fellow.

"Chia Ling comes from a village near Haka," he said, "and I think he is a good man and also he is a Christian. He wants to work for you."

Chia Ling showed us a paper. "I worked for a British officer as an orderly during the war," he said, "and I have a recommendation."

He showed us the letter from some British major. It read, in part, "This cocky young man is faithful and reliable." Chia Ling probably did not understand this dubious recommendation, but we liked him immediately and hired him as a house boy. We agreed on a monthly wage and set him to work repacking boxes for mule travel.

Chia Ling eventually became our second cook. If I took one cook with me on tour, the other would cook for the family at home. Actually the two men, Ram Hlun and Chia Ling, became not only our workers but also dear friends, and they worked for us the whole twenty years we were in Burma. Both were Christians and both became deacons in our Haka church.

We cannot express enough thanks for Ram Hlun and Chia Ling who enabled us to be free from household tasks in order to give our time and strength to the more important work of the Christian mission.

We Begin the Trip

On the morning of Friday, January 31, we woke to the sound of horses and mules chewing corn, and men bustling around saddling the animals. Boi Nol had three mules, a white, a tan, and a black. Another man had horses. Only animals and persons on foot could reach Haka, for no vehicle could cross the Manipur River. The only bridge was a narrow walkway hung from two overhead cables—a suspension bridge, a legacy of British occupation. It was hundreds of feet long, graced with warning signs in English and Burmese reading: "Load limit, two horses." It was impossible to ford the river. Even in the dry season it carried much water, was deep and swift, and filled with huge boulders.

With anticipation we started off with our Chin companions, two riding mules and four pack animals. For almost a year we had worked and waited for this day, and now it had come! Ahead of us was Haka, our future home.

Chapter 13

FIVE DAYS WITH MULES

〜〜〜

On Friday, January 31, we began the fifty mile trek to Haka, starting with a steep nine-mile downhill the first day to a little shack at the suspension bridge. The Manipur River flows through a deep gorge between Lumbang and Falam, then the capital of the Chin Hills. Here we spent the night and prepared for the rigorous climb the next day.

The Manipur River

It is important to understand this river as a barrier to Chin movement. The river begins in the Manipur State of India at a fairly high elevation and flows southward into Burma in a deep and narrow valley straight through the Chin Hills until it turns eastward and into the Myittha River, thence into the Chindwin, and finally into the Irrawaddy, the chief river of Burma. The Manipur is navigable for not a single mile. It is a cauldron of seething water in rapid descent, and in the rainy season it is formidable. When we arrived in early 1947, the suspension bridge on the Lumbang-Falam path was the only way to cross.

The Manipur River quite effectively limited travel north and south, and contributed to the great differences between the Tiddim people to the northeast and the Lai and Laizo people to the south. Not only are the languages different, but so also are the customs and dress.

From the River to Falam

For the nine-mile climb the next day, a rise in elevation of more than 3,500 feet above the river, two riding mules were provided. My legs were not strong enough yet for mountain hikes like this, so I appreciated the strong mule. Betty Lue rode the other mule with Richard also on the saddle, although occasionally he was carried by Ram Hlun or Pente. Our son, one year and eight months old at the time, walked also for short periods. Thus our party consisted of us three Americans, Rev. Lal Hnin, Ram Hlun our cook, Chia Ling our house boy, Pente the ayah, two mule drivers, and the horses and mules. Up and up we went through scrub jungle, passing through one small village on the way, until we reached the town of Falam and the welcoming arch of flowers and the crowd of Christians to greet us.

Falam

Falam was the government center for the whole Chin Hills and considered a town because it had a high school, a hospital, police lines, a jail, a post office, and the British official's house and office. This official was out on tour and we did not meet him. Falam was not large, perhaps no more than 400 houses. The elevation is 4,200 feet, so the weather was pleasant.

We stayed in Falam for Sunday and enjoyed the church worship where special welcoming speeches were delivered in English and Laizo. It was thrilling to realize that Laizo was very close to the Lai language spoken in Haka and which we were learning. We were nearing our goal and our future home!

Three More Days

We started off again on Monday. For three days we traveled on, walking and riding mules by turn, following the old mule road which had been used, no doubt, for centuries. We were on a fairly level road for 7 miles and reached the Mangkhen dak bungalow. Actually that bungalow had been destroyed during the war, so we were in the old servants' quarters. This place was the only rest bungalow that was near a village. There were no Christians in Mangkhen, so we simply bought firewood, a chicken, and some eggs.

On Tuesday we made a long descent to the Pao River, which was merely a mountain stream maybe 30 feet wide. From this river we made the six-mile climb to Pioneer Camp. On this long uphill climb we could see on the right hand the sheer cliffs of Dawn Mountain, as I call it, the mountain that catches the rays of the morning sun.

Pioneer Camp

Pioneer Camp proved to be an amazing place. The government rest bungalow there had suffered grave damage but at least it still stood. The wooden walls were gone and replaced with cornstalks. The floor had a gaping hole 3 ft. by 4 ft. in size where a fire meant for warmth had burned down and through the floor. We put a camp cot over this hole so our son would not fall through and down to the ground. At least this place had a roof, so we felt safe and secure in spite of the primitive living.

These days of our first travel to Haka were days of great anticipation and adventure, and at Pioneer Camp we could hardly restrain our excitement.

First Sight of Haka

On Wednesday, February 5, the third day after leaving Falam, we got our first glimpse of Haka from a spot almost 9 miles away. The road made a long curve to the left. We could see a spot of white amidst the green forested mountain, and Lal Hnin told us that that was the American Baptist mission house, the one called the Strait bungalow, which was presently being used as a government hospital. The Carson house, where we would stay, was not yet visible, he said.

At five miles out we could see the mission compound more clearly and the red-painted roofed building in the government quarter. The scene was beautiful, with Run Tlang (Run mountain) behind and above the village and rising to 7,200 feet elevation.

A few miles out of Haka we came to a lovely archway of flowers across the road. About it were gathered many Christians who had come to meet us and to sing hymns of welcome. They presented us with two chickens, some dozens of eggs, and four stalks of sugarcane. The latter pleased Dick who loved the sweet cane but always became a gooey mess.

The first welcoming archway was on a fairly level road running along the top of a saddleback between hills, a place used for grazing cows and horses. Now we could see two villages. The smaller one was New Haka down the hill to the east, and the larger one, Haka itself, the village where Arthur and Laura Carson had established their mission in 1899. Buildings with corrugated iron roofing were visible; most houses were thatch roofed and hardly visible.

Arrival, February 5, 1947

As we continued, we came to another flowered archway and another group of Christian believers, headed by Rev. Sang Ling, the old pastor who had met us in Tiddim months earlier. The church deacons were with him, and a crowd of women and girls in their beautiful red longyis, and boys in short pants and open shirts. Their songs of welcome resounded, for they had been without a resident missionary for six years.

Betty, Dick, and I, along with Saya Sang Ling and Saya Lal Hnin, headed the procession, while behind us came 200 Christians, young and old. We cannot tell you adequately how we felt to see their joy at the arrival of missionaries after years without them. These were profoundly moving days as at last we reached the village and the people where our gracious God had provided us a home and a ministry.

We paused for prayer for a few minutes at the gate of the fence surrounding the Carson house and then turned and entered, not quite prepared for what we would discover.

Chapter 14

OUR NEW HOME IN HAKA

C oming down the hill from the government road to the Mission
Compound, I saw clearly the smaller of the two houses, the
"Carson Bungalow," and 50 yards from it the larger house, the "Strait
Bungalow," and in the distance, on the more or less level acres, a
low pile of stones which was the ruins of the mission hospital. To
the left a dilapidated wooden building which was the former schoolhouse, now the church, was visible.

The almost thirty acres of the American Baptist Mission
compound with its various buildings, all run-down and some in
ruins, was to be my responsibility.

I gave thanks to the Lord that I was young and not afraid of
work, and blessed with a schoolteacher wife who would carry half
of the load. With that in mind I walked up the four cement steps to
the Carson bungalow.

This was to be our home for fourteen months, until we could get
the government to restore the Strait bungalow to us.

The Carson House

Betty Lue and I saw at once that the description given by Lal
Hnin was correct. The house did have a living room, a dining room,
three small bedrooms, and a separate cookhouse, but the interior was
dark, dirty, smoked, and green with mold, a very depressing place to
live. The reason for disrepair was that the Japanese had removed all

roofing tins to build shelters in the jungle, protection against bombing, and the house was roofless and unused for over a year.

Ram Hlun had preceded us into town and had a fire going and afternoon tea ready for refreshment after our long journey. The local Christians had loaned us a table and two chairs so we had something to sit on. We had our two camp cots and Dick's wooden playpen for his bed. No other furniture was in the bungalow until coolies carried in the teak furniture from Lumbang weeks later.

The interior of the house was dark when the windows were shut, as there was no glass, only boards. We had to use candles and a kerosene lantern until we could put glass into the windows. The house was also rather cold, as it was in the shadow of a hill, and the sun did not warm it until after 10 a.m. in the cold months.

In the next two days Betty, Chia Ling, and I scrubbed and washed the walls and floors of the whole house, using up two long bars of laundry soap. Eventually we painted the walls of the dining room, which had no windows, and that made the room more attractive.

The Compound

A Haka Chin Young Woman

When Arthur Carson purchased the 30 acres of land in 1899 he chose wisely. Heavily forested in pine, it became an oasis of green in a denuded town and was a boon to Chins living downhill as a source of water. Incidentally, the government forbade the cutting of trees above the main road, so the mountainside, rising to 7,200 feet elevation, was a water supply for the whole village.

About 6 acres of the compound were fairly level and on this were built the two mission houses, a hospital, a school, and many outbuildings. Some of this now was in ruins. It was my lot as resident missionary to restore as much of this as possible—but first the main job for Betty and me was to learn the Haka Chin language, also called the Lai language or dialect. To this we set our energies.

In later years we discovered that when the pioneer missionary, Arthur Carson, built this bungalow in 1902, he had the help of some Chinese carpenters for a while, as no Chins were carpenters. But the Chinese left after a dispute over wages, and Arthur did much of the carpentry on the house himself. In pre-war days it must have been an attractive home with the bay window to the east affording a view of the village pathway. We found the house depressing but livable. One concern of mine was the roof. When the roofing tins were restored to the bungalow after the war, it was impossible to put them into their original location, so there were hundreds of nail holes to be patched. For lack of anything else, I used tar and burlap to patch the holes. Later I found an aluminum-looking mastic which made more permanent repairs.

The Cookhouse

The cookhouse in the rear of the bungalow was fairly good, being of wood frame with walls and roof of corrugated iron tins. Cooking was primitive—two bars of iron over an open wood fire. Later I made a brick oven like those used in colonial America, where the wood is burned inside the oven to heat it and then the coals raked out. Our oven made delicious bread, rolls, cakes, and even pies. Ram Hlun had been cook for Chester and Florence Strait, the former missionaries, and he improved even more under Betty's tutelage.

Richard in Haka

Our son Richard was now old enough to wander on the mission compound. The two houses were fenced to keep out animals, but the six acres of level area was unfenced, and horses, cows, and water buffalo roamed at will. We were afraid for Dick's safety at first, but Pente was a dependable ayah and watched over him carefully. Soon Dick made friends with Chin boys in the neighborhood and thus found companionship. His particular friends were Van Awi, the oldest son of Ram Hlun, and Tawk Ling, an orphan boy from Chia Ling's village. With our son watched over well, we were free to study the language.

British Officials in Haka

The British officer in Haka when we arrived was Mr. Hay-Neave. We never learned his first name; typical British reserve. He was joined later by a Mr. Martin. Hay-Neave was a lonely man. His wife died when a German submarine torpedoed her ship when returning to England during the war. He never remarried, to my knowledge, and he considered Haka equivalent to exile to Siberia. Occasionally we had dinner together. He did own a radio and we, without music of any kind, loved to go to his place and hear some classical music.

I have a high estimate of the men in the British colonial service. In general, they were honest, did not take bribes, and attempted to administer justice equitably. Hay-Neave drank too much and he showed no interest at all in Christianity or the Chin churches. He and Martin could at least have given some financial support to the struggling Chin churches.

We last encountered Hay-Neave and Martin in December 1947 at the river town of Monywa. We were returning from Mandalay en route to Haka, and they were on a river steamer heading for Rangoon and on to England as the British withdrew from Burma. Hay-Neave was drunk and I did not see him, but I had a nice chat with Martin on the bank of the Chindwin River.

Sensing that he was disconsolate at the slow dissolution of the British Empire, I said, "Martin, this won't be acknowledged very much in Burma, but the British did many good things for Burma: the roads built, the railroads and regular service, the waterways system for boats carrying cargo cheaply, the telephone and telegraph system, a good working postal service, and in general, peace with suppression of the dacoits. The Chin people will remember you with gratitude."

Martin thanked me for my sincere encouragement. So he and all the British officials left Burma for good as the country embarked on its own independent course.

Chapter 15

THE CHURCH AND CEMETERY

〜⮞

O n our trip in to Haka, Lal Hnin and Ram Hlun tried to describe
the condition of the Haka Baptist Church building, and it was
a sad tale they told.

So Betty and I were taken down to the church by the pastor, Rev.
Sang Ling. "It needs a lot of repair," he told us. He was right, as we
could see at a glance as we approached. The unusual bell was most
remarkable and the first thing you see as one nears the church.

The Church Bell

The church "bell" was the iron shell of a dud bomb. The bomb
was a cylinder about two feet long and eight inches in diameter. It
hung by wires from a wooden framework outside the church, and a
heavy wooden club was stuck into the end of the shell. When beaten
with the club, it made a very loud unmusical sound, a raucous noise
which seemed to offend the ears of the village dogs. Sang Ling told
us that as soon as the bell was sounded, nearby dogs would begin
to howl as if in pain, and the dogs farther away would take up the
noise, so that within a few moments all the dogs in the village would
be howling. It was a very effective, if not beautiful, way to proclaim
the time of services in the church. Incidentally, we learned that the
bell was also used to toll for deaths, and beaten very quickly and
continuously for a fire alarm.

The Church Building

The old schoolhouse, now a church, was on the level part of the mission compound about 150 yards from the bungalow. It was 24 by 56 feet in size, in dreadful condition. The roof leaked, the foundation and floor were rotten, and at least half of the outside siding had been pulled off by Japanese soldiers for firewood. Inside were backless benches for pews. There was a raised platform in front, a few chairs, and a pulpit painted white with a painted cross to mark it as the preaching spot. There were side windows with shutters, but no windows had glass.

Although the church was a depressing sight, there was one very bright and meaningful wall hanging. It was a banner made of black and white handwoven cloth adorned with a cross, and lettered with this Bible verse in Chin:

> Be faithful unto death
> And I will give you the crown of life.
> Revelation 2:10

The banner hung on the wall behind the preacher and was a visible reminder of the need for faithfulness in the non-Christian Chin culture.

The church is really the body of believers, not the building itself. In the case of Haka and its surrounding villages, I learned, the progress of Christianity had been very slow and at one time the early missionaries were ready to proclaim the area as "too hard hearted" to ever respond to the gospel. However, the mission did persist and during World War II it seemed that the tide turned and the people responded much more to the message of the pastors.

The Sunday Service

After we had been only a few days in Haka, it was Sunday and time for Sunday School and the worship service. The time for people to come was announced by the noise of the church bell. People were coming to the mission compound from several directions, many of them hiking up from the lower quarters of the town. The women were colorful in their handwoven red longyis and red shawls, their finest clothing. Most men came in short pants and shirt, and occasionally we saw a man in a loincloth and traditional white blanket with the black stripe.

We entered and saw the central aisle. On the left side sat the men and on the right sat the women, many carrying babies and infants slung in a blanket either on the back or to one side. Many of the children were asleep, and those awake were fairly quiet. As needed, mothers nursed their infants. Younger children hung around their mothers, some squirming and others playing with other kids. It was a lovely sight to see these people, non-Christian animists not long ago, now worshiping and listening to the Bible messages. I guessed that the attendance was about 75.

The Singing

As for singing, we discovered a beautiful practice. As the people gathered, someone would start a hymn and "line out the words," that is, call out the words line by line in time with the music. Very few persons had songbooks, as the war years had stopped the printing of Christian literature. I soon discovered that the people wanted me to get songbooks for them fast, right away. New songbooks were high on their agenda.

Seating in the Church

Betty sat down among the women on one of the low wooden backless benches. Richard, about 1 year and 8 months, was too young to go with other boys, so he clung to his mother. In time, as he grew and developed, he chose to sit with his Chin chums on the floor in front of the pulpit.

As for me, I found that automatically I, being the long-anticipated white missionary, was a "big shot" and was given a seat of honor, a chair right up on the platform. The deacons and other older men sat in the front row of seats and behind them were the other men. There was a choir composed of young men and girls who sat on two rows of benches over against the wall. Singing was a large part of the church service, and usually done very well. There was no piano or other instruments; singing was a cappella, usually with a tuning fork or a pitch pipe to get the correct pitch.

The Sunday School

The first part of the program was Sunday School. Here we found a custom unknown to us. Rev. Lal Hnin was the teacher, but his teaching was really a sermon, not geared to children and young people. He was not getting his message to the youth at all, a pity, for the young boys and girls often slipped out of the church on some pretext. In due time, Betty explained what a Sunday School really ought to be, and then classes were organized and many teachers were trained to teach boys and girls, men and women. But that change came about slowly.

The Preaching

After much singing and three choir songs, Pastor Sang Ling got up to preach his sermon. Although I had studied hard while in Tiddim to learn Haka Chin, my understanding was still so poor that I could not follow the sermon or even know what in general he was talking about. So I drifted off into reverie, probably with glazed eyes.

Thus I found myself thinking how I could build a new church to replace this broken-down building, one perhaps a bit larger, with new roofing tins and a firm floor, and with good walls to keep out wind and cold. Then I thought about our pastor preaching to the many new Christians, so much in need of instruction in the faith. He was one of the pioneer preachers in the Chin Hills and endured the persecution and the disdain that they often suffered from the people—not so much from the common people as from the chiefs and the upper class of Chin society.

Pastor Sang Ling

The Rev. Sang Ling was a man of almost 60 years with gray hair and the demeanor of an elder statesman. He was gentle of speech and often the reconciler of disputes. He enjoyed enormous prestige in the Christian community and in the village at large. His status as one of the noble class was no doubt a factor in his great effectiveness as a pastor and leader of the Christian church. His oldest son was named Sui Mang; and as in the Chin culture a person goes by the name of his eldest child, we called our pastor Sui Mang Pa. That means father of Sui Mang. In the same way, we called his wife Sui Mang Nu, meaning mother of Sui Mang. This is the common and correct way to address those persons who are fathers and mothers.

Sui Mang Pa proved to be a teacher and helper to Betty and me. We grew to respect and love him until his untimely death in 1953.

The Christian Cemetery

Pastor Sang Ling also showed us the Christian cemetery which was downhill from the church and in the grove of pine trees. When we saw it first, it was overgrown by brush and weeds, not often used because Chins often bury their dead in the courtyards of their homes. However, it does contain the grave of a little American boy, Harry Cope, son of Dr. and Mrs. Cope, born in Haka in November, 1911, and died in Haka in October, 1915, just short of his 4th birthday. The Christian cemetery is not large, perhaps fifty feet by one hundred feet in size, and surrounded by a low stone wall.

The Missionaries' Cemetery

Sang Ling took us down also to a small level place on a knoll in the pine forest, maybe a hundred yards from the Christian cemetery. Here are the graves of Arthur Carson and J. Herbert Cope enclosed in a stone-walled area about twenty by thirty feet in size. Carson's grave is of cement enclosing a flat stone outlining the map of the Chin Hills and his name and dates of birth and death. Dr. Cope's grave is also of cement with a slate stone showing a cross and holding a bronze plaque giving his name and dates. This place is a holy place for the Chin believers, for it was Carson who initiated the mission in 1899 at Haka and Cope who initiated the mission in 1910 at Tiddim. They are revered as bringers of the Good News of Jesus and His love.

Chapter 16

A DIAMOND RING

T he matter of window glass for our house was very important. Because our home was shaded by a high hill to the east,
the morning sun did not hit the house early, and it was too cold to
open windows and let in the sunshine. We longed for glass in those
windows.

Window Glass for Haka

We knew that window glass was on the way. I had purchased
glass in India and had it boxed in 50-pound loads. This glass was in
Lumbang, to be carried in by coolies.

Three weeks after arriving in Haka, and before the glass arrived,
I had to go to Tiddim to attend a very important meeting of the
Chin Hills Baptist Association, which that year was attended by
pastors and other important leaders of the churches throughout the
Chin Hills. I could not miss it. With two Chin companions I set out
walking the 100 mile trek, and being single, not with the family, I
traveled fast. I was gone 19 days, my first solo trip. I had left Betty
alone to pay the porters who carried in the loads from Lumbang, a
difficult task for her because sometimes the carriers rejected paper
money and insisted on coins, difficult to get.

On my return home, I was overjoyed to see that the living room
with its bay window was bathed in sunlight from two windows which
now had glass. During my absence, Betty and Chia Ling had opened

a box of glass and were able to put glass into two windows, using little nails to hold the panes. But they could do only two, because the other windows were of a different size.

Wrong Size Glass

When I bought the glass, I used measurements given me by Chins who did not realize that windows of the Carson house were of different sizes.

The panes of glass were one half inch too wide and one half inch too long. They had to be cut down. I had no glass cutter—the need for one had never entered my head. And no one else in Haka or elsewhere in the Hills had a cutter. We needed that glass cut down in size to make our house livable. What to do?

Then a thought came to me—a diamond. A diamond can cut glass, and the best professional glass cutters use a diamond tipped cutter rather than a steel wheel.

Betty saw me eyeing her engagement ring. "What are you thinking, Bob?" she asked.

"Betty, I wonder if your diamond ring could cut that glass," I said.

She looked troubled at the very thought of sacrificing her ring, but recognized that we could not go on living in semi-darkness. "Go ahead and try it," she nobly said.

"I'll try it and if I spoil it, I'll get another ring for you," was my promise, knowing quite well that it would be a long time before I could make good on such an expensive promise.

The Ring Cuts Glass

I got a straight-edge and after some experimentation found that the diamond, held at a certain angle, did indeed score the glass beautifully. With care I was able to break off the unwanted edges. With my wife's diamond ring I cut every piece of glass to size and was able to complete glazing the windows in the Carson bungalow, really transforming the house. Nothing bad at all happened to the diamond and Betty still has the ring.

In addition to having proper windows, the house was brightened by curtains that Betty made and by some pictures we hung on the walls. Thus an empty and dark house was being transformed into a beautiful place to live.

Our Neighbors

House is not a home until it is set within a context of neighbors and friends. We had our Chin servants, first of all. Ram Hlun, our cook, lived in a shack on the compound a bit west of the church. He had children and his older son became Dick's good friend. Chia Ling, our houseboy, lived in our house in a tiny room on the back. He was single, so he appreciated living so close. Pente lived with her uncle who lived not far away, down beyond the bazaar. Our gardener, Ram Thio, an older man who lived just beyond the bazaar line, was important for supplying garden vegetables on which we depended so much. Sometimes we could buy onions, potatoes, squash, and cabbage, but we had to raise tomatoes, carrots, beets, peas, and sweet corn in our own garden. These four workers were on the mission compound and in or around our house daily.

Beds and Furniture

The Simmons Beautyrest mattress and box spring, which were in our Calcutta freight, finally arrived in Lumbang. Men refused to carry these, as they were too squishy and wobbly. Finally Betty persuaded a group of women to go and carry these, promising extra pay. We also gave extra pay to a man who carried our galvanized tin bathtub purchased in Mandalay. It was oval, about 36 inches in length. The man complained that it struck his knee at every step as he carried it on his back. We agreed; he deserved extra.

When finally our teak furniture arrived, piecemeal, one item at a time, our house began to look home-like. Now we had a dining room table, four chairs, four living room chairs, a coffee table, a chest of drawers, and a wardrobe (called an almirah in Burma). We also had the double bed and Dick at last had a proper bed. Thus more comfortably housed, we turned our attention full time to language study with Saya Lal Hnin. Teachers and preachers are often referred to as "Saya" and we used that word. The word for a female teacher is "Sayamah."

By now we were used to being called "Dickypa" and "Dickynu," meaning Dick's father and Dick's mother. This is Chin custom.

Chapter 17

TO WEIGH A WIFE

By June of 1947 we were feeling comfortable in our home, and with Ram Hlun cooking our meals and Chia Ling working around the house we were freed for mission activities. We began to work full time on language. With Lal Hnin as our teacher we devoted 8:00 to 11:00 a.m. each morning and 1:30 to 3 p.m. every afternoon Monday through Friday to language. Our home-made Chin-to-English and our English-to-Chin dictionaries grew larger and we were better able to understand the grammar. We were working to pass the first language exam, which we took in early 1948. It was the rainy season, when Haka gets from 60 to 100 inches of rain, so we stayed close to home and to our books.

We were thankful to have as texts the New Testament in Chin and a songbook of 327 songs. Aside from these, made by former missionaries, we had nothing else written in Chin.

Expecting a Child

By mid-June of 1947 Betty Lue felt the first stirrings of life in our expected child and calculated that the baby would be due about November 10. This was a source of delight, for we wanted Dick to have a playmate. All went well and for the most part Betty was in good health.

During her pregnancy for our first child, our doctor in Chicago had weighed her regularly and cautioned her not to gain too much weight. This time we had no Dr. Hibbard to check on her; we had no doctor at all. But Betty wanted to keep track of her weight to avoid any trouble. In all Haka there was not a single scales capable of weighing a person. She was afraid that it might not be possible to keep track of her weight.

This matter weighed on my mind. What could I do? All we had was the baby scales, a balance that weighed to 22 pounds. Then the thought came, maybe I could make a beam balance like those used in the bazaar when selling onions, potatoes, or other things. These were steel beams usually two feet long, pivoted in the exact center, and on one end hung a basket for the items and on the other end was a basket with the weights, usually weights of one viss (3.6 pounds), one half viss, one quarter viss, etc.

The Two by Four Beam Balance

Of course! I could make a beam balance. "Betty, I think I can make a beam balance big enough to hold you," I said. "Will it be safe? And will it be accurate enough?" were her questions.

So with her approval I started. I found a strong piece of two by four lumber one yard long. I put a steel pivot in the center. At one end I made a sling to hold Betty. On the other end was a bamboo basket to hold the stones. On our baby scales I weighed out a pile of stones, one by one, marking the various weights, as 10 pounds, 5 pounds, etc., down to little stones of a pound or less. The completed scales was tied by a rope to a beam in the ceiling of our back porch.

The pivot was actually a sharpened steel blade resting on a steel cradle, so that the balance was accurate enough to measure differences of two ounces.

I was very cautious the first time I tried it out. I weighed myself first, and it worked okay. I then was sure that it would hold Betty Lue. A fall would be disastrous for her: she might lose the baby.

Success!!

Our back porch was in open sight, and a crowd of curious villagers assembled to see the amazing spectacle, a woman getting weighed like potatoes or rice in the bazaar. Betty sat in the sling and I put stones into the bamboo basket until her weight and the weight of the stones were equal and the bar balanced. Then I added up the weight of all the stones and announced the total. The villagers cheered. No doubt some Chins thought I was an idiot to make my wife get into a contraption like this, but at least we could record her weight regularly.

It was a hilarious time for the Chins every week as we did this.

As it turned out, Betty did not get overweight. Our food supply was never enough to allow us to overeat, and we had very little sugar, cakes, pies, candy, or fats. What we did eat, and loved, was rice and curry. Ram Hlun made delicious curries with chicken, eggs, beef when available, or vegetables, and so our diet was typical of India and Burma. We did have cooked millet almost every morning for breakfast, and occasionally oatmeal.

Amateur Dentistry

In addition to the fun of weighing my wife, we had another amusing experience that summer. A high Burmese official, the Deputy Commissioner who lives in Falam, came to Haka on some business matter. He was the highest ranking official in the Chin Hills. I do not know what impelled him to come down the hill to visit us, but he did arrive unannounced one morning.

He arrived just in the middle of some dental work! A gold crown on one tooth had fallen off and Betty was in the process of restoring it to my mouth. My dentist uncle had earlier supplied us with some repair cement, and Betty had mixed the cement and was ready to replace the crown. I had a tire pump in my hand and was pumping air on my tooth to dry it. Just then the Deputy Commissioner came!

Chia Ling announced his arrival, and Betty quickly said, "I can't stop in the middle of this, Chia Ling, please let the Commissioner in," and continued her work. So this high Burmese official came in. I was pumping air, and then Betty put on the cement and replaced the gold crown. While it was drying, Betty cordially invited the Commissioner to sit down on what was the only available seat at the moment, an upturned hard case suitcase.

The Deputy Commissioner sat down and respectfully awaited the end of the dentistry. Then we enjoyed a nice conversation in

English and we served some refreshments. We laughed many times over this incident and how the Burmese official was undisturbed by our amateur dentistry.

Chapter 18

A DAUGHTER IS BORN

A s we were expecting our second child in November, there was no thought of having the baby born in the Chin Hills because there were no adequate medical facilities. We decided to go to Mandalay. Two lady missionaries there, Alice Thayer and Phyllis Hamilton, had sent invitations for us to stay at the American Baptist Mission Girls' School to await the birth of our second child. Betty mended two mosquito nets for Chia Ling and Lal Hnin who would accompany us to Mandalay. I made a little camp cot for Dick, and I arranged a palanquin for Betty. This was a litter made by lashing two stout bamboo poles to a deck chair. Ten men handled this: eight men to carry in relays of four, and two men to carry their food and clothing. Betty intended to walk as much as possible, but needed the litter for the uphill climbs.

This would be Betty's first trip down into Burma proper, and we hoped to go also to Rangoon to attend the missionary conference to be held there beginning October 1.

The Trek to Fort White

On Monday, September 8th, about 10 a.m., we left Haka. We made quite a procession. We were 6 travelers, 4 mule drivers, 3 mules, 3 horses, and the 10 coolies to carry the palanquin. Our companions were Lal Hnin, Ram Hlun, and Chia Ling.

Betty walked seven of the twelve miles to Pioneer Camp, and Dick walked a few miles but was carried by Ram Hlun or Chia

Ling most of the way. We continued this way for almost a week, making one stage (about 10 miles) per day. Thus Betty did not get too exhausted, and no doubt the physical exercise taken in moderation was good for her.

On the fourth day we reached Tashon, a village between Falam and the suspension bridge over the Manipur. That night I had a high fever and got delirious. I was not sure, but perhaps it was a touch of malaria. I was too weak to walk the next day the long uphill to Lumbang, so I rode one of the horses and the animal's loads were distributed among the hikers.

On the next day, after a night's rest at Lumbang, I felt better and Betty felt strong enough to walk once we had reached the level ground about six miles from the next dak bungalow, Pine Tree Camp. The ten men who had carried Betty up and down the steep mountains were no longer needed. We paid them well for their careful handling of the litter and they returned to Haka.

Betty walked the remaining six miles to Pine Tree Camp where we rested on Sunday. Christians from a nearby village gave us two chickens, two dozen eggs, and some potatoes. We had a little church service with those Christians.

From Pine Tree Camp Betty walked all the way to Bamboo Camp and then on to Fort White, reaching it on our ninth day of travel. Frank Nelson knew of our itinerary and was at Fort White to meet us. Betty had done well on the trek so far, covering 81 miles, most of it on foot.

Fort White to Mandalay

We all had a fine time at the Fort White dak bungalow chatting after our absence of over seven months. On the next day Franklin drove Betty, Dick, Lal Hnin, Ram Hlun, Chia Ling, and me down to the plains where we put up in the local Baptist church which at that time had a floor, a roof, and only two walls. Actually, Frank asked me to drive the jeep which I did at 5 miles an hour the whole way because of the roughness of the road. I was almost fanatically careful not to expose Betty to undue bumping and jarring.

If the road had been good, Frank would have taken us down to the town of Kalewa on the Chindwin River, another 38 miles. But it was the monsoon season, the rivers were flooded, and there was a bridge out on the Kalewa road. Thus, from this point onward, the back road to Mandalay was actually water.

Burmese Country Boat

On Thursday the 18th, Frank Nelson and Ram Hlun turned back to the hills, and my party now consisted of Betty Lue, Richard, Lal Hnin our language teacher, and Chia Ling as our cook. We went to the Myittha River flowing nearby and which was in flood, and engaged a country boat to take us down the river to Kalewa. This is a large dug-out canoe, perhaps four or four and a half feet wide and twenty to twenty-five feet long, and handled by two or three boatmen. A bamboo mat awning was over the central part, where also hung a smelly pot of *ngapi* (fish paste), which to us is stinky but is a staple to the Burmans.

Betty Lue, who does not swim, looked at the swollen river and at this frail craft and wondered if it would be safe. We had no life preservers, and I too was concerned for safety. "Betty, we will just have to trust in God and these boatmen to get us through," I said.

On the Flooded River

We embarked and the men shoved off, using poles to guide the boat through white water spots. We came to one rapids that the men thought too dangerous, so they pulled to shore; we got out and walked several hundred yards to quieter water, where the boatmen pulled up for us. This happened twice—walking around rapids. The lower part of the river was quieter, and we arrived safely in Kalewa, travel worn and wet, and with some sodden luggage.

Five Days on Tugs

Next came three days aboard a tug on the Chindwin, with rice barges lashed on the side. Where the Chindwin joins the Irrawaddy River, at the town called Myingyan, we changed to another tug for two days upstream on the Irrawaddy. We were deck passengers sleeping on the deck like the multitude of Burmese passengers. Thus, on the 16th day of travel, we reached Mandalay safely on Tuesday,

September 23. We heaved sighs of relief that Dick, ever active at the age of two and a half years, had not fallen off the boats.

The missionary residence at the old A.B.M, Girls' School was a delightful haven after the rigors of living on deck and eating very simple food, and here we rested. Alice Thayer and Phyllis Hamilton welcomed us with open arms and we prepared to live with them until the birth of our child.

Awaiting the Arrival of Ruth

The A.B.M. Girls' School was now in the post-war days a school for both boys and girls. There were about 400 children from age 6 to 12. We enjoyed seeing the children and the daily chapel service. Language study engaged us both, and I spent time at the bazaars buying provisions and all sorts of things for restoring our compound and house in Haka.

We did have time to make a quick trip to Rangoon for the missionary conference. This was Betty and Dick's first time down-country to the big city, and we enjoyed the company of many like-minded persons engaged in mission work of all kinds—medical, evangelistic, agricultural, and educational. The American Baptist Mission (ABM) was the largest mission in Burma, beginning in 1813. Back in Mandalay after this trip by train, we continued with language study. We had almost a month yet of waiting and study.

In the Chin Hills we were surrounded by a 100% Chin-speaking population; we almost never heard Burmese spoken. We tried to learn some Burmese some years later, but it was more or less a failure. We never learned the Burmese language and that was a detriment to us in later years.

It was for the purpose of having good medical care for Betty that we came downcountry. We checked early with the Mandalay General Hospital, of course, and met the doctor, an Indian. The pre-war hospital had been destroyed by bombings and now the hospital was in what formerly was the Diocesan Girls' School. That is why our daughter was born in a school.

The Birth of Ruth Kristin Johnson

I took Betty to the hospital about 4:30 on the afternoon of November 17. Dr. Nundy, the Indian Civil Surgeon, did not put in an appearance, so Betty asked about him. "Oh," said the nurses, "Dr. Nundy is around and will come if needed, but actually Daw Saw Kyun, head of the midwifery section, will be in charge." This surprised us, because, as Betty pointed out to the nurses, we had come 16 days journey to have a capable doctor at the delivery.

The delivery room was a large empty room with a table covered with a red rubber sheet. The nurse asked Betty to get up on this, but Betty needed a step. "Oh," said the nurse, "here's a box for you," and she shoved over a wooden box for a step-up. Although the furnishings were crude, the nurses were really nice, even knowing English, and Daw Saw Kyun did show up to take charge.

Our daughter Ruth Kristin was born at 8:10 p.m. that day, a beautiful child of 6 pounds 12 ounces, with blue eyes and blonde hair. This child, with her golden hair and blue eyes, was to become a source of never ending wonderment to Chin villagers who knew only black eyes and jet black hair. When Ruth was 9 days old, we took her home to our room at Alice Thayer's home, and celebrated our American Thanksgiving Day.

And we gave thanks to God for the gift of this precious child.

Chapter 19

RUTH'S LONG TRIP HOME

～～～

A Steamboat on the Irrawaddy and Chindwin

We wanted to get home to Haka by Christmas, if possible. Thankfully, we learned of a boat going all the way up the Chindwin to Homalin, which is beyond Kalewa. I tried to get a cabin passage on the *Serang* but was too late; all cabins were filled, I was told. So I bought deck passage tickets for my group.

As I was paying the money, a well-dressed Burman came up and we started talking. "I heard you talking," he said, "and you have two children?"

"Yes," I said, "and one is our newborn daughter, and we are going to Kalewa."

As we talked more, he learned of our final destination, and told us that he was a judge and was going to Homalin to take up his duties there in the court. He thought a bit.

"Actually, my cabin will be empty for two days," he said. "I prefer to take my family by car over to the Chindwin, to Monywa, and catch the boat there. I will be glad if you can use the cabin for the first two days."

I eagerly accepted the kindly official's offer, for the journey would be for six days on the boat.

The *Serang* was going the whole way, so we had no problem of trans-shipping , a great boon. With Lal Hnin and Chia Ling's help, I got all our baggage and freight aboard. With all the food, glass, cement, building materials, medicines, paint, 50 sheets of corrugated iron roofing tins and flat tins, and a barrel of gasoline, it was almost 3 tons of needed supplies. The building supplies were most important, for with them on hand we could repair the East Bungalow and move into our permanent home.

Ruth Begins Her Travels

We boarded the *Serang* on the evening of December 2 and the boat took off at dawn. Thus Ruth Kristin began her long trip home when 16 days old. It was nice to have the use of the judge's cabin for the first two days, and Betty was able to wash the baby's diapers in moderately clean water.

Approaching Monywa on Thursday, we moved into one of the two rice barges towed alongside. The captain kindly arranged a place for us in the bow of one of the barges, under a steel overhang. I laid down our corrugated and flat tins to make a clean floor. On these we put our three camp cots and the new little wicker basket for Ruth, with the pretty quilted pad Betty had made. Chia Ling cooked our food in the ship's galley, and we ate picnic style on the floor of the barge.

The Cave on the Barge

Around our little living area we piled boxes, bales, and our drum of gasoline, making almost a cave in which to live for four days. Ruth slept well, and Dick had some toys to play with in our "cave." It was surprisingly comfortable, considering that there was no toilet, no water, no table, no storage space, and with such a low roof that we always had to walk stooped over. Toilet facilities were nothing but a crude backhouse or latrine hung over the stern of the barge. It was a primitive way for a family with a newborn child to travel, but it was the only way home, and we made it a fun voyage. Even the fact that a barrel of gasoline provided one side of our little cave did not deter the enjoyment of our barge ride on the Chindwin with a healthy son and a lovely new daughter.

Kalewa to Tiddim

Kalewa is a Burmese town at the junction where the Myittha River coming down from the Chin Hills flows into the Chindwin. There were no Chins living there and no Christian community. We had finished six days on the river, and now we were again on roads—for a very short ride. I hired two trucks to carry our goods to the little hamlet of Kyigone, 18 miles on the road to Kalemyo. That was as far as the trucks could go, due to a destroyed bridge. We spent an overnight in a cowshed by the riverbank. The cows were gone, but there was plenty of manure. We cleaned it out as best we could and piled straw on the ground. The children were quick to fall asleep, and we sat around a little fire with Lal Hnin and Chia Ling and contemplated the pleasures and problems of travel.

The next day we hired three country boats to take us and all the freight the remaining ten miles to Kalemyo. There we met Frank Nelson who had come down to meet us, being a bit worried about our welfare. At this point we gave money to Lal Hnin and Chia Ling to hire oxen or mules and coolies to transport as much of our freight as possible to Lumbang. Frank then took Betty, the children, and me in his jeep to Tiddim.

We spent a week in Tiddim with the Nelsons. Dick now could speak English well and got along famously with Lois and Karen. Frank and I occupied ourselves with repairing the Dodge truck, the 15 cwt. we had purchased in Rangoon in 1946, installing a new crankshaft in the engine. We also made several jeep trips to the plains, hauling up Church World Service relief clothing and medicines as free gifts to the Chins from American Christians. This was part of the freight I had brought up by river boat.

While Frank and I were away on these trips to haul medicines and clothing for the people, Betty Lue and Phileda had plenty of time to talk together of things of particular interest to women: children, health matters, cooking, and housekeeping. They also helped to sort out and distribute these relief items to the people.

To Haka for Christmas

On December 19 Franklin drove us by jeep to Lumbang. There I found Lal Hnin, Chia Ling, and also Ram Hlun who had come from

Haka. Altogether there were no less than 23 men and 12 horses on hand to move us on to Haka. By now the Haka people knew that their missionaries were intending to stay and work. Their former doubts were gone and they were willing to help us.

It took us the normal five days to go the fifty miles to Haka. Ruth Kristin was the center of attention for everyone we met along the roadside.

So, after our long absence, we reached home safely on December 22, just in time to take part in the happy Christmas services and the big feast enjoyed that year by about 300 people on the mission compound. A water buffalo and a large pig were killed for the feast, and everyone rejoiced in the season of Christ's birth. And we rejoiced in the birth of our healthy and beautiful baby girl, and showed her off to all.

Betty Lue and two children on a village path. In the rainy season, the roads and paths are muddy and slippery.

Chapter 20

THE EAST BUNGALOW
OUR NEW HOME

The Government's Promise

The British official in Haka when we first arrived, Mr. Hay-Neave, made us a promise that the larger bungalow, the one called the East Bungalow, constructed by Dr. Hjalmar East in 1907, could be returned to mission use in early 1948. On the basis of this promise the mission made a grant of 8,000 rupees for restoration, and I purchased building supplies in Mandalay and took them upcountry on the boat in December, when we brought Ruth home.

Then there was a period of indecision by the government. My pleas went unanswered until Betty, in March when I was away on tour, visited the Deputy Commissioner and explained our predicament, that the large house was the one used by East, Cope, and Strait and was the logical one for us, also that the government was using our house without permission and without paying any rent, and that now we were a family of four, planning to stay a long time. Her plea was successful and the D.C. kindly granted us our wish. We fixed April 8 as the day of moving and exchanging houses. The East Bungalow had been used by the government as a hospital and medical clinic for over five years, and we knew that it needed much restoration for our use.

The Johnsons Move to the East Bungalow

Fortunately, the hospital did not use the upstairs of the East house, which was really nothing but an empty attic. It was much cleaner than the downstairs. Even so, for over a week before we moved, we cleaned and scrubbed the whole upstairs of the house and had a Chinese carpenter make windows for it. We planned to live in this large attic until we cleaned the downstairs.

On April 8, 1948, we made a complete trade with the government hospital. We moved our family and belongings up into the second floor attic, and the hospital moved patients, furniture, medicine, and everything into our vacated house. I had already begun to construct a cookhouse to replace the one destroyed during the war. But it was not ready, so for weeks after our move we cooked outdoors on open fires.

A Brief Description of the House

The easiest way to think about the East Bungalow is to think of a Midwestern farm house, a two-story wooden house about 40 feet square, that is, about 1,600 square feet.

Quite large. The basement was like a pit dug into the ground. There were no wooden posts; the house rested on a stone perimeter and two stone pillars. Think of the main floor as divided into two halves. On the east side were three bedrooms. On the west side were living room, dining room, and one small storeroom and a pantry. A small bathroom 9 ft. by 9 ft. was added on one end. A nice porch about 7 feet wide and 40 ft. long, the breadth of the house, was on the front, on the north side and consequently usually cold and windy. The walls were of plaster—bless you, Dr. East! Plaster walls keep out wind and cold. The remains of the cookhouse were outside, on the back of the house, a separate building, in oriental fashion.

The roof of the house was of corrugated iron sheets and painted red. The outside walls were of pine clapboard and painted white. The roof and the house had been riddled by bullets and there was much need for repairs. There were three fireplaces, none very efficient, and so the house was cold in winter. We converted one corner bedroom into an office and medicine dispensary. The whole house needed a lot of loving attention.

The Clean-Up

When we moved in, the downstairs was wretchedly dirty and smelled horribly of human dung, urine, and medicines. We could never allow Dick and Ruth to do more than to go through it en route to or from our upstairs quarters. The first job was to clean, scrub, and disinfect the house, and we began shoveling out dirt, especially from the bathroom. I mean that literally, using shovels to clear out dirt and trash.

The next step was to move our family out of the house, seal the windows and doors as tightly as possible, and burn formaldehyde candles to kill vermin and, we hoped, the germs of infectious diseases. For most of a day we thus disinfected the house.

Then we devoted a week to scrubbing, washing with soap and hot water, and removing layers and layers of old wallpaper from the plaster walls. We hired an Indian woman and a Chin man to help in this operation. By the time all the scrubbing was done, we began to feel a lot better about the house.

Unlike the missionaries in the early 1900s who could not find a Chin carpenter, now several men were capable of doing repairs, and we hired them to rebuild the rotting front porch and patch bullet holes. We painted the house inside and out, and by the end of May our house, now known as the Johnson Bungalow, had been transformed. We were immensely pleased with our house. Perhaps it was too large, but then, it was big enough to take in groups of twenty or thirty for meetings or large meals. It was a nice place for our children and their friends to play on rainy days.

The Cookhouse of Rammed Earth

The lack of a cookhouse behind our house inspired me to try something new, never before done in the Chin Hills, that is, to make our cookhouse of rammed earth, not wood.

If successful, I believed, a rammed earth building could last indefinitely providing rain was kept off. I had some bulletins from the United States describing the process.

So we found a type of clay soil nearby which, when pounded hard, compacted almost like cement. With heavy planks to make the forms, I hired a crew of four men and began. With heavy pounders we pounded the earth between the planks until it rang. Foot by foot we built upward to a height of seven feet, leaving openings for two doors and two windows. These walls were 15 inches thick.

We completed the cookhouse with a conventional wood and corrugated iron sheet roof and a hard-pounded floor. I built a brick oven like the one made earlier for the Carson bungalow, but we still used iron bars over a fire for cooking until we were able to bring out a proper cook stove for our second term.

I hoped that the successful use of rammed earth for the cook house might inspire some Chins to build that way also. To my knowledge, only one man tried it and gave it up. "Too much work, it's too hard to do," he told me. So that attempt to introduce a new technique in building turned out as a failure.

However, using rammed earth, I did construct a hostel for men coming to our Bible School, and later I made a garage and a small cubicle building for developing films.

With the move into the large bungalow, cleaned and repaired, and with the addition of the cookhouse, we could look around the American Baptist Mission compound and be satisfied with what had been done. We had been in Haka for a full year, except for the months downcountry for Ruth's birth, and we were getting fairly fluent in the language. Richard was almost three years old and had good friends in Van Awi, our cook's son, and Tawk Ling, a relative of Chia Ling. Ruth was still a babe but very good and in sound health.

The A.B.M. Compound

The mission compound showed the war's devastation. The Emily Tyzzer Memorial Hospital was in ruins; only the stone steps remained. The schoolhouse/church was half-stripped of siding and the foundation was rotting. The former servants' quarters behind our house, a stone building, was usable and we were making repairs. Two other outbuildings were in bad shape and needed repairs. The outlook for repairs to all these buildings was dim, for lack of money. However, we were thankful for the mission grant of 8,000 rupees, about $2,500, which helped us make a good start on restoration of the East bungalow, now our home.

Chapter 21

BOB'S RICE-POWERED WASHING MACHINE

~~~~~

Living as we did in a remote corner of a country struggling to recover from a devastating war, it was necessary for me to make some "Rube Goldberg" inventions. We needed certain things that were just not available from stores. My first attempt was to build a washing machine.

Laundry in Haka

While we were with the Nelsons in Tiddim, we took advantage of Frank's Jeep-Powered Washing Machine and did our weekly laundry up at their home. But when we got to Haka, the only implement to help us was a washboard. I helped Betty wash the clothes, which was a big job, and saw for myself what a tedious job it was to rub the clothes up and down the corrugated board. No matter that washboards have probably existed for centuries, and people have used these without complaint, it was not for us.

"Betty," I said, "we have washed clothes this way for long enough. Maybe we need to hire someone to do this, preferably an Indian woman if we can find one, to wash the clothes for us."

"Having a dobhie (Indian washerwoman) is out of the question," she answered. "They wear out the clothes too fast. They beat the clothes on a rock! We can't do that."

"Maybe I could make something that will work," I said.

Betty looked doubtful. "Well, I rather think you can't make one," she said. "You have no jeep, there is no electricity and no electric motor, and no parts for a washing machine."

The Machine

I discovered that one bazaar man had a 30 gallon steel barrel in his shop, an open ended barrel he used for grain storage. I bought it. That barrel, three pieces of pine board, and a rope made my washing machine.

I set the barrel on a platform to bring the barrel rim up to waist high. I put a piece of 1" by 6" pine board upright in the barrel—a piece 4 feet long. Another piece of 1 by 6 lumber 15 inches long was screwed at right angles to the bottom of the upright board. A smaller piece of wood, about 1" x 3" long, was tapered at one end for a hand-hold and fastened horizontally to the long board to serve as a handle. A rope suspended the long board to a beam in the woodshed. The action was the same as the dasher in a Maytag open tub washer.

The machine was hugely successful. We put gallons of hot water into the barrel, added clothes and cut-up bar soap, and pushed to and fro on the handle, which turned the bottom board. which sloshed the water back and forth just fine.

On this machine we washed for eighteen years without a single breakdown, and with two improvements. When the steel barrel rusted out after some years, we replaced it with an aluminum barrel, actually half of a 55 gallon aluminum barrel used to carry gasoline to China by airplane during World War II. The second improvement: Betty's sister sent us a hand wringer for our washer. This was better than wringing clothes by hand. Since we used hand effort to operate the washer and wringer, we called it a rice-powered washing machine.

A Stove and Stove Pipe

Haka is at 6,000 feet elevation and thus is cold in winter, water even freezing in December and January. When we moved to the large house, a heating stove was needed. There were none on sale in Burma, as far as we could find. So I determined to make one.

Again, a 55 gallon steel barrel came into use. I made that into an outer shell to hold a small steel drum which was the actual firebox. Of course I had to cut out and hinge doors in both barrels to put in wood and take out ashes. The purpose of "double walls" was to keep the outer shell from getting red hot. And this stove needed stovepipes.

Stovepipes

Commercial stovepipes sold in America come with crimped edges so two edges can interlock tightly and smoke cannot escape. But I had to start with flat sheets of tin. With pliers I was able to bend the edges. But how to curve the flat sheets into round pipe and then clinch the edges?

Anticipating this problem, I had brought up from Mandalay a 4 ft. long piece of railroad track. By putting this heavy steel rail inside the pipe, I could hammer the edges together to crimp them tightly. My stovepipe worked well and did not leak smoke. Of course, making the 90 degree angle corner piece was more difficult, but we managed to install this crude drum-like stove into our corner bedroom, and that room became our winter living room because it could be warmed.

After our first furlough, we brought out a nice Heatrola heating stove to replace the crude home-made one.

Richard's Tricycle

One day Dick came to me with an urgent request. "Daddy, can you make me a bicycle?" "No, son, you are too young for a bicycle, and anyway, I have no parts to make one for you," I replied.

But as I thought about it, maybe I could make a tricycle for him. I figured it out in my head what to do and told him, "Dick, I think I could make one with three wheels, but it could only go downhill," Our son seemed satisfied and I got to work.

The two back wheels came from the baby buggy we had for Richard as a baby and which we had brought out in our freight. The front wheel was another wheel from the baby buggy. This wheel was held in a wooden yoke which was fastened to the body of the cycle with a steel door hinge. It had a seat and handlebars.

This ungainly tricycle was an instant hit in the village. It could only go downhill, but that was okay, for the mission compound had a nice slope downward from our house to the church, and Dick rode downhill with great glee. Boys followed him and got their turns to ride. It was an unqualified success and cost nothing to make, just using items we already had on hand.

Running Water in the Bathroom

When we moved into our home, it had no electricity, no heating (except some fireplaces), no plumbing, and no running water. We thought it would be nice to have some running water for a washbowl in the bathroom.

I had purchased a ceramic washbowl in Mandalay, and this I installed on a wooden cabinet against the wall facing the cookhouse, which was the nearest source of water. I had an open-topped small barrel holding perhaps 6 gallons. This I fastened to the outside of the bathroom, a bit higher than the washbowl inside. I then drilled a hole in the wall so a pipe could go from the outer barrel to a faucet in the washbowl. It was our gardener Ram Thio's job to keep this outer barrel filled with water.

Our "running water system" did work, although there was almost no water pressure. It was nice to enjoy running water, even though it was a limited supply.

By the way, the bathroom was really a 9 by 9 ft. shed attached to the rear of the house. It had a door to the corner bedroom, the room which was our winter living room, and another door to the outside. Water from the washbowl fell through a pipe straight downward to the ground. Water from our oval tin bathtub, however, was dumped out the door to the outside and ran away in a ditch. For Haka, what we had was considered quite modern plumbing!

Chapter 22

START OF THE HAKA BIBLE SCHOOL, 1948

~~~~~~

Strait's School and Successors

D r. Chester Strait and his wife Florence ran a school for training pastors for four years in Haka, 1927 to 1931, and graduated thirteen men. These men were the pioneer pastors and leaders of the growing churches. The next fifteen years saw a tremendous increase in the number of Christians and organized churches. The Chin Christians wanted such schools again at both Tiddim and Haka to help fill the need for trained pastors and preachers.

Franklin and Phileda Nelson were able to get their Bible School started in 1947 at Tiddim, but for us who needed time to learn the language an extra year was needed. In consultation with the Haka area preachers we agreed to start our school in Haka in June, 1948, keeping to a limit of 30 students, using Haka Chin as our medium of instruction and running for about 5 months, June through October, for 3 years.

The Physical Equipment

I doubt if many schools began with less in the way of equipment and possessions than did the Haka Bible Training School in 1948. For a hostel we had only a dilapidated stone building 18 by 36 feet in size, divided in two by a rough wooden wall. One room, formerly used by an Indian sweeper, had a leaky thatch roof. The other room, unused, had a broken down and useless thatch roof. The floor in both rooms was earth, and everything was incredibly dirty.

As for equipment, we had a quart of ink, a few notebooks, some pots and pans for cooking, and one blackboard made of wooden boards painted black. There was no library, no furniture, no lanterns, no kerosene, and very little food for the men. During the course of the year, we were able to buy some locally made tables and benches, some lanterns and candles, and were given some used blankets. Each year we were able to secure more equipment to make life more tolerable and study easier.

Rice Supply

We began to purchase rice in early March. For lack of a better place to store it, we put it on the porch floor of our home. Later, when we moved to the large house, we transferred a ton of rice to the upstairs attic and eventually made a circular mat wall about 3 feet high and 8 feet in diameter to hold all our supply. Our attic floor was weak in places, so we chose a spot on top of a downstairs wall lest we collapse the floor.

Americans usually buy rice in 1-pound or perhaps in 5-pound bags. Most cannot conceive of how much rice a Chin man will eat per day. We gave a ration of 2 "pounds" of rice per day. Actually, what the Chins call a "pound" is really the amount of rice held by a condensed milk can, which comes to about 9 ounces. Thus, we figured on a ration of 35 pounds of rice per man per month. When cooked, a can measure of rice becomes a huge plateful. Over this is poured the "ti hang" or curry, which is the soup made of spices, potatoes, vegetables, and sometimes eggs or meat.

We told the students that the school would go to the end of October or until the rice gave out. As we eventually had 41 men, the rice was used up more quickly, we had no money to buy more, and we had to end the school on September 24.

Preparing the Hostel

On May 15 the men began to arrive. We put them to work for two weeks fixing the hostel. The broken-down stone shed was cleaned out, the wooden partition removed, the thatched roof repaired, and over the roofless portion we tried an experiment. As we had no roofing tins and none could be bought, I tried a temporary expedient which indeed lasted through the first year. I had some heavy cardboard called straw-board and a large quantity of tar. Could we make shingles by dipping the cardboard in melted tar? It was worth a try and we had no alternative. We made a wooden roof and then dipped the cardboard in melted tar to make shingles and nailed them in place. It worked!

In this, the main hostel of the Bible School, 26 men slept, 13 on each side on sleeping platforms running the length of the building. We could not give them beds; they had only wooden platforms elevated from the dirt floor. Each man thus had a space about 6 feet long and 3 feet wide on which to spread his bedroll at night. They were cramped for space but took it with good grace.

Thirteen other men were housed in the stone building just behind our bungalow, which Dr. Strait had used as a chicken house. Here we could make no sleeping platform for lack of boards, so the men had to sleep on mats spread on the ground.

The men also constructed latrines and a cookhouse for the main hostel and prepared a garden for which Betty had already sown seeds earlier.

Classes began on June 1. In thankfulness for their help in preparing the quarters and getting the school off to a good start, Betty and I killed a small cow which cost 70 rupees (about $17) for a feast of celebration and thankfulness to the Lord.

Our Students

Whereas in Tiddim the Nelsons planned to teach in the English language and therefore accepted only 4th Standard passes, we knew that in Haka the educational standards were too low and that we would have to teach in Haka Chin. This made it possible for us to accept students with lower education. We decided to admit a number of pastors, preachers, and helpers who were doing good work and needed the training we could give, even though some had no formal education at all, so long as they knew how to read and write. In the case of persons who were not already employed in Christian work, usually younger men, we required at least 3rd Standard pass.

Our students ranged in formal education from zero to 4 years in school. Twelve came from the Falam area and used languages other than Haka Chin, which they all learned. However, in tests they often reverted to their native dialects, adding to the problems that Betty and I had in grading papers. In age they ranged from the low 20s to the 40s. In experience they ranged from almost new converts to pastors who had worked for ten years or more in the church. Almost all were deficient in arithmetic. There were even a few to whom we had to teach addition, subtraction, multiplication, and division. Some were slow writers and poor spellers, and it was difficult for these to keep up with the class.

Why should arithmetic be taught in a Bible school? We knew that these men had to keep track of money and ought to know how to keep the record of income and expenditures and how to give receipts. I also wanted them to know how to figure the area of buildings and calculate the amount of lumber and roofing tins needed.

Classes

The school day began at 8:00 with a fifteen minute chapel service. From 8:15 to 11 they had four classes: (1) Health and Music on alternate days, (2) Epistles of Paul, (3) Practice Preaching, and (4) Arithmetic and Bible Geography, on alternate days. Lunch hour was from 11 a.m. to 1 p.m., followed by one hour of Life of Christ and one study hour, supervised by either Betty or me.

After 3 o'clock the men were free, although on two afternoons a week Betty Lue added a class on how to change the staff notation of music to the tonic solfa, a subject of great interest to the more musical students. The extra music classes were voluntary.

We had four teachers. Betty taught health and music, Lal Hnin taught arithmetic and Bible geography, and I did all the others with help from Pastor Sang Ling who acted as interpreter for some of my classes.

At first we hoped that Rev. Sang Ling could teach the course on the Epistles of Paul, but he did not have the library resources to enable him to do so, so I taught the class mostly in English with Sang Ling interpreting and helping me. All other classes were taught in Chin. Thus Betty and I were forced to use Chin constantly. Without doubt it was a good thing for us, for we learned the language thoroughly, including the religious vocabulary.

Soccer, Free Time, and Dinner

After classes were over for the day, the students generally went out to play soccer on the rocky and uneven field just above their hostel. I usually joined them for the exercise and for the fun of fellowship with these future pastors. Even when it rained, we kept at it and always had a lot of fun.

Then toward sundown the men ate their second and last meal of the day. Occasionally they would have a chicken or some pork or beef given by Christians to add to their curry, but on the whole their meals were rather poor in quality, perhaps less than they would have had at home. Betty had started a garden for them, but to be honest, they were not diligent in keeping up the garden or even going to pick what was ready. Instead, they hoped we would buy beans, onions, cabbages, etc. from traveling sellers. We sometimes did this but were upset when the men seemed too lazy. Of course, we were running into a culture problem, for in the villages it is the women who tend the gardens. Men work the fields (rice, corn, beans, sweet potatoes, millet), but women care for the little gardens near the house.

I should mention here that it is customary for Chin Christians to bring gifts of produce into the church on Sunday morning as part of their offerings to the Lord. In Haka, corn, beans, pumpkins, cucumbers, rice, potatoes, mangoes, even chickens and eggs, were piled in front of the altar every Sunday, especially during the rainy season. These gifts were shared with Bible School students, pastors, missionaries, prisoners in jail, and with the poor of the village. From this source also the Bible School students received food.

The Cook, Ku King

One young man named Ku King came up with students from the Zotung area in the south of the Haka field. He had never been in school and was not chosen by his area to attend the Bible School, but he came anyway, just hoping that we would enroll him. He was zealous for the Lord and declared that he would do anything if we would let him in. We could not formally enroll him, but we decided that he could work as cook for the school and attend classes as an auditor—that is, not for credit and not for graduation.

We liked Ku King. He was a big, good-natured, earnest fellow and hard working. He turned out to be a good cook. Not only that, to us his name sounded so much like the English word "cooking" that it seemed a natural job for him! He stayed all three years, was never counted as a graduate, but afterwards he went down to his home area and became a very effective evangelist. Betty and I felt that in some ways he was more successful than some of the graduates, which perhaps proves that God can use persons whom we in our human "wisdom" pass over.

The Lack of Books

The two most important religious books to the Chins are the songbook and the Bible, usually in that order. Former missionaries had worked hard to give more literature, but the ravages of time and war had just about wiped out the supply of books, even for students in the Bible School. Among our students there were 11 men who had no copy of the New Testament and there were 10 others who had to borrow copies from their friends. Books such as Strait's Sunday School lessons could not be located. How could we effectively teach the Bible to those who didn't have the Scriptures or any other book? At first, those who had Bibles had to share their books with the others. As for helps, we wrote on the blackboard every word to be copied in notebooks.

Although we had to start our Bible School without even New Testaments for all our students, we knew that there were Haka New Testaments down in Rangoon. The British and Foreign Bible Society edition was completed and ready to come up to the Hills.

Red-Letter Day—Arrival of New Testaments

I had written to Harold Willans, the secretary of the British and Foreign Bible Society, early in the year asking him to try to get at least 25 copies of the New Testament to us as soon as possible. Rev. Willans asked Major Kap Zong of the First Chin Rifles to have a soldier coming on leave bring them up. We had no idea when he would arrive.

In June we heard that a large shipment of Bibles had reached Pamunchaung, 80 miles from Haka, at the base of the Chin Hills. They were left in the custody of the chief clerk in charge of government supplies. As soon as I heard of their arrival, I sent Boi Nol, the mule driver who usually went with me on tours, with his two mules and another driver with two horses to fetch the books.

In the meantime, while they were gone, a soldier arrived in Haka Khuathar, a mile from the main village, with the package of 25 New Testaments. The news came late one night. Early the next morning I sent two of the Bible School young men to Khuathar to get the parcel.

The school was in session and my wife was teaching music when the New Testaments came. I walked down to the church with the package on my shoulder, and at the appropriate moment as the music ended I began to beat the church bell in a paean of gladness. I beat the bell for one or two minutes so all Haka village would know and then went inside to the waiting men. They were all smiles. This was the day for which we had been waiting and praying, and at last, on June 21, the books were here. The men rose and sang the Doxology—"Praise God from Whom All Blessings Flow ."

Some tears of joy were visible as we gave 21 Bibles to the men who had none and to those who had borrowed theirs. The four remaining copies we allotted to one of our preachers, Pa Hrek, to send down to the Matu area where he labored, far to the south, 15 days journey on foot.

What a happy day that was! It was also our seventh wedding anniversary that day, so Betty and I bought another cow and had a feast for our students. Perhaps that was the origin of the custom that we followed all the rest of the time we were in Burma—ever after that we always killed a cow or a water buffalo for our wedding anniversary on June 21 and distributed the meat to the villagers and to the schoolboys on the mission compound.

About a week after the arrival of the first package, Boi Nol and his companion arrived with loads of books and these were soon followed by other loads.

Distribution of the New Testaments

Of the 1,500 copies coming to the Hills in the first shipment, we distributed 500 to the Falam subdivision and 1,000 to the Haka area on a strict rationing system to ensure that distant villages were not forgotten. The complete New Testament in Haka Chin sold for three and a half rupees, about one dollar, each. This low price was made possible by the subsidies paid by the British and Foreign Bible Society. Thus, almost any Chin who wanted a copy was able to purchase one.

How badly were they needed? As an example, in the Zokhua area which I had toured in March I discovered that in Lamtuk village there were 3 New Testaments for 139 Christians, in Hrawn Vun 11 Christians had neither Bible nor songbook, in Cinkhua 1 Bible for 137 believers, and in Hmaikha one third of a New Testament for 113 Christians.

To avoid repetition I often use "Bible" and "New Testament" interchangeably. Although this is technically inaccurate, it makes better reading this way. Actually, the complete Bible of both Old and New Testaments was not published in the Haka Chin language until 1979.

Special Consideration for the Matu Area

Among our students were Sayas That Dun and Pa Hrek, Haka area men who were really missionaries to the Matu people in the south. They now had about 200 believers in the Matu subdivision, and to encourage evangelism there, we allotted 50 copies of the Scriptures for them, praying that the Lord of harvest would continue to open the doors of their hearts to the gospel.

Financing the School

Both the Reference Committee in Rangoon and Dr. Howard in New York had made it clear to me that the mission could give nothing for our Haka Bible School except what was already in my evangelism budget. Whatever we did, we would have to do ourselves with no special financial help from the A.B.M.

The Nelsons had made it through their first year of the Bible School in Tiddim in 1947 on the same basis, and we were determined to run our school on faith also, knowing that this was the key to evangelism and church growth in Chinland.

At the end of the 1948 school year we calculated that it had cost a total of 3,815 rupees, not counting the value of some hundred tins of free rice given by Chins (a "tin" is the common kerosene tin holding 5 U.S.A. gallons, or 4 imperial gallons). Of this amount, Chins donated Rs.1,775, I took Rs.865 from the Haka Evangelistic Account (i.e., from the mission budgeted amount), and Rs.1,175 came from various gifts and specifics from America and from personal contributions from Betty and me.

I think that the mission looked a bit askance on the numerous regional Bible Schools which were springing up just then in Burma. Could not the tribal people attend the fine theological schools at Insein and Rangoon? Why start up so many little schools?

Such thinking did not take into consideration the great cost of sending hill people down to the big city, nor the problem of language, nor the weaning of tribal people away from commitment to return to their isolated villages. Frank Nelson and I could see validity in sending down our top scholars and most promising young people for the big schools, but not the sending of the many who had to carry on the village work. So we were determined to conduct our schools in the Hills. We think the results have proved the validity of what we did, in that our little schools grew into the present Zomi Theological College located at Falam.

Close of the School

Our school closed on September 24, one week earlier than we had anticipated. We had run out of rice and out of money! We celebrated the successful end of the school year with another feast of roast beef, and then, after the men had all left, Betty and I with the two children took a day off and had a picnic. After that we turned with a will to finish the repair and painting of our house which we had been unable to do for press of work during the busy days of Bible School.

.

Chapter 23

MY HARLEY DAVIDSON

First Sight

I first saw the Beast when Frank Nelson, Hau Go, and I got to Rangoon in October, 1946, for a mission conference. Later I came to call it The Beast, but when I first saw this Harley Davidson motorcycle, dusty, dirty, and a muddy olive-drab color, I saw a powerful vehicle that would magically transport me up and down the hills of Burma.

Bill Hackett, one of the Burma missionaries, bought this surplus U.S. Army motorcycle in India and carried it into Burma on his truck. Now it could be given to someone willing to use it effectively in Christian work.

Six months earlier I had gone through the Naga Hills of India where I learned that missionary Bengt Anderson was using a motorcycle. So in my mind's eye I could visualize myself astride this powerful motorcycle whizzing from village to village bearing the gospel to the Chins. Already I had learned the slowness of foot travel — perhaps ten to fifteen miles a day at great cost of sweat and weariness.

A Mission Gift

So I asked for the motorcycle. The Executive Committee of the mission asked me to explain my need.

"Well," I said, "some of you know what the Chin Hills are like: steep mountain ranges, villages widely scattered, often ten miles apart, narrow mule paths or even just foot paths, and only one jeepable road, and that road links only about 8 villages. But there are many, many villages which can be reached by motorcycle."

"What about repairs and oil and especially gasoline up there?" they asked.

"I'm handy with tools," I said, "and as for gasoline, we can always in a pinch have it carried in by mules. Each mule can carry two five-gallon army gas cans."

No one asked for the Harley, so it was given to me.

Now, to get our stuff moved up to the Chin Hills, Frank and I bought an old U.S. Army "weapons carrier" truck. Much bigger than a jeep, it was rated as a three-fourths ton truck but could carry a ton easily. We decided to carry the motorcycle and all other provisions and building materials we needed up country on this weapons carrier.

But before I could try out my new motorcycle, I came down with my first case of malaria and was in bed for five days. I was very weak. I could not get up even enough strength to test my motorcycle. However, Bill Hackett said it was fine and I took his word.

Trip Back from Rangoon

Frank and Hau Go loaded the truck without much help from me and we took off for Mandalay on a paved one-lane road. There were no problems the first two days. Then we went on to a town called Ye-U, the end of the paved road. We took off going ever north and west, heading for the Chindwin River town of Kalewa. We were following a dirt road hewn through the jungle by the British when they evacuated Burma in 1942. The road was not too bad, but bridges were out and we had to slog through the deep sand of eight dry riverbeds. In one of these we stalled and broke the main driveshaft. We were broken down, stuck out in the jungle, 46 miles from Kalewa, and about 5 miles from the nearest human habitation.

By this time I had recovered from malaria and was feeling good enough to face this challenge. "Frank," I said, "we're in luck. We won't have to walk out. We've got the motorcycle!"

"We'll reach the river in half a day, by nightfall," Frank said.

124

We unloaded the Harley and prepared to go.

I pumped and pumped the starter, and Frank did the same until we wearied. The motorcycle would not start. It was frustrating to have a machine ready to save us a long hike, but we had to give up and prepare to walk.

It was now too late to start hiking. We camped for the night, very thirsty. The next day Hau Go and I went back five miles to arrange for an ox cart to bring out a barrel of drinking water. We rode back on the ox cart, and then Frank and I started walking. We had to go light, carrying only some food, canteens, the broken driveshaft, and a light blanket each. We camped for the night on the sand of a dry river bed and drank water from a mud puddle. But we made it out to the river safely and eventually reached home. We found a replacement driveshaft from an abandoned truck, and after many vicissitudes we recovered our truck and the motorcycle.

I stored the Harley in the town of Kalemyo at the base of the Chin Hills for almost a year, until again our family came down to the plains for the birth of our first daughter in Mandalay.

Now it was time, at last, to get my motorcycle going. Then it was that I discovered that some thief had stolen the battery.

The Battery Problem

We hunted everywhere in our part of Burma to find a battery that would fit into my American motorcycle—with no luck. There was none to be found.

Some bazaar Indian learned of my dilemma, and offered to help. "I'll build a frame to use a small car battery," he said. In desperation I agreed, and we got the smallest 6-volt car battery made, a heavy thing about 7 inches in each dimension. My new friend welded a 7-inch cube of steel and bolted it to the right side of the motorcycle. I was dubious about this heavy and bulky thing weighing down one side of the cycle. Furthermore, I worried that I could get my right leg and foot caught under this wicked-looking contraption in case of an accident. But I accepted it and now called my Harley by what it had become, the Beast.

Speedy Motorcycle Bogs Down

I put the Beast on a truck and hauled it as far as the end of the truckable road, a village called Lumbang. The road went six miles down to the gorge of the Manipur River. I managed to drive the Beast downhill with no problem. Then I crossed the river on the Manipur River Suspension Bridge, a scary walk pushing the cycle on the swaying suspension bridge.

Now the family had to travel a narrow, twisty road six miles uphill to Falam, then the capital of the Chin Hills district. Betty Lue rode a mule and held our infant Ruth in her arms. Our son also rode a mule, and our pack animals followed making quite a procession.

I cranked up the Harley and, feeling quite good about the fine machine, I shot off in a cloud of dust ahead of my family. All went well with the wind whistling in my face until I reached the first switchback in the narrow road.

The engine of the Beast was beginning to labor under the climb. This machine was made for speed on the level, not for the mountains, I realized. So I came to this first sharp turn. The road was too narrow and too steep uphill to make the turn in one sweep. I had to stop. I turned my motorcycle by pushing it forward, back, then forward again, getting it pointing in the right direction. "Wow," I thought, "this is tough!"

With the motor running again, I started off with the back wheel spinning in the gravel. I went to the next hairpin turn and stalled again. And so it went, with the engine failing because of buildup of heat. I could not go fast enough to cool the engine.

To solve the problem of the sharp uphill turns, I had to hire four coolies to follow me. I was able to proceed for a while on the straightaway, but coming to a hairpin turn I stopped, cooled the engine, and read a magazine to while away the time until the coolies caught up. Then away I would go until the next turn. What a drag the Beast had become! Betty Lue and my mule drivers thought it all was hilariously funny. The "speedy missionary" sat at each turn waiting for the coolies to catch up! I felt exactly like a chump.

So it went. I got to Falam eventually and on to Haka on slightly better level roads, and parked the Beast behind our home with a sigh of relief.

Failed Trip to Sakta

Then another problem struck. The battery went dead and I had no charger. I solved this problem by wiring four flashlight batteries together to get a 6-volt current. This worked, and the Beast came to life. I figured that the regular battery would get charged up as the engine ran.

I told Betty that I would try to run the 20 miles south to the village of Sakta to visit Pastor Za Ling who was ill, and I would return the same day. After all, 40 miles on a motorcycle should not be hard.

I rode the Harley out of town about 4 miles and then the road narrowed so that I found myself riding on the edge of a precipice, just inches from the road's edge, so that my right leg had nothing solid under it if I should tip to the right. When a motorcycle slows down, it tips easily. In a flash I realized that if I tipped to the right there was absolutely nothing to keep me from going over the edge and sliding down the mountainside with the heavy motorcycle on top of me. And being pinned under a hot engine and maybe with battery acid spilling on me? And I was alone, no companion to help in case of accident. What stupidity!

Very shaken I managed to roll past that dangerous spot. The Beast had conquered! "I can never ride that thing safely," I said to myself. "I'm a nut even to think of using it in such mountainous country."

My Harley Davidson, a good machine for the plains, was useless to me, and not only useless but dangerous in the Chin Hills. In those years there were no special mountain motorcycles such as we can buy now. My vision of speeding the Gospel of Jesus was gone; I would go the old fashioned way—walk from village to village.

The end of the matter was that I managed later on to get the motorcycle back to Mandalay. I returned it to the mission, and washed my hands of the whole affair.

Chapter 24

THE FIFTY-YEAR JUBILEE

The Chin Christians realized that 1949 would mark their 50th year of evangelism and Christian witness among their people. So together with the two missionary families they planned a great celebration. This would take place in Haka, where Arthur and Laura Carson established the mission in 1899. They also wanted to hold this festival as close as possible to the day that the Carsons entered Haka village. They decided on Thursday, March 31, to Sunday, April 3.

No Debt Reduction

Franklin and I suggested a special name for this occasion— Jubilee. The name comes from the Old Testament where the Jewish people observed a festival every fifty years. It was for them a time of release from debt. We were amused that some of the Christians eagerly embraced the idea of a release from debt and could hardly wait for the Jubilee to cancel their debts. We had to explain carefully that what happened in Old Testament times did not apply to us in the church age, so they would have to pay their legal debts.

Preparations for the Jubilee

Haka villagers and folk from the surrounding area began to collect food to feed the multitudes—rice, salt, tea, sugar, and kerosene for lights, wooden posts and boards to construct what is called a *basha* in India and a *mandat* in Burma. This is a rough, temporary structure, mainly a roof to keep off the hot sun. It has no walls. The one we built was large enough to afford shade to about 3,000 people seated on the ground, and the roofing was thatch, boards, old roofing tins, and perhaps some leafy boughs. When finished, there was also a large platform, a pulpit, and a large banner behind the platform. Two bamboo poles carried aloft the Burmese flag and a Christian flag.

The Karen Rebellion

Frank and I had sent invitations to down-country missionaries to come to the Chin Hills to join in the festival, and several agreed to come. But just at this time fierce fighting broke out in Burma between certain rebellious Karen people and the Burma government. Karens are one of the many ethnic groups inhabiting Burma, and they, the Karens, are numerous, making up about 9% of the population. This conflict became known as the Karen Rebellion. The Rangoon suburb of Insein was a Karen stronghold and was at the center of the conflict. The disruption of river and rail travel throughout Burma made it impossible for any of our American friends to come for the Jubilee, and it turned out that the American attendance was only six: Franklin and daughter Lois, Betty Lue, Richard, Ruth, and me. Phileda Nelson and Karen could not come because they had an American visitor friend in Tiddim who was ill and needed her care.

The Crowds

People began gathering on Wednesday, a day early, and on Thursday the crowds were an endless flow. We had urged all those who could bring their own food to do so, but it seemed that few heeded, bringing mostly clothing in their baskets. I was worried about the food supply. I went down to find Saya Zo Maung doling out rice to those crowded around him. "How much are you giving?" I asked. He replied, "Two viss to each family." That was over seven pounds. I suggested that Zo Maung reduce it to one viss (3.6 lbs.), with more later if possible.

I found a very harried Saya Isaac trying to find places for people to sleep. Isaac filled up as many Christian homes as possible, the church, the soldiers' barracks, all the schools, and yet hundreds had to sleep in the open under the stars. The number of travelers came to almost 4,700 and the official tally of the festival was 5,128. What a change since the Carsons came, when the Christians numbered zero!

Why a Jubilee?

If someone asked why so many thousands of people came to this festival, I can answer that they came for perhaps three reasons. First and foremost, the religion centering on Jesus Christ was relatively new to them. Many were very new to the faith, coming out of the old Chin animism, and they would be strengthened by contact with thousands of strangers suddenly become brothers and sisters in Christ. Secondly, many Chin people, especially women, travel very little, sometimes never farther than the nearest villages, and know almost nothing of the whole Chin Hills, much less the country of Burma. So a trip to the Jubilee, even though it meant two, three, or five days travel each way, was a sort of milestone in an often humdrum life. So it was exciting. Third, the young people, the youth, found it exciting to see youth from other areas. And it was a wonderful place for church choirs to sing in front of a huge crowd. Fourth, Westerners such as us with white skin and strange ways, who lived in a big white house, were an attraction to some, just as we go to see animals in a zoo.

The Open House

In regard to this fourth point, people were so eager to see our house that we made a special time on Saturday morning for an "open house." Betty opened the front door at the appointed time and the crowds rushed in, so fast that Betty got pinned against the wall by the door. We had figured that our visitors would look around and then file out orderly. That did not happen. The people came in and stayed until the whole main floor was burdened and we were afraid the floor would collapse. Thankfully, I had locked the door leading to the upstairs, or surely that weak floor would have collapsed with injuries to the people.

Richard and Lois and little Ruth were so frightened by the crowd that they crawled under a bed, with Dick shouting, "Don't take my toys, don't take my toys," when visiting children picked up and looked curiously at his playthings.

The fiasco was ended when Ram Hlun reached Betty and gave her our harmonium (small keyboard pumped by hand) and shouted to the visitors, "Follow Dickynu outside and she will play music for you. Follow her!" This Pied Piper strategy worked, and Betty Lue gave a concert outside on the lawn as the crowd gathered outside.

The three days of meetings were inspiring, the weather the whole time was delightful, the food proved enough to feed this great multitude, and various preachers encouraged the Chin people to continue in the true faith of Jesus. One of the best preachers was a Karen teacher, Saya Aung Dwe who was then the Deputy Inspector of Schools for the whole Chin Hills. Another former teacher, Saya Shia Khaw, gave a testimony to the grace of God in his life; he was the first convert and the first one baptized in the Haka area, in 1906.

A Baptism at Jubilee Time

A moving event of the Jubilee was the baptism of 373 new converts in the little pond up by the government offices. This took place on Saturday afternoon. Those baptized were from various villages and had delayed baptism until this Jubilee festival. Eleven pastors entered the lake for the baptismal service, and Rev. Sang Ling baptized the first one, an aged lady, and the pastors continued, as the crowd on the lakeside sang hymns. Frank and I stood close, just to the west of the lake, and we both had tears in our eyes as we saw the beautiful event. Men and women, some old, some young, confessed their new-found faith in Jesus Christ as Savior and Lord. We thought of the Carsons, fifty years ago at this very spot, quite alone and rather forlorn. At that time a Christian church did not exist here, there was no school, there were no Christians. They could not have envisioned a mass baptism like this nor the throngs gathered to praise God for these days of Jubilee.

Some Church Numbers

From the time the former missionary, Chester Strait, arrived in Haka until the Jubilee was about twenty-five years, 1925 to 1949. Near the close of the Jubilee some numbers were given out to show the spectacular growth of Christianity in the Chin Hills in that brief span of time, 25 years:

Organized churches, 13 in 1925; 142 in 1949
Pastors (ordained men), 3 in 1925; 26 in 1949
Preachers (unordained men), 9 in 1925; 48 in 1949
Church membership, 1,289 in 1925; 18,466 in 1949
     (only baptized persons counted as members)
New baptisms in the year, 125 in 1925; 2,727 in 1949.

Much of this increase came during World War II, when it seemed that the hardships of war awakened the hearts of the people to the new truth of Christ.

An Evening to Remember

When Chins gather in large church meetings, such as this one in Haka in 1949, the last evening is always long, exciting, and a place for anyone to get up and sing or make a speech, and for choirs to compete for top singing honors.

Sunday night at the Jubilee was capped with a 4-hour-long celebration, from 7 to 11 p.m. No less than 20 choirs took part and many pastors had a chance to give messages, and laymen and laywomen also could tell what was on their minds and hearts. It was indeed a great scene, ever etched in my mind—thousands of people under the mandat, seated on the ground, light from a few pressure lanterns and from some flickering pine torches, and all eager to hear what was said, except for small children who went to sleep in their parents' blankets or in their arms.

I took time around 9 p.m. to go apart from the tabernacle, away from the crowd, and up a road overlooking the town. I went about a half mile distant from the Jubilee celebration. It was very dark, as Haka has no street lights or other open lights. It was very quiet up on the hillside. No animal sounds, no dogs barking, no noise from a motorcycle, car, or truck, for they had not reached Haka yet. It was so still that I could hear clearly the hymns being sung in the mandat. Not only the sound, but even the words were clear to my ear. The stars were very bright and it was a beautiful, almost heavenly, scene.

I found myself shedding a few tears of joy. What a wonderful work that God had called Betty and me to do in this lonely part of the world! I thanked God for His grace and blessing, and prayed that all the Chin people would come into this light, the light of Jesus the Lord.

Chapter 25

THE "CUT-OFF" YEAR, 1949

⟿

Isolation in the Chin Hills

I have termed the year 1949 as the year of our isolation. This will be incomprehensible to the Chins, for were not their missionaries surrounded by Chin friends? Who could be lonely in Haka? Who could be lonely in Tiddim?

The answer is: the Johnsons and the Nelsons were lonely in their villages, surrounded by Chins, because we were for months cut off from news of loved ones at home in the States and from our colleagues in Rangoon. It was depressing to go week after week, month after month, without a single letter from our loved ones. Normal rail and steamer services in Burma were cut off by the civil war. Occasionally letters from the mission office in Rangoon and the U.S.A. might get through, carried up by some soldier coming on leave and usually flying by military plane to Mandalay and then onward.

A Private Postal System

But these were so few and erratic that finally the Nelsons and we inaugurated our private postal system to India. In early August we hired a coolie to make one round trip a month from Tiddim to Kangpokpi in Manipur State where the Andersons lived. He carried out our letters to John Anderson who posted them. Our mail from America, now addressed to us in care of the Andersons, was picked up

135

and brought to Tiddim, from whence ours was mailed down to Haka. There was no break in mail service within the Chin Hills, thankfully, so Franklin and I could keep in touch. When our mail system via India was finally under way, we kept it up for almost a year.

Depressing Times in Haka

The worst depression I suffered came in September, 1949. We had been without mail from home for two and a half months. Our money had run out and the mission had no way to get more to us. We were borrowing from the Christians, just on our promise to repay. It was the middle of the rainy season and that too conspired to make me feel gloomy. Betty managed to keep in better spirits than I did, which is probably a fault that I should confess. God is faithful, and I knew and believed that, but those were grim days, I recall.

To Ease the Depression

During 1949 the Johnsons and the Nelsons watched our supply of flour go down to nothing. There were no bakeries in the Chin Hills. We had to bake our own bread, rolls, cakes, pies, cookies, doughnuts, and whatever else we needed. Both families delighted in having pastors and other guests in for the British custom of afternoon tea, usually about 3 p.m., and we liked to serve something with the tea. Therefore, the lack of flour was a serious blow to our hospitality.

The Johnson Milling Company

To eke out our dwindling supply of flour, Betty and I resorted to grinding and pounding corn, rice, and millet. We found that muffins made of four parts of millet, one part wheat flour, and held together with some eggs, were very tasty. We came to depend more and more on that. As for real bread, we rationed ourselves to one slice per person daily. Then, to help the Nelsons a bit, we started the "Johnson Milling Company."

It happened that in Haka we had a large corn grinder, left behind and cast out by someone during the war. We managed to fix it enough so it worked. We also had a coffee grinder. With these two instruments we began to make cornmeal and millet-meal and we mailed weekly parcels of this to the Nelsons. It was of course a bit of a joke. We needed some relief from the depression caused by lack of communication with home folks and our colleagues down-country; so we sent parcels from our mythical milling company and wrote whimsical letters to our co-workers in Tiddim. One of my favorite jokes was to write and ask Nelson what time it was. In reply, in his letter he would say something like, "It's now a quarter to five." Amazingly stupid things like this relieved the tensions of life for us during that difficult year.

Actually, thinking about the time of day, everyone was running on "sun time." There was not a single working radio in the village to get correct time. Everyone's clock or watch read differently. So we simply noted noon by a sundial and let it go at that.

An Airdrop at Haka

My spirits lifted tremendously when the government was finally able to make an airdrop in Haka on October 6. The twin-engine DC-3 circled our village three times and dropped 18 bundles. We had hoped there would be foodstuffs, particularly flour and sugar, but the drop was mostly soldiers' clothing and shoes. We did, however, receive a packet of mail and learned that our mission was printing an edition of 5,000 of the Haka songbook. These, plus the 3,000 of the first printing, would give us enough to last out the first term, we thought with joy.

Currency Rate Change in Burma

At this point I note that in October, 1949, the official rate of exchange of the Burmese rupee went from 3.3 to Rs.4.75 to the U.S.dollar. This meant that our missionary salary, always quite small, was suddenly increased in its buying power. The same number of dollars now brought more rupees. The mission society did try to give us enough to live modestly and to educate our children.

We Pass our Second Language Exam

On Nov. 5, U Thang Sun, the headmaster of the Haka post-primary school, gave us a good hard exam that took almost two and a half hours. Part of the test was to give a 10-minute speech in Chin on an assigned subject. My subject was: "Why do some people baptize by immersion and some by sprinkling?" Betty's subject was: "How can the women of the Chin Hills help to spread the gospel?" When it was all over, Thang Sun declared that we both had passed. He explained a few words that we had not known, and then he gave us a present—a pound of white sugar. White sugar! A treasured gift, for we had not seen white sugar for months.

We both were surpassed by our children. Ruth, almost two, knew scarcely any English but was speaking good sentences in Chin. Dick, then four and a half years old, spoke Chin better than we did and with perfect accent. He also knew English quite well and made almost no errors in grammar, having never heard English spoken incorrectly.

Good Things During the Year

Yes, there were some bad things during 1949: the lack of letters; the lack of money because of the breakdown of the postal system, causing us to borrow from the Christian church; the rumors that all missionaries in Burma had fled the country; that Haka would be attacked by a Communist army gathered at Gangaw, ready to invade the Hills; and that we, the missionaries, should be ready to leave Haka and flee to India.

In spite of these negatives, we came to the end of the year counting our many blessings. The Jubilee celebrating the 50 years of Christian work was a very successful event. Most of the worrisome rumors about warfare coming to the Chin Hills proved untrue. Our private postal system to India was going great and letters and parcels were coming in from the States. The mission was finally able to get money drafts to us so we paid our debts. And the second year of our Bible School came to a successful conclusion.

Another Teacher for the Bible School, David Van Bik

Our new teacher for the Bible School was proving to be a jewel. David Van Bik, a Haka Chin from Thantlang village, came to us after three years of study in the Presbyterian Bible School in Cherrapunji, India, so he knew English well. He took over my classes in theology and the Epistles of Paul, because he could, as a native speaker of Chin, express the biblical material much better than I. He also knew Lushai from the war years when he was in the Lushai Hills of Assam. He knew Burmese too, of course. With these languages it became possible to begin translation of the Old Testament.

Beginning Bible Translation

We already had the New Testament translated by Dr. Chester Strait in pre-war days, but we had nothing of the Old Testament. Therefore David Van Bik and I began to translate the book of Genesis in our spare time from teaching. It is more accurate to say that David did the translation and that I was his scribe, writing down every word. We did not get far, a few verses a day, but it was a start on Genesis.

Concerning our Bible School in 1949, Betty Lue taught full courses in Health and Music, and I taught Life of Christ, Bible Geography, and Church History. Van Bik taught Theology and other courses we thought would be helpful to young pastors. We all, the three teachers, were satisfied that our students were learning how to be effective witnesses for Christ to their own people.

Chapter 26

WE LOSE A SON

The Nelsons Visit Haka

Phileda Nelson had not been able to attend the Jubilee at Haka and had never been to our village, so it seemed a good time in early 1950 for the Nelsons to come south and visit us. In addition, it provided a chance for Frank and me to tour some villages together as a team, which we had never been able to do earlier.

At this time Betty Lue and I were expecting our third child, and we calculated that the birth would be sometime in April.

Remembering our difficult trip with coolies for Ruth's birth, we thought it would be a much easier trip this time because it was the dry season.

In mid-January we all started out together, the Nelson family of four and my family of four, traveling on foot, horses, and pack mules the fifty miles to Lumbang where Frank had stored his jeep at the end of the motorable road.

It was important for me to attend the Association meetings in Haka and again at a village on the India border. My idea was then to go north to Tiddim, and with Betty Lue, Richard, and Ruth proceed downcountry to a hospital at either Moulmein or Mandalay for the arrival of the child.

Betty and Children to Tiddim

So at Lumbang I said goodbye to my wife and children and turned back to do the Association touring. Frank took his four, my three, and our cook Chia Ling in his jeep to Tiddim to await my arrival sometime in late February or so. I marvel at how those old wartime jeeps could stand up to the constant overloading.

After leaving Betty and the children, I returned on foot to Haka and enjoyed some stimulating meetings with hundreds of people gathered from widespread villages. Every church group wanted to have their Association meet at full-moon time to make it easier for travel, but thankfully the Chins were willing to stagger the dates a week apart so I was able to make 2 or 3 Association meetings each spring.

Thus it was that I enjoyed a weekend at Fungkah village near the India border, and then continued to tour villages, preaching at each. I reached the village of Tlangpi, 150 houses and a strong Christian church. I had been on tour 8 days, some of it through rain, and hadn't had a chance to wash clothing. So I was washing out some clothes when a Chin handed me a letter he had been carrying for days, saying that it was urgent. He was obviously a runner who had come in a hurry from somewhere.

It proved to be in Betty's handwriting, but the message brought a tidal wave of sadness. I read it again through tears. "Bob dear," it said, "I am all right now, but our little son was born prematurely and lived only a half hour. The Christians of Tiddim have buried him with a cross of flowers at his grave."

The letter went on to say that the little fellow had been born at 3 a.m. on February 5. She was writing the next day, so I felt that she was probably all right. But nothing could assuage the anguish that I felt to lose this dear little son.

Hurried Trip to Haka and Tiddim

I was too devastated to continue the tour. My inclination was to rush directly to Tiddim by the shortest path, but I soon realized that this would be stupid. No, I had to return to Haka to get our passports, our money, pay salaries, and close the house for what might be a long absence.

My traveling companions and I immediately packed up and started for Haka. We spent the first night at Farrawn. The second night we had to camp outside the village of Thantlang because it was taboo (in Chin, khua a chia) because of animist sacrifices going on.

We slept along the roadside, in the open. On Friday, a hike of 20 miles took us home to Haka. I expected to find some mail; there was nothing from Tiddim.

Later I was to learn that Betty and Phileda had tried to send a wireless message to me about the death of the baby. In those days, a telegram from Tiddim went first to Kalemyo. Kalemyo sent it to Falam. The Falam postmaster then mailed the message to Haka. A long process, involving days of time. As I recall, the wireless message never reached me at all; it must have been lost en route.

The baby was born and died on Sunday, Feb. 5. I received word on Feb. 15, eleven days later. By the time I got home, handled all the business needed there and got my papers and funds, started out again and got to the Manipur River crossing, it was Feb. 21. I was so tired from hiking 25 miles that day that I probably didn't notice where I spread my blankets, for the next day when I reached Pine Tree Camp, my bedding and mosquito net were alive with bedbugs. I spent half an hour killing them.

On Feb. 23 another long hike took me to Fort White by 4:30 p.m. just as it began to rain. A truck came along carrying teak lumber to Tiddim. I quickly grabbed a cup of tea and two chapattis at the local teashop and got on board the truck, leaving Ram Hlun behind to come later, as there was no room for him on the truck.

A wild rainstorm came up and fog so thick the driver could not see. He stopped a mile short of Kennedy Peak, at an elevation of probably over 8,000 feet, where I spent a miserable night, cold and wet. I tried to dry out by the fire. I recall the night with special horror because I was so worried, for people along the road were filled with rumors about my wife. They had heard the bad news about the baby, and some thought my wife was still alive, some that she was dead. The rain, the freezing cold, the fog, the loneliness of being with men speaking no Haka Chin, and the rumors—indeed it was a night to try my soul. I prayed as never before. All I could do was to sit up, wrapped in my blanket, trying to keep warm near the fire the men had kindled on the roadside.

Arrival in Tiddim

My truck reached Tiddim at about 9 a.m. on Feb. 24, and Ram Hlun arrived about the same time on another truck. I hurried up to the mission compound, almost dreading to find tragic news. What a joy when Betty came out to meet me, alive and getting over the experience! But she was slim again and the realization of our loss flooded our souls as we wept together. "He was so little, Bob, but so perfect, even little fingernails," she told me. "He tried hard to make it, but he was just too young."

The premature birth had come while Franklin was on tour, and only Phileda Nelson was there to help. She did not even have a kerosene pressure lantern working; it was broken. She delivered the baby by the light of candles and a kerosene wick lantern. Phileda was not a nurse, but she did wonderfully. I felt so grateful to her.

Peter Johnson

Betty and I named him Peter. He tried hard to live and would undoubtedly have lived if oxygen had been available. Modern medical care would certainly have saved his life. But we were in the Chin Hills and such things did not exist. We could not blame anyone or anything. Certainly we did not blame God. Rather, God gave us grace to accept it as one of the hard things that sometimes comes to believers. All we can do is to bow our hearts and say sincerely, "The Lord gives and the Lord takes away, blessed be the name of the Lord."

The Grave

Later Betty and I went down alone to the Christian cemetery on the hillside below the main road, among the pine trees. We did not want Dick and Ruth with us, for it was necessary for us to weep a while together. She showed me the fresh little grave and told how the Chin Christians tenderly buried our little son, and how the girls put a cross of rhododendrons on the grave and the Tiddim pastor conducted the funeral service. Later they made a cross of teak wood to mark where he lay. While I was in Tiddim, I carved his name and the date: Peter Johnson, Feb. 5, 1950, on the cross.

I was drained emotionally by the events of the past two weeks, but gradually the sadness faded and I was left with thankfulness that I had two healthy children and a wonderful wife who was recovering her strength. So God was good, is good, and ever will be good to us.

A Means of Christian Witness

I cannot end this story of the death of our child without telling how the Lord has made many good things come out of our loss.

Many times women came to our house to talk with Betty about this and that. They revealed to her the loss of their babies either prematurely or while still very young. Betty told them that she could sympathize with them, for she too had lost a baby at birth. Often the women would say with astonishment, "Do you mean that you really lost a baby?" When Betty said "Yes," they often would say, "We didn't think that American women, and especially missionary women, ever had miscarriages, or still births, or lost a young baby." Then Betty would tell them of her experience and explain that God did not put a special hedge around her to ensure that she would never have any sorrow; rather, she, an American woman, entered into the same suffering the Chin women suffer. It was a new and revolutionary idea to many Chin women, and often a means of grace, for then Betty could tell of the God who gives comfort to the bereaved and sorrowing.

To India and Back Home

The roads were dry and the dangerous Kalemyo-Tamu road had been cleared of bandits, so Frank proposed that we go with our families to India where Betty could see the mission doctor in Jorhat. We did so, both families in the one jeep. The Jorhat doctor suggested that Betty needed some vacation, so our family went up into the Himalaya Mountains, to Darjeeling. We returned to Haka refreshed and healthy, and in time to take up our work in the Bible School, the third and last year for this class. At this time we decided that our furlough should begin in 1951.

Chapter 27

THE HAKA BIBLE SCHOOL FINAL YEARS

~~~~~

The second and third years of the Haka Bible School in 1949 and 1950 brought to a successful conclusion for 32 men three years of study to prepare them for the rigors of Christian ministry in the southern part of the Chin Hills. The Bible School at Tiddim likewise concluded in 1950, with the graduation of 28 men and 2 women. One of the women was the wife of Hau Go, our able colleague who became the first General Secretary of the Zomi Convention. The other later married Rev. Kam Khaw Thang, who became the translator of the Bible into the Kamhau (Tiddim) language.

These two schools were for a crisis situation, as the rapidly growing churches needed trained pastors, even those of lower education. Frank Nelson and I always had the vision of a permanent Bible training school for the Chins, located somewhere in the Hills, and taking in new classes yearly and graduating others yearly. This was to be a project, we thought, when we returned from furloughs in the States in 1953. We dreamed of teaching on a higher level and using English as the medium of instruction. This dream came to pass, but in a different form than we had anticipated.

The Second Year, 1949

The students arrived in Haka in late May and prepared their old stone house for occupancy, cut firewood, and tended their garden started earlier for them by Betty. We began classes on June 2 but limped along for a week until David Van Bik arrived to teach his classes. He had been ill with pneumonia. Van Bik moved into our front upstairs room which he occupied for about a year.

Rev. Lal Hnin taught the Book of Acts; I taught the New Testament Epistles (Hebrews to Revelation) and Church History (Pentecost to the Reformation); Betty Johnson taught Music; and Van Bik had the important task of teaching Theology. In addition to his teaching duties, Van Bik taught Betty and me language from 12: 30 to 1:30 daily and worked with us on translations from 1:30 to 3 p.m. During much of this latter period we continued work on our Chin dictionary, searching out new words and their meanings.

The students continued their program of evangelistic touring on certain weekends during the five months of the school, and many people were strengthened in their faith and many others made decisions for Christ for the first time.

Living in a country which had been ruled for decades by the British, we thankfully adopted the custom of afternoon tea. All teaching and literary work ceased at 3 p.m. That was the magical hour when we had tea. After tea and maybe some cookies or small rolls, it was time to do other things, such as working with my hands to get a rest from mental labor. We often wrote letters then, for that did not require much hard thought.

Tests and the End of School

The last week of October brought the time for final tests. Monday of that week was Betty Lue's 33rd birthday and I noted she made a banana cake with brown sugar icing which we ate at supper. I had no present to give her, and that made me feel bad. But the civil war was still on and nothing was coming through to us.

On Thursday the Bible School men came in to our house for a "lentecelhnak" or a fun time. We had a rollicking good time when Van Bik, Ram Hlun, and I put on a "shadow operation." This abdominal operation was done behind a sheet so only our shadows were seen by the audience. I pulled a screwdriver, a pair of pliers, an iron chain, etc., from Ram Hlun's stomach. Most of the men had never seen that stunt done before and were convulsed with laughter.

The Third Year, 1950

Classes for the third year began on June 5 and the students and subjects were much like the previous year. Van Bik continued in Theology, Lal Hnin taught the four Gospels, I continued in New Testament and Church History, and Betty Lue taught Music and a new subject, Sunday School Methods. I added a class called Odds and Ends. That was my title for a class to teach a lot of miscellaneous things that either were requested by the students or things I thought they should know. Under this heading I taught them a bit of astronomy (sun, moon, stars, planets), a bit of painting (varnish, enamel, lead and oil paint, etc.), how to make an attractive cross for a church, how to tie knots in rope, treatment for snake bite, and the like. Does a class like this seem a stupid waste of time? One who criticizes would have to know the eagerness of the Chins to learn some of the simplest things about science and the larger world.

Music Classes and Tonic Solfa

Betty's class in music undoubtedly was a most helpful course, for it seems that music was often the key to opening the hearts of the Chin people. The Chins use the tonic solfa system (doh, re, mi, fa, sol, la, ti, doh) and there is a way of writing this music using periods, commas, colons, and semicolons to indicate the time. Betty had never seen the solfa system until she came to Burma, but she learned it and eventually was able to change many songs from the staff notation into the solfa. Six of the more musical students learned this skill from her and thereby gave a tremendous boost to Christian songs and hymns being known far and wide in the Haka subdivision.

The Problem of Tempo

We tried hard to teach simple conducting of songs, hoping that the song leaders could get the singers to keep up the proper tempo, keep up the pace, and not let the songs drag. This dragging of songs was a common fault of hymn singing in the churches, and often someone would call out "faster, faster" which helped the tempo for a period.

In discussing this problem of tempo of songs, some of the students asked me directly, "Bawipa, can you get us a machine or something to beat the time for us so we can learn?"

"Well," I said, "there is something called a metronome to do that, but it is very costly."

"About how much?" they asked.

"About fifty dollars or more," I answered.

"It would be nice if every pastor had one," the students said, "but maybe you can get one for the school."

This got me thinking. We can't afford real metronomes for every student and pastor but maybe we can do something with a pendulum. A pendulum swings slower or faster according to its length, I reasoned. So why not use the simplest thing for a pendulum: a piece of iron or even a stone suspended by a string?

The students and I had a fun time learning how to measure tempo by this simple apparatus. I gave each student a yard of string. Each found a small stone and tied his string around it. By trial and error we learned that a string length of 20 inches made 84 swings per minute. We learned that a string length of 27 inches measured a beat of 71 per minute. Each beat was a quarter note.

Over a period of time I determined the optimum speed or tempo of the commonly used songs in congregational singing. I wrote the numbers in my songbook, and had every student copy these numbers into his personal songbook. Our string pendulums were crude affairs, but they did work fairly accurately. Since the students did not have rulers to measure length, I made each one a yardstick so he could measure string length. The "string length" is measured from the middle of the weight.

A Piano in Haka

A few of the more enterprising students wanted to learn to play the piano—and thereby hangs a tale.

Our local doctor, Dr. Sheriman, who was really what was called an L.M.P. (licensed medical practitioner) bought an old piano for

Rs. 300 from a Karen teacher named Sein Pe who left for Rangoon in mid-June. The piano was unusable, being broken and terribly out of tune. We made a deal with Dr. Sheriman. If he loaned it to us for about a year, until we left on furlough, we would repair it and tune it. He agreed, and the Bible School students carried it down to our house.

The piano was in bad condition. I spent part of a week repairing broken parts and making new parts for it. We had no proper wrench for turning the pegs, but I managed to fashion a tool for that purpose. I had no ear to tune it, but I was the man who turned the pegs. Betty told me when to tighten and when to loosen the strings. What a pleasure to have music in our home! We enjoyed the instrument until we went on furlough. Actually, none of the men learned to play, but they at least had a chance to see what a piano was like.

Graduation Day, October 1, 1950

On Sunday, October 1, the church fairly groaned with the press of people. There was a record attendance of 555. Every nook and corner was full. We even had mats right up to the preacher's feet, and people to the right, to the left, and behind him. There were nine anthems including three by the Bible School students, and it was a wonderful occasion.

The 6 best students academically received gold seals, 18 average students got silver seals, and the remaining 8 received red seals. Actually, the red seals were so attractive that the persons receiving those were quite happy.

Just before graduation, Betty and I gave a dinner party for all the students and had a fun and game night. The year thus ended joyously for the students, and as they departed on Monday for their homes, many thanked us sincerely for their three years of study. We too thanked the Lord for the opportunity to prepare these many men for their ministry. Over the years we have followed their progress with great interest, for it is largely due to these men that the seed planted has finally resulted in the abundant harvest.

Chapter 28

SHAKING HANDS WITH LIAN HMUNG

Ｏne Saturday when I was down in the village visiting people, I met pastor Sang Ling. This was shortly after arriving in Haka and I was trying to learn to speak the local language. After chatting a while, the pastor asked me if I would shake hands with his son Lian Hmung the next day at church, at the morning worship service. I said, "Yes, of course, I will be glad to do that."

Later I thought about this rather unusual request. I knew that Lian Hmung was an army officer and perhaps because he was leaving Haka soon for the army service, his dad wanted me to be sure to say farewell to him. At any rate, I soon forgot the agreement to shake hands with his son.

On Sunday morning the church building was comfortably filled, which was a good sign that the Chins were coming to hear the gospel preaching. It was quite hot and of course everything was all in Chin—songs, announcements, preaching. I was sleepy and it was hard after an hour and a half of the new language to avoid being bored. Yes, I was bored and wished for the service to end. Finally the sermon was over and I expected the end of the service. But Pastor Sang Ling said something that caused a stir in the audience. A man on the left side of the aisle and a woman on the right side arose, and came down the central aisle together toward the pulpit.

Then Pastor Sang Ling turned to me and said in English, "Bawipa, it is time now for you to perform the wedding of Lian Hmung and Nu Tial."

I was astounded. The last thought in my mind that Sunday morning was about wedding ceremonies. The pastor must have seen my jaw drop in surprise because he asked what the matter was. "What did you say I would do?" I asked. "Oh, perform the wedding ceremony for my son as you said you would do," he replied.

Well, I was in for it. Suddenly it dawned on me that the words "kut tlaihnak," literally "shaking hands" were the words used for the wedding ceremony. What I erroneously thought to be a simple request to shake Lian Hmung's hand was really a request to perform the marriage ceremony for him. I was ignorant of the Chin idiom and hence was in this predicament.

I had no book, no preparation, not even a clear thought on what to do. How did the marriage service begin? Could it be done without a ring? What about translation of certain difficult words? I drew a deep breath, pulled myself together, and drawing on my memory of the marriage service in my native language, I started, managing to keep one thought ahead of Pastor Sang Ling who translated it sentence by sentence. I have always loved the traditional English marriage service in use for hundreds of years, and this I tried to follow as much as possible as I tried to recall it.

All this took place at the conclusion of the morning worship service. The bride and groom who had been sitting apart through the whole service and had come forward for the wedding, seemed pleased with what had taken place. I felt better—nothing had gone seriously wrong.

After it was all over and we were at the dinner table, Betty laughed at me. "Did you listen to what the pastor said?" she asked.

"No," I said, "I was too busy thinking up the next sentence to listen to him."

So she enlightened me. "When you said, 'Marriage is not to be entered into hastily,' Sang Ling translated it, 'In marriage you must promise to love her, not hate her!'"

Perhaps Pastor Sang Ling expected me to understand his request to perform the wedding service and be ready for it. Or perhaps he just assumed that the missionary is always ready to preach and to conduct funerals, marriages, baptisms, and communion services at a moment's notice. Not only Sang Ling, but all the pastors, expected me to speak without warning.

I was not the only one. The Chins expected the same thing of my wife. We often were simply assigned, not asked in advance, to speak or do certain jobs. I remember that even our children were not exempt. Richard, for instance, returned from India during his vacation time from high school, and was simply assigned to speak to the Young People's service that very afternoon. It was common for us to be asked to sing a solo, a duet, or a song by the whole family, all without warning.

To us it was a sign that the Chins accepted us and treated us as brothers and sisters in the Lord. We felt a closeness to them, and they felt close to us, close enough to ask us to speak or sing without prior notice.

Chapter 29

SCHOOLING FOR RICHARD AND LOIS

Richard begins School

School began for our son Richard in May, 1950, when he was five years old. He began Kindergarten, and he used the fine materials sent to us by the Calvert School in Baltimore, Maryland. This included little books, coloring books, paper, crayons, pencils, and instruction books, none of which were available in Burma.

His classroom was on the second floor of our house, which resembled a large attic, unbroken by walls except for one wall on the north side of the house which formed a rather large room used as a bedroom for David Van Bik who was teaching in the Bible School. There were upright posts here and there supporting the corrugated iron roof, and these posts became corners of the school room for Dick. I hung up woven bamboo mats for walls. Light came from one window on the south side of the attic. We had a table and two little green chairs, because little Ruth, too young for school, also insisted on attending. Betty put her to work coloring and cutting out pictures.

A Disciplined Classroom

Betty Lue was the teacher, and the pupils called her "Mrs. Johnson" while in school, not Mom or Mother or Mommy. Betty tried to make our school in Burma as much like an American school as possible, and so she insisted on this formality. We were also careful of her time and did not allow visitors to interrupt during school hours unless it was a dire emergency. She did, however, have a recess period and would see visitors then. Subsequently in later years we maintained this schooling rigidly, almost never postponing or canceling classes, and we think that this enabled our three children to get excellent schooling at home. Betty Lue was a professional teacher before becoming a missionary, so that helped. Before marriage she taught four years in a rural school in Illinois, having grades 1 through 8, and she had another year after marriage while I was in the U.S. Navy in the South Pacific during World War II.

Teaching Through Seventh Grade

Actually, Betty taught all our children up through seventh grade, except for the years of our two furloughs. Thus the children were fortunate to have almost a one-on-one experience with a gifted teacher, and they learned to speak English correctly. In later years, when answering questions on grammar, they always could give the correct answers, because the incorrect forms just sounded funny.

We Gain Another Pupil

In October of 1950 we received a sad letter from Franklin and Phileda. Mrs. Nelson's pregnancy was not going well, and Phileda was bedridden and unable to teach her two girls. They asked if we would please take the girls to Haka and if Betty could teach them.

Fortunately I was home at the time, not out on tour, so immediately I set out with my cook Ram Hlun. We walked 78 of the 100 miles to Tiddim and indeed found Mrs. Nelson in bed. Karen did not want to leave her parents, so it was just Lois, ten years old and in 5th grade, who returned with us to Haka. Frank drove us to Lumbang in the jeep, so we had only 50 miles to walk. Lois rode a horse loaned to us by a government official. We reached Haka on September 28 and learned later that Frank, returning to Tiddim from Lumbang, had great difficulties passing over a landslide near Bamboo Camp.

Lois in Haka

Lois was with us for two and a half months. She was an energetic and friendly girl and made friends among the local boys and girls in spite of the language problem. Of course, with Dick and Ruth she talked English, although to tell the truth, little Ruth was more fluent in Chin than in English. Lois was with us for Christmas and enjoyed the wonderful Christmas singing and dramas at the church.

Her Return

While Lois was with us in Haka, Franklin and Phileda decided that in view of her deteriorating health it was necessary to seek medical help in a hospital in Rangoon or the mission hospital in Moulmein. So they flew to Rangoon, to the mission Guest House. Franklin returned to the Chin Hills to continue work, and so it was that at Christmas time the Nelson family was divided, Lois in Haka, Phileda and Karen in Rangoon, and Franklin in Tiddim.

In early January things were not going well for Mrs. Nelson, so she wrote her husband of the continuing problems of her pregnancy. Frank then decided that he would get Lois and join the others down-country. He and his cook Lian Khen started for Haka to get Lois, but the gear box of the jeep failed and they could reach only Fort White. The two men then starting walking, hoping for a vehicle to come along, but nothing came. They walked, carrying their food and blankets, and after a long hike reached Pine Tree Camp, a two-stage trek. The next day they reached Lumbang at 10 a.m., a shorter hike, but Frank was totally exhausted and ill. Unable to go farther, he asked Lian Khen to go alone to Haka. Lian Khen left Lumbang immediately and hiked the 50 miles to Haka arriving Sunday noon, January 6. Frank had not been able to tell us of his plan to come to get Lois, so we were surprised when his cook arrived tired and hungry. I was away on tour, so he told Betty the news of the Nelson family and that he had come to get Lois, and that Frank planned to go immediately with her to Rangoon.

Lois quickly packed her few possessions and got ready to depart on the next day. Betty found a riding horse available, and on Monday noon Lian Khen, Lois, and the horse driver departed for Lumbang. They traveled fast, sleeping Monday and Tuesday nights along the roadside with fires to keep wild animals away. They reached Lumbang on Wednesday and the ten year old traveler, safe and healthy, was reunited with her father. As Frank's jeep was broken down, Lois, Franklin, and Lian Khen walked all the way to Fort White, a three-stage journey, on foot. Leaving the jeep behind, Frank and Lois found a truck to carry them to Kalemyo where they had to wait five days for a plane to Rangoon. So on January 16 the Nelson family was together again.

Safe Arrival of the Nelson Baby

The Nelsons continued on to Moulmein to the mission hospital and welcomed their third daughter, Phyllis Margaret, on April 14, 1951. She weighed 8 pounds and 12 ounces, a chubby, healthy little girl. The siege of illness was over and the Nelsons prepared for the end of their term and the sea voyage home to the States.

Chapter 30

TOURING THE MOUNTAIN VILLAGES

B etty Lue and I were considered "evangelistic and general missionaries" by our mission. The first part refers, of course, to preaching, establishing churches, training pastors and leaders, and preparation of Christian books and literature, including translation of the Bible. The "general" means that we were to do everything that needed doing in agriculture, medicine, construction work, etc. It is a broad category, and we certainly had to be ready for any job.

For me, village touring was an important phase of my work, for only by seeing at first hand and meeting the Chin people in their little villages could I really know them and win them to the Christian faith.

Tour to Farrawn

I had been in Haka only a few months when it became necessary to make a tour westward, toward the India border, to the village of Farrawn to help settle a quarrel among churches about the use of church money to run a school. Farrawn was about 40 miles distant. I left home on May 21 and returned on May 28, just one week. With me were my cook Ram Hlun, Rev. Lal Hnin as interpreter, and Boi Nol, the muleteer. It rained every day, so the trip itself was strenuous. Every village of more than ten houses was required by the government to construct and maintain a little rest house where visiting government officials can stay while traveling, so Farrawn had such a little house, in which I stayed. Ram Hlun cooked my meals in the adjacent cookhouse. Villagers supplied firewood, water, and chickens and eggs..

Although the weather was inclement, the tour was thoroughly enjoyable to me, for now, I felt, I was doing the very thing the mission society had sent me out to do. The split among the churches was healed. One of the good memories of this first long tour was the fine choir of the Farrawn church, singing anthems and hymns in beautiful four-part harmony, with no musical accompaniment. I especially admired their choir leader. This barefoot gentleman kept time with the big toe of his right foot. I was fascinated by the movement up and down of his toe. Only the big toe moved. Later I tried this feat privately and was quite unable to move my toe properly.

Commonplace Tours

Every year during the dry season (late October through May) I made village tours of a week, two weeks, and longer. One trip to a village on the India border was for 19 days, and it was 100 miles each way. Mountain ridges run for the most part north and south. This means that east to west travel involves long climbs and long descents. Chin villages are not large, from 50 to 150 or 200 population and are 5 to 12 miles apart. They are joined only by footpaths or horse and mule paths. The Chin Hills are really mountains, rising to over 10,000 feet in one place, and 7,000 and 8,000 feet mountains are common. Haka itself is at 6,000 feet altitude and therefore is cold in the winter season.

It was a lovely custom of the Chin Christians to come out along the roadside to welcome me as their new missionary. They often gave gifts, such as sugar cane, eggs, or occasionally a chicken. Often the eggs were so many, more than I and my tour group could eat, that I could pack some in banana stalks and find a traveler going to Haka to deliver them to Betty.

Eggs at Tikir

One special time stands out in my memory. I was on a 16-day tour of the Thantlang area southwest of Haka and reached the village of Tikir. Seemingly the whole village was lined up to greet my party on arrival, and I shook hands with each and every person. Soon I had 5 eggs in my left hand, and someone produced a hat to carry the eggs. That hat filled up, then another. Ram Hlun was wearing a stocking cap and we filled that too. It stretched longer and longer. What a lot of eggs! When I reached the rest house, I counted the eggs. Ninety nine!

During dinner I thought of one of the stories Jesus told and I thought that perhaps now I would be able to make a little joke in Chin. That night we held the usual preaching service in the church. I began, saying, "This afternoon I came here and you gave me eggs, many eggs. How wonderful to have that many eggs, all safe in my washbasin. Do you remember the story that Jesus told, about the 99 sheep safely in the fold, but one sheep was lost on the mountainside? The shepherd was worried about that one lost sheep and went out searching for it and found it. Now, brothers and sisters, here I am with 99 eggs. But I am worried about the one lost egg. Where could the one lost egg be?"

As I spoke this in Chin, I noted that the people chuckled and seemed to understand my story about the lost egg.

Early next morning a man came and gave me an egg. "Here is the lost egg," he said.

Another man came, then a woman, and then more, each with that lost egg. Finally, when there no more coming, we counted the eggs again. There were 113 eggs!

We Lose a Little Horse

One year in early April I set out to tour the Zophei and Lautu area southwest of Haka. I walked about 4 miles, feeling sicker with each step. Ram Hlun saw my faltering steps and insisted that we turn back. I managed to reach home and collapsed on the bed. Betty was down at the weekly women's meeting in the village. When she arrived home, she began to treat me for malaria. It was several days before I had strength enough to walk upstairs to the attic and do any work.

I was able to start again on April 21 for a 10-day trip, but changed to a different area, the MiE circle of churches, where Rev. Nawl Kling was pastor. Because of my weakness from malaria, I decided to rent a riding horse, unusual for me during my first term of service. The mare I rented from a local owner had a yearling colt which followed the mother everywhere. All went fine until we got to Ruantlang, the village nearest to the Burma plain.

Ruantlang had been moved that very year to a new site. The people had cut down all the trees in the village area and there were hundreds of little pointed stumps, from a foot to two feet high. During the evening the colt slipped and fell upon a sharp stump which pierced the abdomen. Some Chins saw this and called Chia Ling who was my cook on the trip.

At about 7:30 in the evening, Chia Ling called me just as I was ready to go to the little church for a meeting. He looked almost terrified. *"Bawipa,"* he whispered, *"rang fate a ril a chuak."* I knew immediately what he meant. The colt's intestines were coming out. The poor animal! We caught the colt and tried to repair the damage but he kicked too much and made the wound worse. "We'll have to kill the horse," said Chia Ling and the other Chins at the scene. "How can I kill that beautiful little colt?" I whispered.

The scene is forever etched in my mind. The bright stars, the quiet night, the flickering pine torches which illuminated the beautiful little animal, and those pleading brown eyes. I raised my shotgun. I lowered it. "Is there no other way?" I asked. "There is nothing we can do to save him," they all said.

We all had grown to love the frisky little colt. "God forgive me," I said, and I pulled the trigger. More villagers came and we buried the animal after the evening service. In the morning we travelers sorrowfully left Ruantlang; the bereft mother horse almost refused to leave without her colt and neighed piteously.

When we got home to the saddened owner, the church elders discussed the payment to be made. I paid half the value of the colt, my share coming to 200 rupees, about 65 dollars.

Although I made many short and long tours during our first term, I did not try to take the family along. I now tell the story of a trip with the family, one that came close to disaster.

A Family Trip with Horses

As our furlough time approached after five years in Burma, Betty Lue and I wished to take the whole family, children and all, on a typical village tour, using packhorses, riding horses, and so forth. We had dreamed of the day when we as husband and wife could go <u>together</u> on preaching trips, for we knew that the village women, so very isolated, had never seen a white woman and would appreciate very much the appearance of "Haka Siangbawinu," as she was called. We were sure that it would be a great impetus for them to accept Christ as Savior and Lord and join with their husbands in establishing truly Christian homes.

We Begin an 11-Day Tour

So in early 1951 we made a trip as a family to Tlangkhua to attend an Associational meeting where over 2,000 Christians attended. We started off on a Tuesday with four pack mules and two riding ponies. Richard rode one horse led by an attendant. Betty Lue and Ruth rode the second horse. The weather was cold and at the first night's camp water froze.

The fourth day took us through Mualkai to our destination of Tlangkhua for the Association. Along this road we had a frightening experience.

The Runaway Horse

Dick was now a few months short of six years old. He felt at home riding the horse and asked if we would let him ride alone, holding the reins. We felt that indeed he was capable and permitted it. The man who normally led the horse walked behind. As we walked up and up the ascent to Mualkai, Dick's horse suddenly balked. We do not know what caused it—a snake or perhaps a scorpion. The horse ran out of control up the hill and poor Dick began to fall off. We had not realized the danger of this before, but because his legs were too short to reach the stirrups, he had put his feet into the loop of the leather straps holding the stirrups. As our son fell from the horse, his left foot caught in the strap and he was dragged, upside down, along the road.

I was numb with fear as I chased the horse and finally caught up with him a hundred yards or so uphill. I thought the flying hooves might have killed our dear son, or that his head might have been dashed on the rocks. I grabbed Dick and pulled him free. He was crying. His heavy woolen coat was over his head. Thankfully, praise God, he was unhurt, aside from some scratches. The woolen coat protected his face, and the place where the accident happened was sandy, clear of rocks. But what a scare!

Never again did we let him ride alone until he was a few years older. And I vowed that we would bring out a proper child's saddle with hooded stirrups, so that never again could his foot be caught. We never forgot the lesson learned that day, and we did buy and bring out a child's saddle in 1953.

As we traveled on toward Tlangkhua, our companions told us of gruesome tragedies on horses, how one man fell off and was impaled on a sharp bamboo, and how one little Chin boy was dragged by his foot through a river bottom and was killed on the rocks, exactly as our young son had fallen. How thankful we were that we still had our firstborn son!

At the conclusion of this eleven-day tour, we realized that "whole family touring" was not the best thing for us, at least while the children were small. Most of the villagers had never seen white people before, and the children especially were objects of curiosity. The bamboo walls of our shelter were peepholes for hundreds of children. Washing up or taking a bath proved difficult or impossible. And I will not mention the problems of an inadequate latrine.

Teaching with Phonograph

On one of my trips to Rangoon I purchased a phonograph, which the British call a gramophone, and seven records. These were 78 r.p.m. records, considered antiques now. The phonograph was a sensation in the villages. Literally every person in the villages came to hear this marvelous machine that made music. One of the best records was sung by Bing Crosby, "Try a Little Tenderness." I always told the listeners, "This is not exactly a Christian song, but it has a Christian message, which is to be tender and loving to your wife and children."

166

So I played the Tenderness song, among others. But I never had the nerve to play the flip side. It was "Sweet Georgia Brown."

Chapter 31

FURLOUGH AND A BABY

Our furlough in the United States began in 1951; the Nelsons' furlough began the same year. We both had stayed about six months longer than normal because we wanted to bring the Tiddim and Haka Bible Schools to completion. With the students graduated and already engaging in pastoral work, we felt free to leave Burma. We asked Hau Go, back from two years in seminary in Philadelphia, to carry on the work and begin what we meant as a permanent theological school for the training of pastors.

Welcoming Hau Go Back to Burma

Betty Lue and I met Hau Go in the village of Hmawntlang in early April shortly before we went to Rangoon for our departure. Back from two years of study in America, he looked fit, and as for his clothing, I had forgotten how nice new American trousers, shoes, shirts, and coats could look. Everything was new and clean, and up-to-date in style. Five years of knocking around in Burma had done my things in. My pants were patched on the knees and frayed at the cuffs. Shirts were about worn out. My shoes were almost falling apart. It was indeed time for us to go home to America.

Sailing on the *Prome*

Franklin and Phileda with Lois, Karen, and baby Phyllis, and Betty Lue and I with Richard and Ruth sailed together on the *Prome* of the Henderson Line on May 23, 1951. The ship had been delayed for two weeks which gave us some time in Rangoon to study literacy under Dr. Frank Laubach, a visiting expert in the field of teaching illiterate people to read. Thus we did not mind the delay.

The *Prome* proved to be a "happy ship," for we had comfortable cabins and the vessel steamed sedately, making stops at Ceylon (now Sri Lanka), Aden, Port Sudan (where the ship loaded 4,300 bales of cotton), Port Said, and Plymouth, England. It was a British ship and manned mostly by Indians, so we enjoyed rice and curry every day.

We also enjoyed the Nelsons' company on board, and we had 34 days until reaching England to discuss future plans for our families after furlough. We expected that the two families would return to Burma in September, 1952, and start a Bible School, a high school, a hospital, and a new mission center for these projects. That was our dream and vision.

I have mentioned that Frank and I had become fast personal friends, never having to differ in theology or biblical understanding. We were close enough to joke together. On shipboard, I would greet Frank with, "Hi, Nothing Remarkable, it's a nice day." Frank would rejoin with, "Good morning, Negative, how are you?" We would laugh uproariously. These names for each other came from mission doctors' reports on our health. One doctor examining Frank checked on his brain and nervous system and noted "Nothing Remarkable" on Frank's chart. The doctor who examined my brain and nervous system wrote "Negative" on my chart.

Back Home in the USA

My father met us in New York and soon we were with relatives in Chicago. We continued on to Decatur, Illinois, and there met Betty's mother and sisters. Her father had passed away during our term in Burma. We stayed some weeks in Decatur.

Betty Lue and I went to Chicago in September to attend the Northern Baptist Theological Seminary for six months. I brushed up on Hebrew, useful for the translation of the Old Testament that David Van Bik and I were doing. I took courses in biblical studies and theology also. Betty took courses in Christian education and

New Testament. Richard went to first grade in a public school, and Ruth was in a nursery school run by the seminary. During all the months of furlough I kept busy with "deputation visits" to churches where with the aid of color slides I told of the work among the Chins. Furlough was thus for us not a vacation; it was a time of work, traveling, telling the story of missions, and of renewing family ties.

Vigorous Deputation Speaking

During my first term in Burma I made extraordinary efforts to make color slides to show on our return to the States. This was in the late forties and color film was difficult to get and even more difficult to get processed. Furthermore, my camera made pictures approximately 2 x 3 inches in size. The pictures were of superlative quality and in beautiful color, but I had to do the developing myself in Haka. At that time, Rangoon was too hot for good color developing. At any rate, with Betty's help I developed all the film and made them into 3x4 inch glass slides, heavy to carry but beautiful on the screen. Churches loved it, and so many invitations to speak came in that I was kept on the run from April to mid-December. In those days, color slides were still a rarity and the response to my messages and pictures was gratifying.

Birth of Martha Anne

Of course, the birth of our second daughter was the event of the year 1952. We were in Decatur, Illinois, at Betty's mother's home. Richard was in second grade now and Ruth Kristin in kindergarten. The children were well and happy and looked forward to meeting the new arrival.

Martha Anne Johnson was born on Oct. 21st. It was a blessing to have a fine hospital in Decatur with skilled doctors and nurses, for Betty Lue needed a blood transfusion after the birth. Well cared for, Betty recovered quickly and proudly brought home another blonde-haired girl, but this one had dark brown, almost black eyes.

The doctors and the mission board ordered us to wait at least three months before starting back to Burma, so Martha could get the proper shots and we make sure of her fitness to go abroad.

Purchases for the Second Term

Through the gifts of relatives, friends, and churches, we were able to make a number of purchases, which we hoped would make our life a bit easier in Burma and our Christian ministry more effective.

For safety, and remembering the near tragedy when Dick fell from a horse and was dragged, we bought a Western-type child's saddle suitable for a young boy or girl. This one had hooded stirrups so a foot could not slip through and be caught.

When leaving Burma we gave our portable typewriter to David Van Bik who was entering the Burma Institute of Theology at Insein, a suburb of Rangoon. In America we bought two office-type machines, one used and the other a new long platen Olympia with a special dot-under-T key.

Two stoves were also part of our freight. To replace those two iron bars over an open fire which served us during our whole first term, we purchased a wood-burning cook stove. We also took out Betty's mother's Heatrola, a first- class heating stove, with a brown porcelain jacket and a sturdy cast iron firebox. This was designed to burn coal, and no coal was available, so we had to use wood, cutting every stick of wood to a length of 12 inches or less.

I also carried out two firearms this time. One was a powerful hunting rifle of .30-06 caliber, capable of felling deer, bears, leopards, and even tigers. Those dangerous animals were not numerous any longer in the Chin Hills, but they did exist. The other gun was a simple one barrel shotgun, one with a visible hammer. Through the experiences of our first term, when I had a hammerless shotgun, I had learned that many Chin villagers could not use a hammerless shotgun safely.

Radio

An important purchase was a radio. We had been without one for years and longed to get the news and some music into our home. We bought a Zenith Trans-Oceanic portable radio, with shortwave bands. It was excellent, except that batteries were very expensive and had to be ordered and mailed out from the U.S.A. This was before the days of the transistor radio.

Printing Press

For years we had dreamed of establishing a printing press in Haka for producing Christian literature. We did not have the money to invest in a big machine, so I bought a Kelsey, 6 by 10 inch size hand press. I also got the needed equipment: rollers, lead type, type cases, ornaments, spacers, ink, etc., and very important, directions on how to print, for we were raw amateurs. The Kelsey worked by hand, pushing a lever. It was fairly slow and could only print up to 6 by 10 inches in size, but it was not a toy, it actually did print successfully. When set up in Haka, in our attic, we began what has become the Deirel Press with its own building, large foot-operated printing press, large cutter, and equipment.

The Crosley Farm-O-Road Vehicle

The most expensive item of equipment we took out to Burma was a small vehicle called a Farm-O-Road, a sort of pint-sized jeep. I doubt that many Americans will even recognize the name. It was made for a few years by the Crosley Corporation but evidently was not a commercial success and so went out of production.

I bought this small vehicle deliberately because it was only 48 inches wide and therefore was the only jeep able to cross the Manipur River and the Pao River suspension bridges. A regular-sized jeep was too wide for the bridges. The Farm-O-Road had a 16 horsepower 4-cylinder engine. It had a 3-speed transmission and a reduction gear, giving a total of 6 forward speeds and 2 reverse. It had small wheels, but in the rear there were dual wheels, so there were six tires on the car.

This vehicle was a gift from a church in Los Angeles. Their generosity made it possible for our family to get in to Haka and out to various villages much more easily and cheaply than by foot and with horses. We used the Farm-O-Road for all six years of our second term, finally selling it and getting a full-sized Jeep for our third and last term, for by then new bridges and new roads had improved transport in the Chin Hills.

The Estey Organ

One day the ladies in the Women's Circle at church asked Betty if there was anything she wanted to get for the coming term in Burma. "Ask what you wish and we'll get it for you," they said. Betty wasn't sure if they meant something for ten dollars or for a hundred, but she decided to ask for a musical instrument, much needed. "Well," she said, "it may be too expensive, but to tell the truth, we could use an Estey Organ, the little fold-down organ." "We will get it for you," said the ladies, and they did. The Estey Organ folds down into a portable package, and it is foot pedaled. This was a great addition to our freight for Burma.

Packing for Burma

We collected all of "our stuff" in Decatur and packed for shipment by freight. The big object, of course, was the Crosley Farm-O-Road. A local company made a wooden box large enough for this vehicle. When I saw how much extra room there was in the box, I added things like shovels, spades, hoes, rakes, and lots of stovepipe. That last was needed to replace the homemade stovepipe I had made years ago.

These extras thrown into the box were to cause me trouble in Rangoon. The customs official gave me a good scolding for loading undeclared objects into that box, but he did not fine me. Some things are learned by trial and error.

Chapter 32

OUR RETURN TO BURMA

The Atlantic Crossing and Onward

Farewells to family and loved ones are difficult when one is going away for years, but this time things were better. We knew where we were going, even back to the same house as before. We now knew the language and had countless friends in Burma. The reports from the churches were encouraging. The government was building and widening roads and bridges for easier transport. So we went out from America with high hopes and with the prayers of thousands.

The fastest ship on the North Atlantic at the time was the *S. S. United States,* and on that ship we crossed the Atlantic in six days. The sailing date was January 31, 1953, and we were told that the ship went at 35 miles an hour.

On February 13 we boarded our old friend, the *Prome,* at Liverpool, sailed the same day, and steamed sedately at a comfortable 10 or 12 knots to Egypt, through the Suez Canal, to Port Sudan, Aden, Colombo, and on to Rangoon. The *Prome,* a freight/passenger ship of about 8,000 tons, seemed quite delightful to us as we even knew some of the officers who were on our previous sailing.

Again as in 1951, there was the laundry problem. There were no laundry facilities, so Betty washed clothes, including diapers for Martha, in the cabin washbasin, then hung them up on lines stretched out in the cabin after the captain made the usual morning inspection. She turned on the fan and we went on deck until the clothes were dry. Evidently Egypt was angry with Britain for some reason at this time, so we were refused fresh water at Suez and we had a water shortage until reaching Port Sudan. The same was true of vegetables, so we ate cabbage and cauliflower, cauliflower and cabbage. But we all survived!

Rangoon at Last

At last the journey drew to an end. On the morning of March 19 we saw the muddy water that told us that we were in delta of the great Irrawaddy River. We anchored for the turn of the tide and then in the early afternoon we began the run up to Rangoon. The mangrove swamps on the shore, the palms and banana trees, the thatched houses of the people, and then, at last, off in the distance the golden dome and spire of the Shwe Dagon pagoda, all spoke to us of the familiar Burma scene.

We were back in Burma for our second term. Our absence had been longer than anticipated—1 year, 9 months, 27 days—because of the arrival of Martha Anne, but we were all in good health and intended to stay for the full term of five and a half years. As it turned out, we did stay the full term and one year more, due to the press of the work.

How good it was to be back, this time to be welcomed by many Chins living in the Rangoon area and by the missionaries to whom now we were dear friends.

But there was a dark cloud. Franklin and Phileda Nelson had to delay their return. We still maintained hope for their return for several months, but our hopes were dashed; the Burma government did not issue stay permits for them, and they were not able to return to the Tiddim area work.

Preparations in Rangoon

In Rangoon Betty and I had the usual rush. This time it was to get things through customs, visit the police, get licenses for guns, ammunition, and the radio, get registered as foreigners, try to get extensions of our stay permits, open bank accounts, visit with many Chin friends, buy provisions in the bazaar, repack baggage for transport by mules and coolies, and send 3 tons of equipment off on the river steamer up-country. The Farm-O-Road was not due in Burma until sometime in May, so we knew that we would have to wait until after the rainy season to bring it up to the Chin Hills.

When we ourselves flew on April 5 from Rangoon to Kalemyo, it was Easter Sunday, a most unhappy time to be forced to travel. But those were the only reservations available on the airplane which now had twice a week service to Kalemyo.

Kalemyo to the Manipur River, Jeep Troubles

From stories about jeep breakdowns in Burma, one might conclude that jeeps are most awful vehicles. Actually, when in proper repair they are dependable and versatile, very useful vehicles. But the problem in Burma was the inability to get spare parts, clean gasoline, proper oil and lubrications, etc., so that gradually they began to fail mechanically. This happened to us on our return to Haka.

David Van Bik had flown to Kalemyo a few days before us, and arranged a jeep to transport us to the Manipur River, to the crossing called Vaar, below Lumbang village. David then went on ahead. We did get the jeep on arrival at Kalemyo. The driver was a Burman who could not speak a word of English or any of the Chin languages, and our Burmese was halting. All went well as far as Fort White, where the road turns southward toward Falam. At this point something went wrong with the transmission. The jeep could go only in low or high; second gear was out. We managed a dozen miles and then the low gear went out. Now our driver had only high gear. Thankfully the road was mostly level, but there were a number of hills where both Betty and I had to get out and push the jeep. Even Dick and Ruth had to help push.

At last, after nightfall, we reached Lumbang, expecting to find Ram Hlun and Chia Ling there and perhaps a meal on the fire at the dak bungalow. Alas, there was no one to meet us and the bungalow was locked.

The jeepable road now reached the Manipur River, 6 miles farther down, so we decided to go there, thinking that our cook and houseboy would certainly be there. The road was so curvy that we found many switchbacks where the jeep had to be backed up to round the curve. Then we discovered that the gears would not back the jeep. We had only one gear—high forward! Therefore it became the job of Betty, Dick, Ruth, and me to push the jeep back and uphill so it could make the sharp turns. We had run out of drinking water and were hot, tired, thirsty, and despairing when we finally reached the Manipur River and found neither Ram Hlun nor Chia Ling. We had telegraphed them ten days previously—why had they not come to meet us?

The Vaar to Falam

Some man had a thatched shed at the river. He gave us tea to drink, but had no food.

Anyway, we were too tired to eat. Poor little Martha, only four months old, was so thirsty that she drank a whole cup of sweetened tea right from the cup! No one there could speak Haka Chin. We felt forlorn and depressed, but we managed to lay out some blankets, hang one mosquito net for the three children, and pass a wretched night. We had no mosquito net for ourselves. It was probably there at the Vaar, exposed to mosquitoes at the low elevation, where I contracted the malaria that almost killed me a few weeks later.

To Home at Haka

That was a most difficult Easter Sunday. If the jeep had not failed, we would have arrived in daylight and possibly gone up to Falam, for now a motor road existed from the river up to Falam. It had been opened to jeep traffic just 2 weeks previously.

The next day turned out better. We managed to get some breakfast at the river, crossed the Manipur on a tiny raft, and then found a jeep on the other side to take us 9 miles on a new road the 4,000 feet ascent to Falam. The Chinese driver went up at 15 miles per hour, which seemed perilously fast for the narrow, twisty road, but we arrived safely. In a few hours we were met by Chia Ling. Our reaction was, "Thanks be to the Lord!" At last here was someone to whom we could talk, someone to help us with meals and the remainder of our trip.

To Home at Haka

We found that neither Ram Hlun nor Chia Ling ever received our telegram or a letter about our coming. The communications had broken down completely. Chia Ling decided to leave home and come to Falam almost on a whim, or maybe a vision. He was followed a day later by Ram Hlun. Soon we had both men to help us and all went well the rest of the trip, which we did with pack horses and on foot. Martha lay in her bassinet which was tied to a bamboo pole carried by four men, always trying to draw herself up to look over the side.

Thursday, April 9, was a beautiful day in the Chin Hills. After we passed the cliffs of Dawn Mountain and neared the familiar Run Mountain on which Haka lies, our hearts beat more quickly. From miles away the village is visible across a valley, and for miles we could see our house shining white in the afternoon sun. A large party of Christians came out to greet us and escorted us in to the mission compound. Thus, after 10,000 miles and 76 days of travel we were home once more. I went upstairs to look at my tools; Dick and Ruth hunted up their old toys. And Betty? She checked up on the cook-house and did those innumerable little touches that make a house into a home.

Eventually we got the house to Betty's standard of order and cleanliness, and prepared to settle down for a long second term.

Chapter 33

CHANGES AND CHALLENGES, 1953

A New Church Building

When we returned to Haka, it was to a mission compound much the way we had left it two years earlier, except that now there was a new two-story church building which was to be dedicated in June. Rev. Sang Ling was still pastor of the church, and we rejoiced that during our absence many good things had happened to the Christian group, including the conversion of the young chief in Haka, Edward Mang Kio. The Christian work both in the village and in the whole area was moving forward well.

We had the same three men as before as helpers: Ram Hlun, our cook; Chia Ling, our second cook and houseman; and Ram Thio, our gardener. Our former ayah, Pente, now married to Chia Ling. had two children and hence no longer worked for us.

Black Water Fever; Bob's Malignant Tertian Malaria

I had been home only about a week when an illness struck me that almost took my life in late April.

I think that I picked up the disease through mosquito bites at the Vaar camp, the Manipur River crossing, where our family had to stay overnight on the way in to Haka. Just about ten days after that overnight camp I came down with fever. I spent six days in bed with temperatures of 103 degrees, reducing gradually. I was on a liquid diet only, and became weak. However, we did not think that it was malaria, for it was not the typical malaria pattern.

During those long days and nights of fever I remember thinking, What about my wife and three children? What will happen to them if I die? My Christian faith was tested.

I was then up for about three days, able only to read and write some letters, and then came down sick again, this time more virulently. My temperature went up to 104 and occasionally to 105 for long periods of time, and I was deathly sick. Thankfully the Civil Surgeon from Falam, an Indian named Dr. Kain, happened to come to Haka for a tour and came down to our house and cared for me.

What Kain gave to me I do not know. It was a huge white tablet. Whatever it was, it broke the fever and I almost dissolved in sweat. Betty had to change pajamas, sheets, and mattress cover. But it felt so wonderful to be free of the terrible fever. Dr. Kain said that my illness was malignant tertian malaria, a particularly dangerous disease, life threatening. Thank the Lord for His mercy—I lived to carry on our work.

First Jeeps to Reach Haka

While I was thus so ill, the first jeeps reached Haka village on Sunday, April 26. It was a magnificent day for a celebration and as most people were not out in the fields, it proved to be a magnet to attract crowds. Most of the Haka women had never seen a wheeled vehicle (aside from my ill-fated motorcycle), and even most of the men were applauding the sensational arrival of the three jeeps. Two were from the Public Works Department, making a trial run, and one jeep was privately owned. The P.W.D. had put 100 coolies to work for weeks on the road to make it usable for small vehicles, and the bridge at the Pao River (halfway between Falam and Haka) had been slightly widened to allow a jeep to cross with one inch to spare on either side.

As for me, I was ecstatic. Now my little Farm-O-Road also could get to Haka, and the government had done the road work; I did not have to worry about how I could afford to fix the road!

Nowadays the Falam-Haka road has a new alignment and is 46 miles long. In 1953 the road was just a widened mule trail and much shorter, 34 miles, but also much steeper and more dangerous.

The Children Begin School

Upon our arrival in Haka, Betty Lue lost no time in starting the children's school. We arrived on a Thursday; she began school for them on Monday. Dick was in 3ʳᵈ grade and Ruth in first. We again used the Calvert School courses, as indeed we did all through their schooling until finally they went to India many years later.

At this time Betty dedicated the hours from 8 to 11 a.m. to their schooling, following a rigid schedule. She asked villagers not to visit during those hours. Only in cases of real emergency did she relax the rule and handle problems or talk to visitors. When the people understood the rules of school for us, things did work out fine and our children had the constant attention that they needed for good learning. We had the joy of seeing all our children do exceedingly well not only in the Calvert School home-study courses but also in subsequent schooling.

Later on, in higher grades, Betty, who was always called Mrs. Johnson in the schoolroom, started classes at 7:30 a.m. and finished at 11:30 with a 15-minute recess.

General Fund Committee in Falam;
Decision on the Bible School

On my 38ᵗʰ birthday, May 1, I was able to eat a bit of soup and was thankful for that. The malaria had weakened me dreadfully and I was afraid that I might not be able to get to Falam for a very important meeting of a committee of the newly planned Convention in the Chin Hills, the organization to tie together the three Baptist Associations. But I regained strength in time and met with the group of 16 men on May 15. These men represented the three Associations existing at that time: Tiddim Baptist Association, Falam Baptist Association, and Haka Baptist Association. These corresponded to the government Subdivisions in the "Chin Special Division," as the Hills were called at that time. Later, the Special Division became the Chin State.

Our purpose was eventually to unite the Associations into a Convention. We also wanted to establish a theological school to train men as pastors and church leaders in accordance with the plan that Frank Nelson and I had considered during our first term.

So two important decisions regarding the new and permanent Bible School were made at the Falam meeting: (1) The Bible School would be started in Tiddim on July 1, 1953, with students limited to 15—five each from Tiddim, Falam, and Haka areas—who had passed 6th Standard, with English as the medium of instruction. (2) The teachers would be Rev. Hau Go and Lun Cung Nung, the latter a 1950 graduate of the Nelsons' school.

We can consider May, 1953, as the inauguration of the Chin Bible School which has grown now to a thriving institution, staffed by Chins, and granting degrees, now called the Zomi Theological College. A mighty oak has grown from a small acorn.

The Word "Zomi"

It was at this meeting that I really first became aware of the use of Zomi in regard to our Chin work. Two names were being used for the new organization being formed. These were "Zomi Baptist Convention" and "Chin Hills Baptist Convention." The Committee at Falam specifically voted that the latter name be used so the government would be aware of the Chin nature of our organization in the petition to be sent to the government regarding the Nelsons' return.

I cannot recall the word "Zomi" being used during our first term. It was especially desired by the Tiddim people, and the other groups acceded to their wishes. Although the word in reverse, Mizo, referring to the Lushai people across the border has been accepted by the Indian government and the name of the Lushai homeland is officially called Mizoram, to my knowledge the Burma government has never accepted the name "Zomi" for the Chins. Also, because other people in general do not recognize the name, our mission usually adds the word "Chin" to the official name; thus, "Zomi Chin Baptist Convention" is found in reports and articles on the Christian work in Burma.

Dedication of the Haka Church, 1953

The official name of the two-story wooden church constructed in 1951—1953 was the Carson Memorial Baptist Church. It was dedicated with great joy on June 21. Betty and I thought that a tea for celebration would be enough, but the Chins firmly wanted a great feast, in spite of the rainy season. Sure enough, we had rain the whole weekend. The Chins killed three cows and that, together with the cow we killed for our wedding anniversary, provided a sumptuous feast for a great crowd on Saturday.

On Sunday, for the dedication, there were 525 people in the church service and there were 11 choir numbers. I gave a sermon, and then Pastor Sang Ling preached for 50 minutes, making it a long but impressive service. One group of girls sang a song in 4-part harmony in English. Betty sang with them to give them confidence.

We thought that this fine wooden church building would serve us for many years. We could not imagine that in just a few years it would be too crowded and that we would have to shore up the floor to keep it from collapsing from the weight of the people, and that in only eight years we would have to start building a much larger church! Thus God was blessing.

We Become Purchasing Agents

Upon our return to Burma, I was elected a member of the mission Executive Committee which met four times yearly in Rangoon. I went as a representative for the Chins, to present financial and other needs. Due to the long time involved in travel, I managed to get to only three meetings per year for each year of our term. With these frequent trips downcountry, I became an unofficial agent for many Chins, and I bought and brought up paint, hardware, nuts and bolts, tools, corn grinders, meat grinders, and medicines, etc. We charged only the purchase cost plus a portion of the transport cost. This is how we got involved in a revolving medical fund.

The Revolving Medical Fund

One of the many good things that we were able to do for the Chins during our second term was to begin a revolving medical fund program of selling medicines. The money came from a grant of $3,000 by the mission for the Chin Hills. Tiddim got half, to be shared with Falam, and Haka got half for our larger and more remote area.

I brought up a large quantity of medicines, about Rs. 7,000 worth in July, 1953, and we established our medicine sales in the front room of our house, which was my office. I had some shelves built and we began to supply simple medicines to the people at cost. We charged only enough above the bare cost of the medicines to cover the cost of transport and the salary of a young lady to be the seller.

Why Missionaries Sold Medicines

The reason we began this service was that too many people were either unable to secure the medicines from the government dispensary or from bazaar sellers, or that they were victimized by unscrupulous sellers. In particular, traveling sellers were coming over from the Lushai Hills and taking money for worthless chalk tablets or other counterfeit medicines. Anyone coming to our dispensary knew that he would not be cheated and also that he would get proper directions on dosage, etc.

A constant stream of Chins came to our door daily for medicine. In addition to helping with their health needs, it also offered us the opportunity to tell about the Great Physician in whose name we came to Haka. It was indeed an evangelistic opportunity opened to us. I cannot begin to measure the many times either Betty or I was called in to counsel with such people, nor how many were turned to the Lord by means of this simple evidence of Christian love.

We kept a meticulous record of every sale and every rupee and anna collected, and later, when the money changed, of every kyat and pya taken in. We insisted on such careful records to protect ourselves against the charge of making a personal profit from the sales. Because it was a revolving fund, we came to the end of our work in Burma in 1966 with the fund still intact, and turned over the money and records to the Chins.

I should mention that many times we were asked to give medicines in exchange for eggs, bananas, vegetables, or other produce. We always lost on those deals as the medicines were always more valuable than the gifts.

Chapter 34

NEW THINGS IN 1953

⤳

Better Mail Service; also Wireless

In the troubled days of our first term the mail service to and from the Chin Hills broke down and almost did not exist for over a year. The Nelsons and we resorted to our own mail service over to India. In contrast to that, the year 1953 brought a speedy and much more reliable mail service. We were able to get airmail letters from the U.S.A. in about three weeks. Parcels also came with regularity. All in all, the mail service to Burma was good. Coolies still carried the mail inside the Chin Hills area. Later, when the postal service began to depend on jeeps and trucks for carrying the mail, the service deteriorated due to landslides, mechanical troubles, and mud.

Wireless service to and from Haka began during the rainy season of 1953. This too was a great help for us. No longer did we have to depend on wireless messages forwarded by cooly from Falam. We could even send telegrams to the United States, but that cost 25 cents a word, so we never used that service.

New Things for Women

During our first term of service Betty Lue was a very busy person, talking with and helping Chin women and girls. This was an area of work almost closed to me, a man. But women would talk freely to Betty and open their minds and hearts freely. The same continued in our second term. I am absolutely amazed at the many activities in which she was involved, the many new projects she started, and the hundreds and even thousands of Chin women that she touched in her ministry.

The morning teaching Dick and Ruth in 3rd and 1st grades took all of Betty's time until lunch, but she did have a 15 minute recess when she talked to people on health matters or personal concerns. In early June she was involved two hours a day in teaching some men from far south of us, in the Matu area. She organized and taught a girls' choir which learned to sing in English. Other chores were, of course, the planning of meals, overseeing the garden, doing the weekly laundry in my homemade washing machine, overseeing the selling of medicines, talking to dozens of villagers daily, and the care and nurture of our children, particularly Martha who was still a nursing baby.

Pre-Natal Care and Baby Care Classes

In June, Betty started a class for women in Pre-Natal Care and Baby Care. The class met at our house every Wednesday afternoon after the regular women's meeting. In this project she worked together with a young lady from Falam who had trained at our mission hospital in Namkham and later at Rangoon and who was posted to the government hospital at Haka. There she was the only trained nurse on the staff. She was a Christian and so Betty asked her to teach the women, but as she did not know Haka Chin at first, Betty became her interpreter. My wife provided all the necessary things for demonstrations, and this work continued for many months. By this they built up the confidence of Chin women in the nurse so that they were willing to come to the hospital for maternity cases instead of coming afterward for repair of the damage caused by the unsanitary practices of village midwives.

The nurse spoke English quite well and her presence was a real boost to the struggling, poorly equipped government hospital which still was located next door to us in the old Carson Bungalow.

Betty an Organ Teacher

In July our Estey organ was carried in. We were delighted that it was dry and in good shape—in contrast to our fine settee that we had bought in England, which got wet from rain in Mandalay and again at the Vaar crossing and thus suffered some rot. As soon as the organ appeared, there also appeared a group of youth anxious to learn to play. Almost before we knew what was happening, Betty was an organ teacher.

Haka Girls Progressing in Education

By 1953 a number of girls had progressed to the 7th and 8th Standards in school. Many wanted to learn English better. So Betty took on a weekly class for them. She reported, "It is nice to be able to speak a little English now and then to some of the girls. They are very shy and hide their faces at first, but after a while they get a little more nerve, and speak out."

Then Betty began a weekly class to teach the girls who were teachers in the Sunday School. Of this she wrote: "We are terrifically busy. I had seventeen here last night for a Sunday School Teachers' Class. They come every week to study the lesson which they will teach on Sunday. There are now 12 classes in our Sunday School, and with substitute teachers that makes quite a group." Then, as though all these activities were not enough, Betty added yet another job: teaching in a surprise Bible School.

Seven Matu Men; Our Surprise Bible School

One day in late May seven men arrived on our doorstep. They were weary and travel worn. "We are new Christians from Matu," they said, "and we want to enter the Bible School. We want to work for God in our area."

"We are glad to have you come," I said, "but didn't you know that the Bible School is starting up in Tiddim?"

They were all crestfallen when they learned that the Bible School would be in Tiddim, not in Haka, and with only 15 students, none from Matu, and that only 6th Standard pass students would be admitted, and that instruction would be in English. Not a one of them knew a word of English. These young men had only 4th Standard education. "We have walked for 14 days to get here, and what can we do?" they asked.

When Frank Nelson and I had divided our work years earlier, Frank took responsibility for Tiddim and Falam areas, and I took Haka and "all south" which included the Matu, Kanpetlet, and Paletwa areas. And here were some men from Matu. I knew that two Chin pastors were sent to Matu by the northern Christian churches in 1945, a year before we arrived. These were Rev. That Dun and Rev. Pa Hrek. These two men studied in our Haka Bible School in 1948-50 and had been able to convert about 700 Matu people to the Christian faith. Now here were six of them, anxious to study. They had almost no money, but hoped to attend the new Bible School. Their food supply was exhausted on their 14-day journey. What could we do for them?

These students had come without any advance warning, and by all normal standards we should have sent them home. But here they were, the firstfruits of the Matu area, men hungry for learning the Word of God. We didn't have the heart to send them back home.

Betty and I talked it over and decided that we would give them six weeks of Bible study in Chin. I took them for three hours every morning and Betty taught them two hours daily after lunch. For her, this was in addition to the schooling for Dick and Ruth and the other informal teaching she was doing.

When the six weeks were up, it was time for me to go to Rangoon to be gone a month. So, still tender-hearted, we couldn't send them home. Betty added my classes to hers and kept the Matu men studying during my absence. She also began them in English, necessary if they were to get into the regular Bible School next year. Thus she continued until other men and women arrived for a new project, the Seven Weeks Bible Study, whereupon the Matu men joined that and continued their studies.

So it turned out that these unexpected students actually had over four months of training in our home. We were able to provide food and some new clothing for them from various gifts we received from America from time to time, gifts which were termed "specific gifts" and were outside the mission budget, so we could use the money any way we wished.

It may be well here to mention that the three southern subdivisions of Matu, Kanpetlet, and Paletwa were marked on government maps as "unadministered areas," indicating how very remote these peoples were, even from government officials, at this time of history.

Chapter 35

"SEVEN WEEKS" AND BIBLE CONFERENCE

U pon our return to Haka in 1953, Betty and I were literally bombarded with questions and requests from the area Christians who were very eager for further instruction in the Christian faith.

"Bawipa, we need teaching in the Bible. We need to know how to run meetings and lead the churches." (The word "bawipa" is given to male government officials, teachers, chiefs, and missionaries as a term of respect. It is often used for God and Jesus. The female equivalent is "bawinu.")

"Bawipa, the Bible Conferences are good but too short, only one week. Can you teach us the Bible for a longer time?"

These were questions asked of us not by pastors but by church deacons and other leaders in the villages who wanted to know more how to conduct services and run their churches well.

The Seven Weeks Bible Study Program

Of course we were thrilled by the chance to help in this way.. This was the very reason the mission had sent us to Burma. We agreed to run such classes and decided on a time late in the rainy season, just before the annual Bible Conference. We called this program the Seven Weeks Bible Study to distinguish it from the regular Bible School which would come to Haka in 1954. These seven weeks of special study and the one week of Bible Conference following it

193

made a neat package of two months of steady teaching, after which would come the open season for touring the villages.

So we agreed to begin. We set the dates as August 17 to September 30. The Bible Conference would be October 1 to 7.

Thus began what turned out to be one of our most successful activities during the remainder of our years in Burma. The Seven Weeks courses, held yearly, became very popular because they filled a real need. Each pastor had a circle of anywhere from 5 to 20 villages under his care, and was unable to get to more than one per Sunday, as they were widely separated. Thus the Sunday church services were largely in the care of laymen who needed help in preaching and teaching. Actually, we widened the scope of our teaching considerably, to take in health, hygiene, agriculture, and music.

Perhaps the annual 7-Weeks teaching and the annual Bible Conferences were strategic for the future rapid development of the Christian churches. I should mention that these were not limited to lay persons. Pastors and preachers often came and profited from the teaching. They were open to both men and women, of course.

One more thing of interest, these Bible courses were run at practically no cost to the mission. Each student had to provide for his or her own living quarters and food. Usually they would stay with friends somewhere in the village. Often there were some people who without financial help would have to return home, so Betty and I helped such persons with gifts from America. Also, every year we bought and killed a cow or water buffalo for the Seven Weeks students. We always enjoyed the Chin cultural reaction to such a gift of meat. Chins might forget to thank us for providing two months of teaching, but they were always profuse in their praise of us for killing a cow!

The 1953 Seven Weeks Bible Study was highly successful. We thought there might be 20 students. There were 66, including the seven Matu men who joined in. I taught three hours a day; Betty took two hours daily in the afternoons. Courses were on the book of Acts, Life of Christ, Parables of Jesus, Old Testament, and Health.

The Seven Weeks Bible Study courses ended with a flair on September 30 and the next day we went immediately into the Bible Conference.

Bible Conferences: an Explanation

Bible Conferences, as Franklin Nelson in Tiddim and I in Haka conducted, were, as the name suggests, a time for church people to confer on religious matters. We used the name Bible in the title to indicate our high regard for the Scriptures as we gathered, pastors and laymen, women and men, for a week of teaching from the Bible. There was always time for discussion and the raising and answering of questions. Discussions were not limited to religious questions; we always had time to teach health and sanitation, child care, good parenting, and things of general interest, such as the decimal system when the new money (100 pyas to the kyat) was introduced by government.

The 1953 Bible Conference

Our first post-furlough Bible Conference was held October 1 to 7 in Haka, this time in our new church building. Attendance was good, 174 in all, and the daily program may be of interest

9:00 to 9:15	Devotions by different leaders
9:15 to 10:00	Book of Galatians, taught by R. G. Johnson
10:00 to 11:00	A "work period" devoted to revision and correction of the Haka hymnal
11:00 to 12:00	Leadership training taught by Rev. Sang Ling
1:00 to 2:00	Discussion time and business meeting
2:00 to 3:00	Christian Education, taught by Mrs. Johnson
Evenings:	Special programs 6 nights out of 8, including two dramas put on by the local Christian Endeavour youth.

The "discussion time" allowed everyone present to talk about the problems of marriage, divorce, bride price, animistic customs, and the like, which needed to be aired and resolved if possible. Also at this time, I presented a simple "Funeral Manual" to give guidance to those conducting Christian burials. These books were greatly appreciated and greatly needed, to be sure.

Every pastor in our vast area was present for the 1953 Bible Conference except one man from faraway Matu. We all were encouraged by reports from the workers in the Kanpetlet district; they now had 60 baptized Christians. I think that I was too busy to notice that Pastor Sang Ling was a little bit tired during his teaching hours. We did not know that this would be his last time with us.

Burma Changes Currency to Kyats and Pyas

During the rains of 1953 Burma changed over to decimal currency. Instead of the old Indian system of 12 pies to an anna, and 16 annas to the rupee, now we had 100 pyas to the kyat.

The kyat still had the same value as the rupee, about 21 cents at that time. Kyat is pronounced as "chat" and pya as "pia," both with the soft Italian "a."

At the Bible Conference Betty and I took time to try to explain the mysteries of writing the decimal system. The decimal point was bewildering to the people. For instance, to indicate 1 kyat and 5 pyas, they wished to write it as K 1/5 or else K 1.5. We explained that it should be K 1.05. When they finally mastered the idea that the decimal point is followed by <u>two</u> digits, they went to their homes able to add and subtract in the new system. But for over a year, we had problems in church finances until finally the old pies, annas, and rupees system gave way to the new.

Chapter 36

JEEP ACCIDENT AT MILE 17

U ntil 1953 no Secretary from the Boston or New York headquarters of the American Baptist Foreign Mission Society had
ever been able to visit the Chin Hills with the sole exception of
Dr. Joseph Robbins who traversed a portion of the Tiddim field in
1933 and was present for the Chin Hills Baptist Association meeting
at Tuimui village near Kalemyo. Until the advent of air service to
Kalemyo about twenty years later it was just too time-consuming
and expensive to reach our remote fields.

Plans for John Skoglund Visit, November 1953

Therefore we were very pleased to learn that Dr. John Skoglund,
our Foreign Secretary in New York, planned to visit the Hills in
October. Due to visa problems in India, Skoglund had to postpone
his visit until November. I learned via wireless that Skoglund and his
party would arrive in Kalemyo by air on November 5. Dr Richard
Cummings of the Home Department in New York and Rev. Erville
Sowards, our mission secretary based in Rangoon, would accompany
John to Haka. I was delighted at the prospect of seeing these mission
officials reach Haka, probably one of the more remote of our worldwide mission stations at the time, and the Haka people began to make
preparations for the visit. They bought a very expensive handwoven
silk blanket, the kind called *puan sen* by the Chins, as a gift to this top
official, and they planned special meetings and dinners.

I was glad for the delay of one month for the visit because it gave roads one more month to dry out after the rainy season. Jeeps had reached Haka in late April, so I knew that jeeps could carry us from the Manipur River to Haka, and I could hire a truck to take us from Kalemyo to the river. My little jeeplet, the Farm-O-Road, was far too small for our party, and I left it parked in Kalemyo in a Methodist missionary's garage.

The Skoglund Party Arrives in Kalemyo

The airplane from Mandalay arrived promptly on time at Kalemyo on Nov. 5. In addition to the hundreds of Christian church members in the area to greet Skoglund's party, there was a great delegation of military and government people out to greet other important visitors. These were the Hon. Minister for Chin Affairs who was a Buddhist Chin from the Kanpetlet area, several Members of Parliament, and some army officers. All those who arrived on the airplane were warmly welcomed by the church people, so it was a pleasant occasion for all.

The best-maintained vehicle that I could find for my party was a truck en route to the new crossing place of the Manipur River, a place called Vaar. All during our first term, we had used the old suspension bridge about two miles farther downstream, the bridge that was limited to two mules or horses and one driver. That was a long, narrow, swaying bridge suspended by two steel cables, and made by the British. In my many crossings there I never saw anyone overload that bridge. One look at the rocks and rushing water far below made believers of the two-mule load limit.

Sitting on the load of boxes and sacks of rice in an open body truck was not the best way to introduce John Skoglund, Richard Cummings, and Erville Sowards to travel in Chinland, but it was the best I could do for them. Ram Hlun was with me as cook, and he made a good dinner for us all at the government rest house at Pine Tree Camp, where we had a pleasant overnight stay. On the next day our truck took us to the Vaar crossing in the Manipur River valley.

The Vaar Crossing

There was no bridge, hence trucks could not proceed. Months earlier, when the river was low, two jeeps had been taken across to the Falam side and were available for hire. One of these would take us on to Haka.

A single cable spanned the river, a distance more than a football field. On this wire cable was a wooden cage suspended by two pulleys, and meant to carry one man at a time across the river. Men on both sides of the river pulled ropes to draw the cage back and forth. It was a scary contraption to ride, and it was best not to look down at the rocks below. We all crossed safely, one at a time, and enjoyed tea at a little shop nearby.

Up to Falam

I hired the better of the two jeeps, driven by an Indian man, and we motored up to Falam, a 4,000 foot climb. It was my first time to experience motor travel on this road, which I had climbed hot, tired, and weary many times. The road was still narrow, and twice the jeep had to be backed up in order to make the sharp corners.

We reached Falam at 6 p.m., rather late, but had a quick supper and went to the church. It was packed for the meeting with these two mission leaders from America. Falam was then the capital of the Chin Special Division, and we were pleased to see that many government people came to the service of welcome.

Over the Mountainside at Mile 17

On the next day, Saturday, Nov. 7, we started off at about 8 o'clock on the last lap of the trip, 34 miles to Haka along the old mule trail, using the same jeep and driver. We expected to arrive by noon. There were six of us in the open jeep: the four Americans, Ram Hlun, and the Indian driver. All went well and we passed over the Pao River suspension bridge and started up the long 7-mile climb toward Haka. About a mile beyond the bridge, at milestone 17 from Falam, exactly halfway to Haka, there was a short but very steep grade. Nobody is sure exactly what happened. I believe, though, that the driver was going in what is called the "high range" and when the jeep engine faltered, he attempted to shift down into "low range" to get more power to the wheels. To do this, he had to use his brakes to prevent a backward slide. But the brakes were faulty—he had to pump the brake pedal to get the brakes to hold, and he did not have time to pump the pedal. The brakes thus failed to hold, and in a twinkling we rolled backward out of control, plunging over an almost precipitous descent. We went right over the edge, and down, down, down.

Dick Cummings and I were sitting in the rear seat on the right side. Our side of the jeep went over first, and as there was no top we probably were dumped out first, rolling with the jeep down the steep hill. I remember nothing but spinning like a top and then that was all. I was knocked unconscious.

When I came to, I found myself lying on my back on a pile of brush or branches. The jeep was ten feet farther downhill on its wheels, jammed against a tree forty feet down from the road. Some people say it turned over twice. Dick Cummings was a few feet away, also prostrate, unable to get up. Ram Hlun, Dr. Skoglund, and Erville Sowards were all on their feet, but injured. Skoglund's ribs were hurt, so that he could walk but could not stoop down or bend. Erville Sowards had a bandage over the bridge of his nose and kept holding his side and wincing at times. But he was able to do the most for me. Ram Hlun was badly hurt with a broken shoulder, we later found, but was able to go uphill several miles to the nearest village to call for help. He was a very brave man, suffering greatly but impelled to call for aid because he thought I was dying.

As for the Indian driver, the one through whose negligence we had the accident, he was unhurt. He went downhill, back to the Pao River, to call for aid from some men working there.

Aid Comes; Back to Falam

The accident happened at 10:45 a.m. About noontime villagers from Hairawn and Tiphul arrived at the scene, a welcome sight indeed in the jungle wilderness we were in. Those of the villagers who were Christians prayed with us from time to time in addition to preparing litters for Cummings and me and preparing food for those who could eat. The decision was made to take us back to Falam to the Civil Hospital, rather than on to Haka where Betty was waiting for us with dinner prepared.

At about 5 p.m. our rescuers were ready to move. They carried us downhill to the Pao, and here Sowards, Skoglund, and Ram Hlun stayed for the night in a little shack, some 50 Chins staying with them to prepare food and keep campfires going.

Carried Through the Night

It seemed that Dick Cummings and I were the most seriously injured. So the Chins decided to carry us on through the night to Falam. It was sixteen more miles, of which the first seven were a constant uphill grade. There were three relays of carriers, 8 men at a time, on each litter. Through those long hours, by the light of flaming pine torches, the men struggled up the mountainside. It began to rain, never heavy, a slow drizzle. We did not have adequate protection, so we both got wet although umbrellas were kept over our heads to try to fend off the rain.

Eight miles out of Falam we were met by a crowd of 50 young men, members of the Christian Endeavour Society and the Boy Scout troop. They brought hot soup and two gasoline pressure lanterns. They carried us on the last lap to the hospital. Dick and I arrived at 2:15 a.m. on Sunday morning. The Indian doctor gave us penicillin, tetanus, typhoid, and morphine shots. It was a relief to get out of wet clothes and into dry blankets. He made the hospital especially nice for us by making a special ward in one of the hospital offices. At this time and until there were enough Burmese doctors trained, Indian physicians came to Burma on a contract basis, and we received their greatly appreciated care.

John Skoglund, Erville Sowards, and the cook Ram Hlun arrived at the hospital at 9 a.m., having come up by a jeep sent out to rescue them. Ram Hlun was in the hospital for a week or so, but John and Erville stayed only two nights, then took the painful jeep trip back to Kalemyo to catch the Thursday plane to Rangoon. It later proved that John had two broken ribs and Erville one. But for Dick and me, it was 17 days before we could move on from Falam.

Betty and the Children Come to Falam

Meanwhile in Haka, Betty Lue and the children awaited our coming on Saturday. She figured that we had had some mechanical problem and were delayed. Finally, in late afternoon, some travelers brought the news that there had been an accident at mile 17. Later in the day Betty received a wireless message. It was enough to chill her soul!

Someone in Falam, upon hearing of the accident, telegraphed my wife with what he intended as an encouragement to her, that God would help me and keep me safe. But his English was faulty, so the message Betty received read:

> Jeep accidented at mile seventeen,
> Johnson hurt worst. May God help him.

To her, of course, that meant that I was probably near death. It crushed her.

As the news spread throughout the village, a crowd of about 75 Christian young men, mostly students, gathered and made immediate preparations to go out to rescue us. The Haka doctor went along too. They actually went most of the way to the scene before learning that we had been taken the other way, northward to Falam. They turned around and returned home, all in all a hike of almost 30 miles.

Betty immediately began preparations to come to Falam to our bedside. It was not easy. She had to round up horses for riding and to carry loads. Also, Dick was sick with malaria just at that time and could not walk; he also needed a riding pony.

Betty Arrives in Falam

The Chins were most helpful and she was able to get going with the three children by Monday noon. On the third day, Wednesday, they arrived. Along the road she had met some Chins who informed her that her husband was so badly hurt that he would surely die, which did not cheer her up! When she came into our ward, not knowing what to expect, she took a look at me and passed me right by—she did not recognize me. No wonder, for my face was swollen beyond recognition and I was still covered with blood from my smashed nose and facial cuts. Evidently I had hit every rock there was on the way down the hillside.

I was overjoyed at Betty's arrival and happy to see Dick, Ruth, and little Martha who had learned to walk during my long absence. Betty quickly took charge of nursing Dick Cummings and me back to health, and although it was cold, being November, and bleak in the private room we had, Betty never complained. She washed my face and encouraged me when the Civil Surgeon, Dr. Kain, set my broken shoulder and sewed up my wounds. The worst was my nose, which, according to Betty, had been split open "like a piece of meat hit with the flat of a cleaver." Falam had no x-ray machine. Dr. Kain did the best he could without it and later, doctors in Rangoon complimented his skill.

Cummings had a broken vertebra and a broken bone in his foot. Movement was hard for him and he suffered. But these seventeen days together in the hospital forged a wonderful bond of friendship as we talked over mission work. Years later, when we both served on the mission staff at Valley Forge, Pennsylvania, we never forgot the Falam days.

The Chin people were wonderfully kind to their injured missionaries. On the first day at least 250 people came to see us, and at night members of the Christian Endeavour Society came in small groups for a continuous all-night prayer meeting. Government officials and many other townspeople came to cheer us up. People brought gifts of fruit, eggs, chickens, and even expensive cans of a cocoa drink called Milo. The Falam church took an offering equivalent to 50 dollars to help take care of us. The pastors and other leaders who were waiting for us in Haka walked to Falam to cheer us all up. They also delivered a beautiful Chin red blanket to John Skoglund.

Down to Rangoon

The day came when Cummings and I felt strong enough to make the trip to Rangoon for further medical treatment. We had spent seventeen days in the hospital, part of the time with Hau Go who came to see us and who then had liver trouble and was admitted also.

Richard Cummings and I caught the regular Thursday plane from Kalemyo to Rangoon. It was the American Thanksgiving Day and I recall that the Guest House had goose for the celebration. My meat had to be cut razor thin, for I could not open my mouth more than a slit. I was still seeing double. That is called "double vision." However, my teeth, which earlier were "rattling around" in my mouth, according to Betty, were firming up.

The Doctors' Verdict: America

Dr. Suvi, the Indian doctor who cared for many of the missionaries, and Dr. Dorothy Gates, our missionary doctor who flew in from Moulmein to see me, decided that I had to go to the United States for hospitalization. The facilities in Burma were not adequate. The injuries were multiple. My skull was fractured from the impact of a sharp rock; the left eye socket bone was fractured; my left shoulder blade was broken close to a joint—a bad place; my nose was broken; and the worst seemed to be that my jaws were broken in such a way that my lower jaw was displaced and my mouth opened more on one side than on the other.

The doctors recommended that America was the place for a "delicate and specialized jaw operation." At that time I could not chew and could not open my mouth enough to get a spoon in. My left arm hung useless.

Betty came down with the children to Rangoon, arriving on December 10, bringing my passport and other necessary travel papers. She had had to return home to Haka with the children, then turn right around and travel the lonely road back to Falam and then down to Kalemyo for the plane. It was made hard for the children and her because I had taken almost all our travel bedrolls and blankets for the expected guests, so they had to sleep in their clothes for lack of blankets.

I left two days later by Comet jet plane for England, then took a Stratocruiser plane overnight to New York by way of Iceland. I marveled at the speed of jet planes, then very new to commercial travel. John Skoglund and Franklin Nelson met me at New York and Frank continued on with me to Chicago. By Tuesday afternoon, Dec. 15, I was admitted to Wesley Hospital and to the care of Dr. Edward Compere, a noted orthopedic surgeon.

I did not know at the time, but my trip to the United States coincided with the death in Haka of our beloved and revered pastor, Rev. Sang Ling. Thus neither Betty nor I was there for the funeral.

Medical Treatment in Chicago

At Wesley Hospital various teams of doctors examined me. At first they seemed more concerned about my fever and double vision than about my jaws. I told them that the fever was malaria and that I had suffered from that on the Comet jet to England. They decided that the blow to the left eye and the broken bones in that area would heal naturally in time.

Dr. Compere decided that surgery on my jaws would not be necessary after all. This was a relief and I praised God for that, for Burma doctors had thought that my jaws would have to be wired.

As the broken jaw bones had healed by this time, Dr. Compere explained that he would "stretch my jaws" by using forceps to force my jaws open. Muscles in the jaw area were in trauma. In simple terms, the muscles were locked in spasm, much as a twisted rubber band will go into knots. Four times, each a week apart, Dr. Compere injected novocaine into my jaw muscles to deaden the pain, then, inserting a metal instrument like a pliers whose jaws opened up as he squeezed, he forced my mouth open. The pain was incredible and left me limp, but it worked—my jaws were broken loose and gradually I was able to open my mouth. I was given a wooden stick to use in continual prying to get my jaws to open more and more.

"When you can open your mouth one half inch, I can discharge you," Compere said. "It will continue to open more and more until you are normal."

Thanks be to God, all went well. My eyesight became more normal. My shoulder healed and I began to regain some strength in my left arm. My mouth returned more to normal and I could eat again. I had lost 30 pounds, but I began to gain and I looked better. Eventually I became almost as good as before, except that the contour of my eyes was changed somewhat and my broken nose never returned to normal. But all in all, I can thank God for His mercy on me and for allowing me to live and continue my work in Burma.

I should mention that Dick Cummings was put into a body cast for his broken back. Eventually he recovered fully from that and from his broken foot. Ram Hlun also recovered and continued to serve us faithfully. John Skoglund and Erville Sowards, injured relatively lightly, likewise fully recovered.

I am told that the foolish Indian driver, who, we learned, had been up most of the night before the accident playing cards and was probably sleepy, later caused a second accident, and some years later he was badly hurt in yet another accident, which left him paralyzed from the waist down.

Financial Worries Dispelled

While I was in the hospital, I worried some about the costs. By the standards of hospital costs today the 1953 costs at Wesley seem absurdly low, $14 a day and 20 percent reduction for being a missionary, hence only $11.20 a day. To me, at the time, a month at that rate seemed a big burden. The mission policy at the time was for the mission to pay 80 percent and the missionary 20 percent of medical bills. That would reduce the medical and hospital bills for me to a low figure.

But the real worry was the high cost of the airplane trip to the U.S.A. and back to Burma, which came to $1,733. Twenty percent of that was a big chunk of money to us, and if I had to pay it all, I would be in debt for years.

As it turned out, the mission society paid for the airplane trip in full and for most of the medical costs as well, and Dr. Compere contributed his skills free of charge. What a blessing to be associated with an organization like the American Baptist Foreign Mission Society! I appreciated then and still appreciate the concern, the love, and the financial integrity of the mission society. I am continually proud to be linked with such a responsible organization.

Discharged from Wesley Hospital

On January 11 Dr. Compere had his last session with me with his awful "jaw stretcher" and said that I could leave the hospital soon, and that my mouth would continue to open more and more until it should become normal. My left arm, which after the accident had hung limp, by then had recovered with therapy until I could raise my arm above my head and move it in all directions. This was important to me, for I am left-handed in most things. My eyesight was almost normal again too. It was heartening to have this good word, and it was heartening also to have had visits from my father, sister and family, and many aunts, uncles, cousins, and friends. I was anxious to get back to my wife and children and the work in Burma.

On January 13, 1954, my 30th day in the hospital, I was discharged on a day when the temperature in Chicago was near zero. But I went out into a warm world of family and friends.

Return to Burma

I did spend a few days visiting the Frank Nelsons, Betty's mother, and some of my relatives before flying to New York on Feb. 2 and on to Burma via London, Rome, and Cairo, Egypt. I was delayed in Egypt by engine trouble, but in the evening of Wednesday, February 10, I landed safely at the Rangoon airport, to be met by my loving wife and children. I had been away so long that Martha was shy and it took a day or two for her to realize who her daddy was.

During my absence of almost two months in the U.S.A., Betty Lue had stayed in Rangoon at the guest house and later with missionary friends She taught the children, read proof on Sunday School lessons for the Chins, and proof of a 350-page book of Old Testament Stories done by David Van Bik. She was a very busy woman during my absence.

Return to Haka

The Union of Burma Airways was using the dependable old twin-engined D.C.3 planes, called the Dakota in Burma, and we were thankful for plane service to Kalemyo and elsewhere. But sometimes the military or the civil authorities would charter whole flights, so the common people have to wait. Two flights a week was the standard now to Kalemyo, the entry port for the Chin Hills. Our family was finally able to get a flight on February 21. Our car, the Farm-0-Road, was parked at Kalemyo, so this was our first time to go in our own vehicle, pulling a light trailer.

We discovered that the Vaar crossing now had a temporary wooden bridge, built during the low water season. So we crossed without trouble and arrived home safely to Haka on Feb. 27. Instead of being away from home three weeks as I had planned, it turned out to be 4 months and 20 days.

All during the accident time and the months of recovery, the Chin Christian group had prayed for my return to health and the return of our family to Haka. Their prayers were answered and we were able to get back home and to the work the Lord had called us to do. Praise His name!

Chapter 37

FAREWELL TO REV. SANG LING

~~~~

During the first days of my 17-day hospital stay in Falam after the jeep accident, many pastors and church leaders came all the way from Haka, 34 miles each way walking, to visit and comfort me. Among them was our pastor, Rev. Sang Ling, grizzled and still active in his old age and full of enthusiasm for doing some village touring with me after I recovered.

"Bawipa, when you get back to Haka and are well again," he said, "let us do some village touring together again." I agreed heartily with him.

Planning a Tour of Villages

"How about a tour south to Kanpetlet area?" he said. "There are a lot of villages there and no church, not even a single Christian. We can do some evangelizing there and maybe send a preacher down to work there and get a church started."

These were sweet words to hear. I had long been concerned about the southern part of my field, the Matu and Kanpetlet subdivisions which were my responsibility, along with the Haka subdivision. This was the area that Frank Nelson and I had agreed upon when we "divided our fields." So when I went to the United States for surgery on my facial wounds, it was with the expectation that upon my return I would accompany Sang Ling and some other pastors to Kanpetlet.

It was perhaps in late December in Chicago when an airmail letter from Betty in Rangoon informed me of the bad news, Rev. Sang Ling had died in Haka on December 13. It was quite a shock to me as I had not thought of him as ill when we made our plans in Falam. His death brought a real sadness to me, and yet a sense of joy that he had entered into his heavenly rest after such a productive life. He was one of the "old men" who labored for God in the early days of the Chin Mission when he was the butt of scoffing and vilification. His stand on the liquor question—no beer, no wine, no strong drink—made him unpopular with chiefs who gained revenue (actually the alcoholic drink, not money) from the use of strong drink in their villages. It was not unusual for him and a fellow pastor to sleep outside a village while on tour because the village was taboo. Sang Ling was a mediating presence in business and planning meetings, and always encouraged prayer and long consideration of problems. To me he often said, "Let us do it slowly, Bawipa," reining in my impatience.

The Rock Slide

Whenever I think of Sang Ling's patience, I remember being with him on a village tour when the local pastor was baptizing some new believers in a stream. We were a crowd of people to witness the baptism. When all was ready, the pastor asked Rev. Sang Ling to pray. Sang Ling was squatting down (i.e., sitting on his heels) on a huge rounded rock. As the old pastor began his prayer, there was a slight tremor in his voice. I peeked to see what was going on. Pastor Sang Ling was sliding down the rock, very slowly, still on his heels, and praying without missing a word. I think that he slid about 20 feet this way, and then struck the ground. He gave a little grunt, but continued his prayer without an interruption. I admired him for his calmness.

The Wedding Manual

Another vignette of Rev. Sang Ling concerns the time he "married" Betty and me. This happened during our first-term Bible School days. David Van Bik and I were aware that our pastors and students needed some training in order to conduct wedding services in a dignified and Christian way. So with David's great help in composing elegant Chin words, I made a "Christian Marriage Manual." We printed the manuals on the mimeograph machine and presented them to the people at one of the Bible Conferences when we had plenty of people in the church.

In form, the wedding manual followed closely the Western pattern common in American churches. Some critics say that the missionaries should not impose such Western customs upon the simple people of the East. I dispute that idea, for the form we used has been used for centuries in English-speaking countries, including the royal weddings in England. The vows and promises of faithfulness and love are priceless and do not belong to only one race of people. So that is what David and I did.

Now, when writing our manual, we came to the part where the new husband kisses the bride. At this point I balked, saying to David that kissing in public is not the Chin custom. David reminded me that just over the border, in India, the Lushai tribe does have the kissing ceremony at weddings, and perhaps some Chins might want to follow their cousins' custom, and so we needed to establish a time when the kiss is appropriate. For this reason, we wrote a time for the wedding kiss, immediately after the vows and declaration of marriage. However, we placed these words in a box to detach it from the rest of the ceremony.

When we presented the Marriage Manuals at the conference, the people wanted to see the ceremony performed. So it was decided that Pastor Sang Ling would be the minister and Robert and Elizabeth Johnson would be the ones to get married. It was a hilarious event and every eye was on us as we walked down the aisle. We had no music, no flowers, no bridesmaids, no real rings to exchange. But the Chins thought it was a great spectacle.

So we came down the aisle and the pastor read through the whole service, and the onlookers cheered us on. "Great, great!" they shouted. Then they noticed that one part of the ceremony had been eliminated—the wedding kiss. "Do it all again, do it all!" said some and they all shouted that Betty and I do it all, including the wedding kiss.

I demurred, saying "That is not in the Chin custom, and we don't want to do anything you, the Chins, do not do," but they were adamant. So we did the ceremony again, in full.

This time my wife and I followed instructions and kissed. And that brought down the house with laughter, shouting, and approval. It was a real fun time for the people of the hills, seeing for the first time this aspect of Western culture.

Faithful Unto Death

Pastor Sang Ling was not a highly trained seminary graduate, but he was a man who loved the Lord and spent his life in communicating the Gospel of Christ to mostly illiterate non-Christians. He had a motto which in English read "I will do God's work until I die. I will not rest. My resting place will be heaven."

Another indelible memory of this beloved pastor is the motto on the banner that hung on the wall behind the church pulpit. It reads: "Be faithful unto death and I will give you the crown of life." Revelation 2:10.

Chapter 38

DOWNS AND UPS IN 1954

~~~~~~

"No" to the Doctor Family

While I was in Wesley Hospital in Chicago in December, 1953, Dr. Norman Abell and his wife Jean came to visit and talk about Burma. They had been appointed as medical missionaries to Burma for the Chin Hills work. Franklin Nelson and I had planned on a renewal of medical work among the Chins and happily the mission board did agree to send out the Abells. We were thinking of establishing a new station five miles north of the village of Lumbang to be a center for medical, educational, and agricultural work. Our vision was to have a hospital, a Bible school, and a high school, with at least three American missionary families.

The Abells were hopeful and full of questions. I told them about Dr. East, the man who built the little Haka hospital in 1908, and about Dr. Woodin who followed but left in 1915 at which time medical work ended. I said that the people were anxious to have a medical missionary again and gave them a lot of advice on what to bring and what to leave behind when they come to the Hills.

When able to travel again, I returned to Burma, rejoined my family in Rangoon, and we went on to Haka hoping to get rein-forcements: the Nelsons in Tiddim for Bible school teaching and evangelism, and the Abells for medical work. The Johnsons would be in Haka as the third American family. Perhaps it would be a good idea to concentrate the missionaries at a new site in the Falam area near Lumbang and work out from there. In that case, Tiddim would be an outstation in the north and Haka an outstation in the south. Everything depended on getting the mission board to take advantage of the Chins' mass movement to the Christian faith and pour in money and missionaries. And of course there would be the matter of getting visas and permission to live and work in Burma.

Such were our grandiose plans for the Chin Hills mission. Norman said that he would like to take some seminary study and come to Burma in fall of 1954. If the Nelsons could return, this would complete our missionary staff.

But none of this came to pass. The Burma government did not give entry visas to the Abells. Some of the high-ranking Chin officials then informed us of the new government policy to permit already established Christian work to continue, but that missions would not be permitted to initiate new work. Inasmuch as mission medical work had come to a halt in 1915, the establishment of a hospital would be considered a new project and therefore not allowed.

The Final "No" to the Nelsons

In spite of the earnest efforts of the Chin Baptist leaders to secure permission for the Nelson family to return to Burma, the final negative word came sometime in December, 1953. The delegation of two Tiddim men to Rangoon and later efforts of a larger group all had failed, and it became apparent that there would be no reconsideration. Why the Nelsons' return was refused and ours permitted, we were never told. It seems to be just one of the obstacles that Christian missionary work had to face. Their absence from the northern part of the Chin Hills left a huge void in our plans for the future.

When it became certain that their way to Burma was blocked, the Nelsons resigned from our mission service in April, 1954. Later, Franklin became a mission executive for the Swedish General Conference of Baptists and had service on other fields.

Rev. and Mrs. Leon Emmert Appointed for Chin Work

When the Nelsons had to drop out, the ABFMS appointed Leon and Martha Emmert for evangelism in the Chin Hills. The mission tried very hard to secure permission for them to come out in 1954, and the newly formed Zomi Baptist Convention, representing all the churches in the Hills, made a vote in April of that year requesting the government to grant them entry visas.

The Emmerts were to be replacements for the Nelsons. Although it seemed to be government policy at that time to permit replacements for departing missionaries, in this case it was denied. Later, Leon and Martha Emmert were assigned to a field in Africa, at that time called the Belgian Congo, later Zaire. Norman and Jean Abell likewise were reassigned to Zaire, which now is known as the Democratic Republic of Congo, usually shortened to D.R. Congo.

The Johnsons Have to Work Alone

I am not sure just when it became clear to Betty and me that there was no hope of getting any new missionaries in for the Chin work and that we would have to carry on alone. Perhaps it was late 1954. By that time the Zomi Convention requests for the Abells and the Emmerts had been denied. It was apparent that the leaders of independent Burma did not wish any more Christian missionaries in their country and that, on the contrary, it would be governmental policy to cut back on foreign religious persons. Although the Karen, Kachin, and Chin people on the whole were anxious for the Baptist missionaries to be there, the dominant Burmans were overwhelmingly Buddhist in religion and it was to be expected that it could be their policy not to welcome Christian missionaries.

Thus Betty and I had to face the prospect of trying to cope with the impossible task of being missionaries for the whole Chin Hills area. Formerly, Frank and Phileda had the Tiddim and Falam subdivisions and Betty and I had the Haka subdivision and south. Even that was too much for us. Now we would have to take over the two northern subdivisions as well and run the Bible School in Haka in addition to our other work. The prospect was overwhelming.

To be true, some earlier missionaries had to work alone in the Chin Hills without American colleagues, but they were alone for short periods of time, a year or eighteen months.

The Johnsons' Responsibilities

Betty Lue and I had to face a similar situation but for a much longer period, 13 years in all. From 1953 when we returned for our second term until 1966 when we left, there were no other American missionaries working with us in the Chin Hills. We alone were responsible to our mission for everything that was done on our vast field. We became involved in just about everything: church planting and nurture, evangelism, fostering the associations and the convention, Sunday School work, the Bible School, literature production, Bible translation, women's work, education, medical, and agricultural work to some extent, writing constitutions, and representing the ZBC at the mission headquarters. All of this was for an area of more than 13,000 square miles, most of it reachable only on foot.

To be sure, we did not work alone. There was a corps of wonderful pastors and preachers. Hau Go was a great help until he had to leave because of illness. Bright young men were coming through the Bible Schools, and even many Chins were gaining university education. But it still remains true that Betty and I were ultimately responsible for the growth and well-being of the Chin churches—in the eyes of the mission.

Two Important "Ups" in 1954

I have described some of the disappointments that came to Betty and me as we faced a future without American colleagues to help share the load of ministry in our vast field. However, several very good things came to pass, things that brought hope to our work. One was the formation of an organization of churches called the Zomi Baptist Convention. Another was the move of the Chin Bible School to Haka to be under our direction and which my wife and I ran, with very important help from some Chin teachers, for five years until it was moved to Falam.

Establishment of the Zomi Baptist Convention

For some years after the organization of the very first church among the Chins in 1906, each little church was isolated from others by distance and language. As more churches were formed, they began to group together in Associations in the Tiddim, Falam, and Haka areas, and finally a Chin Baptist Association was formed to unite all three areas. As time went on, the associations got strong enough to organize with salaried secretaries. Finally, in 1953 the leaders began to plan for a Convention to unite the associations with a constitution, bye-laws, officers, and a paid General Secretary. Thus, in April, 1954, at a great meeting in the village of Khuasak, the very place where Dr. Hjalmar East had baptized the first four converts, over 5,000 Chin Christians gathered to celebrate the 50th year of the first conversions to Christ. (I might add that the baptism of these converts took place in 1905.)

The churches on the Burma plains around the town of Kalemyo formed a new association called the Kale Valley Baptist Association and became the fourth association in the ZBC.

The Z.B.C.—A Great Step Forward

I rejoiced in the formation of this organization, for we knew that foreign missionaries would not be allowed in Burma indefinitely, and it was necessary to produce the leaders who could carry on into the far future. Rev. S. T. Hau Go of Tiddim was chosen as General Secretary, a man highly trained in Burma and who had two years of study in a seminary in Philadelphia.

The Bible School Moves to Haka

What was meant to be our permanent Bible School actually began in Tiddim in 1953 with Hau Go and a graduate of Frank Nelson's school, Lun Cung Nung, as teachers. When Hau Go was elected as head of the Zomi Convention, he could no longer run the school, so the ZBC leaders asked Betty Lue and me to take over the direction of the young school. We had expected the Nelsons to do this, but there was no other solution, so Betty and I agreed. The school moved to Haka in June, 1954. As it turned out, we ran the school for five years, and I helped build wooden buildings for it in Falam, extending our tour of duty a full year in order to complete the building program in 1959. The school has continued for forty-six years under Chin leadership and is now called the Zomi Theological College and has advanced enough to grant degrees.

Chapter 39

SCHOOLING FOR OUR CHILDREN

~~~~~

Missionaries run into very different sets of problems for their children's schooling. Some are able to send them to International Schools locally. Others send them to Christian boarding schools, often at a distance. Others teach their children at home. In our case, we elected to teach Dick, Ruth, and Martha at home until they reached the age of twelve.

Reasons for Our Choice of Home Teaching

Perhaps the main reason Betty chose to teach the children at home was that she was a trained teacher with five years of experience in a rural school, one of those one-room schoolhouses where the teacher has all the grades, 1 to 8. She loved to teach children and felt equipped academically and psychologically to do a good job.

Another reason was that Haka has a healthful climate, was fairly free of tropical diseases, and the prevailing atmosphere on the mission compound and around our house was Christian. Our nearest neighbors were Chia Ling and Pente with all their children, eight by the time we left in 1966, who lived in the stone house 30 feet behind our home. On the compound lived up to 90 schoolboys, almost all of whom were Christians. These all became friends to our children.

A more personal reason was that we loved to have our children nearby where we could supervise their play and study, and guide them in the way of the Lord personally.

There were some disadvantages, of course. Living in an isolated village, they were not thrown into contact with other American children. They grew up speaking Chin as their first language. That in itself is not a disadvantage; in fact, it is a plus. But it is true that our children spoke English as a second language, and Martha did not really speak her mother-tongue until she was almost four years old. When the children did learn English, however, they spoke it grammatically.

When Should They Go Off to Boarding School?

Betty and I discussed the optimum time for them to leave home and go to boarding school (we had chosen Kodaikanal School in southern India). We agreed that if possible we would keep them at home until they were 12. We did this and think that in our situation the decision was correct.

The Calvert Course of Study

Presumably Betty Lue could have made up her own courses of study, but it was convenient and easier to secure the papers, books, and supplies from the Calvert School, located in Baltimore, Maryland. This school provided everything a child needed. Usually mothers taught their own children, but in some situations where two or more families are close, a person could be engaged to teach all the students. Detailed instructions for teaching were supplied. In the Calvert school system, by paying extra fees the students' papers and exams would be graded by a teacher in Baltimore. However, we did not need that extra service and just ordered the books, paper, and other supplies. Our children did well and were able to transfer directly into American schools without hindrance or penalty.

Schooling in Our Second Term

In 1953 we returned to our work, reaching Haka in April. Upon arrival home, Dick was almost 8 years old and in 3rd grade. Ruth was

5 ½ years old and in 1ˢᵗ grade. Martha was a baby of 5 months. Betty began teaching the two older children the week after our arrival and carried them through one grade each year thereafter. Usually she began the school year about March 1 and ended a few weeks before Christmas. Parts of December and the months of January and February were vacation time.

A Typical School Day

Living as we did in a mountain village where the women loved to come and talk by the hour, and where we had people coming by the dozen every day to buy medicines at the dispensary in our home and who often wanted to discuss medical problems, Betty had to make some schedules and rules. If not, she would have been distracted beyond measure.

Thus, school began promptly at 7:30 a.m. with the children fully dressed, hair combed, and ready for study. At that moment "mother" or "mommy" became "Mrs. Johnson" during school hours. A 15-minute recess was given, at which time Betty would talk to waiting people. Classes were usually over by 11:30 a.m. But sometimes, as the studies got more difficult in higher grades, she continued until lunch, or had afternoon classes.

We remember especially a time when Dick was learning algebra. He was manfully struggling to understand clearly one difficult equation, and Betty could see by his eyes that he did not comprehend. "Let's continue," she said, "and we'll just eat lunch later. I think you almost have it." Dick agreed and continued to study a while. Suddenly it was as though a great light suddenly dawned on him. His eyes sparkled and he exclaimed, "I see it now! It is clear and I understand!"

We expected the kids to study and they did. I guess it did not occur to them to do anything else—they had no bad examples to follow. In the afternoon the children were free to play, run around the mission compound, or read. We made it a point to have suitable books around the home and they all learned to appreciate reading.

Dick Goes to Kodaikanal School

During our terms in Burma, our colleagues usually sent their children either to Kodaikanal School in the Palni Hills of southern India or to Woodstock School in Mussoorie in northern India. Both were excellent Christian schools, each run by a consortium of Protestant denominations. We chose Kodaikanal probably because many other Baptist missionaries sent their children there. It was not limited to missionary children, of course. Many business, government, and other parents, including Indian nationals, sent their children there.

Our son flew from Rangoon on January 8, 1958, for his first school experience away from home. There were five others in the school party, and at Calcutta they joined others on the rather long trip by train and bus. He was five days on the trip. I still remember how little our 12-year-old son looked as he walked across the tarmac to the Indian Airways turboprop airplane. Yet he was not little; he was growing up fast. He needed to be with other American boys and girls. We were very proud of our son. Just a few weeks before, at Haka, after profession of faith in Christ as Savior and Lord, he had been baptized by our pastor, Rev. Lal Hnin, along with his good friend Van Awi, eldest son of our cook Ram Hlun, and seven others. We were sure that Dick knew what he believed and that he would be strong in his Christian faith and morals.

Dick had finished 7th grade at home in Haka late in 1957. The Kodai headmaster had warned us that most youngsters taught at home do poorly at first when getting into a large school, and that we should expect he might have to take 7th grade over again. The headmaster was wrong! He had not reckoned on the quality of Mrs. Johnson's teaching. Our son did not have to do seventh grade over. Rather, he did 8th in four months and went right into 9th grade. So, when he returned to Burma in October, 1958, he had finished half of his 9th grade, the first year of high school, with all A's and B's.

With Richard away in India for most of eighteen months before we finished our second term, the big house was eerily quiet with no rambunctious son and friends around. But we had our two daughters and their good friends around the place, and they kept us busy. Betty continued teaching, of course, and by the time we returned to the U.S. Ruth had finished 6th grade and would begin 7th in an American school of 1,500 students; Martha had finished 1st grade; and Dick had completed 9th. We felt that the children had done well and had a good educational foundation.

Chapter 40

THE BIBLE SCHOOL
FIVE YEARS IN HAKA

~~~~~~~

When the Executive Committee of the newly formed Zomi Convention voted to locate the Bible School in Haka, at least for the time being, Betty Lue and I fell heir to the task that Franklin and Phileda Nelson were hoping to take up. We knew that it would be a full-time assignment, at least for the six months from June into December each year. But we really relished that task, for we knew that an educated ministry was essential to building up the church among the Chin people, who were rapidly being converted from their primitive animism to the Christian faith. The problems were, of course, finding enough money to buy rice and other foods, house the students, and get supplies, mostly paper.

The Students

When the students arrived in late May, 1954, there were 16 who had studied in Tiddim under Hau Go and Lung Cung Nung and now were in their second year. (That year, 1953, is considered the start of the permanent Bible School which over the years has developed into a great institution and is located in Falam.) There were fifteen men and one woman. We managed to house the men in that old broken-down stone house, now repaired and quite livable. The one woman was a Haka girl who lived in her parents' home. That solved the housing problem. We held all classes on the lower floor of the 2-story wooden church, the one built during our furlough.

In addition to these students who came to us after their first year in Tiddim, we added six men as "special students," as related in a previous chapter. Four came from the southern Matu region and two were from Haka and a nearby village. They pleaded for entrance, and though they were of a much lower standard of education, Betty and I reasoned that they showed much promise, for they had the zeal to come from afar.

In the earliest planning for this permanent Bible School it was decided that English would be the medium of instruction, because knowledge of English would give the students access to the wealth of books on all subjects and also allow them to get higher education both in Burma and abroad. Regarding the special six, we made no effort to teach them English; we taught them in Haka Chin. The regular students had some smattering of English, but it was minimal. We did teach in English but had to supplement that by explanations in Chin. In mid-term our students came to us with a plea for more instruction in English, more than Saya Lal Hnin could give, so Betty responded by adding another class, a full hour daily in the afternoon in English grammar and sentence structure. Progress was painful, but at least these future pastors and preachers would have a chance to read and study helpful books.

I discovered to my surprise that being left-handed was a boon to me. I had to write every word on the blackboard to be copied by the students. It was tiring work to write with my arm raised, and I learned to write alternately, with the right hand until tired, then with the left hand until tired, and back to the right, etc. Surprisingly, the handwriting looked quite the same with either hand.

What Is a Bible School?

In common speech, a "Bible School" usually means a school especially for lay men and women who wish to learn more about the Scriptures and not necessarily a school for preparing ministers. But in the Chin Hills we definitely were preparing both men and women for Christian ministry of many kinds. Therefore we enlarged the curriculum with all things necessary for a pastor. Thus we added music,

Christian education, missions, preaching (homiletics), health, sanitation, geography of the Holy Land, church history, ancient history, and even such subjects as art, color harmony, and arithmetic.

Teachers for the 1954 year in Haka were Betty Lue, our pastor Lal Hnin, and I. I placed many burdens on Betty, for when I had to go down to Rangoon three times a year as the Chin area delegate to the mission committees, I left her for weeks at a time to fill in for me. As she was also teaching our children, her own classes at the Bible School, and adding mine, it was a crushing load. Thankfully her health in the early years of our second term was good and she survived my long absences.

So that was our humble Bible School in its first year in Haka, where it was to continue for five years until moved to Falam, the capital of the Chin Hills, in 1959, and where it has continued and thrived under Chin leadership.

The Year 1955

When David Van Bik arrived in early 1955, fresh from four years at the Burma Divinity School at Insein (now the Myanmar Institute of Theology), it was a great enrichment to the teaching staff. I continued to teach New Testament, Church History, and Preaching, and Van Bik took Theology and Old Testament. Betty continued to teach Music, Christian Education, and English. In addition to Van Bik's teaching load, he worked with me on Bible translation, taking up where we left off, four years earlier.

American Dinners for Chins

As Chin food and eating habits are so different from Western customs, Betty Lue and I felt that on some occasions, perhaps when in Rangoon, our students might be invited to eat at a British or American home, and face the problem of using knife, fork, and spoon instead of only a spoon or fingers. So we decided to invite them to eat with us, four at a time, at a typical American meal.

We experimented with these dinners, but during the first year we served a more Indian-type meal of rice and curry. The table was set with knives, forks, spoons, and napkins, water glasses, cups for tea, etc., and we urged our students just to follow our examples and not be self-conscious. The men enjoyed these meals and began to understand our strange Western customs.

During the second year of meals, we went to a traditional Western-style meal of meat, potatoes, vegetables, salad, dessert, and tea. This was even more strange, but all enjoyed the experience and thanked us for giving them an idea how to use knife and fork in the Western manner.

Bible School in 1956

The year 1956 was unusually rich in teachers—five in all. David Van Bik was with us for the second year. A Tiddim man, a recent graduate of the Burma Divinity School, Kam Khaw Thang, came to Haka for the year and with David shared classes in theological and religious subjects and English. Kam Khaw Thang went on to become the general secretary of the Tiddim Baptist Association and then became the translator of the complete Bible in the Kamhau language, capping a lifetime of service.

Betty and I were the third and fourth teachers, and the fifth was Rev. Van Lo, a pioneer pastor in his area near the India border. Saya Van Lo taught Burmese. It seems hard to believe, but Burmese, the national language, was hardly known among the Chins at that time. We felt that all pastors should know enough of the language to carry on a conversation with a Burmese official. During 1956 we had 26 students and we graduated 14 who had finished the four years. About this time we gave the school a new name, the Zomi Baptist Bible School, its name for many years.

Graduation Day for Fourteen

Graduation Day for the first class of our permanent Zomi Baptist Bible School was Sunday, December 9. The church was filled to more than capacity with 875 worshipers. The Bible School students had a nice processional and during the course of the service sang two anthems. Our scheduled speaker, Thra Tun Shein, General Secretary of the Burma Baptist Convention, visiting in the Chin Hills at the time, failed to show up due to transportation problems, so Van Bik and I had to fill in at the last moment. As principal of the school I had the honor of presenting diplomas to the thirteen men and one woman graduates. They had finished four years of study and were ready to carry on for Christ in their home areas. All of the graduates entered full-time Christian work, most of them as pastors. Miss Sui Bor was employed by the Haka Baptist Association for women's work, and two men became book printers for the Falam and Haka Associations.

The Last Two Years in Haka

David Van Bik left us in early June, 1957, to go to the United States for two years of study in the Berkeley Baptist Divinity School in California. Our other teacher, Kam Khaw Thang, left us to work as association secretary in Tiddim. So our teaching staff for 1957 was reduced to just three: Betty Lue and I, and a young man who had just finished Divinity School in Insein, James Sang Awi. James was the son of Rev. Van Lo who had helped us with Burmese teaching the previous year.

Our student body was now smaller with 13 men and 2 women. We were glad for the female students, as our mission was constantly urging us to enroll more young ladies. It was hard to find those of adequate education, able to do the work in English. The smaller group was fine for us as we could devote more time to each person, even one-on-one tutoring in English.

We lacked suitable books. So we made our own books. By this time we had a Gestetner mimeograph, a high quality machine made in England, and on this we produced typed copies of some books that we thought could be understood by our students. Even so, I revised the texts to eliminate passive verbs as much as possible, also idioms not understandable by Chins, and stories or illustrations from American culture, such as references to baseball and hockey. With these simplified texts, yet retaining the meaning, we labored to teach English to village Chins.

Seven Weeks Bible Study and Bible Conferences

During the five years we had the Bible School in Haka, we continued the Seven Weeks Bible Study program, usually having 100 to 120 people attend for the seven weeks. These were church deacons and teachers who carried on the weekly worship services in the little village churches in the absence of the pastors. Each of the pastors had from 8 to 21 villages in his "circle." This 7-weeks study was completed with the annual Bible Conference which brought together all the pastors. This was always a wonderful week of preaching, teaching, singing, and discussion of problems. Our Bible School students attended the discussion groups which gave them a good idea of the problems facing the churches.

The Mission Grants Money to Build a Bible School

During our term in Burma, the capital of the Chin Hills was the town of Falam, 34 miles north of Haka by the old mule path and now 46 miles north by the new and mostly level road. Falam was also the location of the offices of the Zomi Baptist Convention. Most of the ZBC executive committee wanted to locate the Bible School permanently in Falam. With this decision, the Falam Christians began work to prepare house sites on the ZBC compound, and over a thousand days' work was given freely to level the hillside for three new buildings. This saved the mission a lot of money.

Our mission then promised a grant of 35,000 kyats (about $7,400) when plans and specifications were approved by our Rangoon Property Committee.

It fell to me to be the architect and draw the plans. I took a full week in December, 1957, and produced 14 large sheets, drawn to scale, and then added up the needed lumber, nails, roofing tins, bolts, glass, hinges, transport costs, and the like. The Property Committee approved and we hired sawyers in 1958 to begin cutting lumber in the pine woods 30 miles north of Falam and across the Manipur River. That river crossing was to give us much trouble in 1959 when we had to haul the lumber by truck and the bridge was destroyed by a flood.

We also ordered two heating stoves from America for the teachers' homes to make them livable during the winter time.

Lengthened Term for the Johnsons

Our normal time for leaving Burma and returning to the U.S.A. for furlough was May, 1958, and the mission strongly urged us to go at the proper time. But I resisted this for two important reasons. The wood for the three buildings to be constructed in Falam had to be cut and seasoned. Also, David Van Bik, already chosen to be principal in my place, was not scheduled to return to Burma until May or June, 1959. So we determined to add one year and end our term about the time of David's return.

Two Houses and a Dormitory/Classroom Building

When classes ended in late December, 1958, I was free to give a lot of time to building the teachers' houses and the two-story dormitory/classroom building in Falam. This took a lot of time away from home. We had capable carpenters, but the problem was trucking in the lumber cut 30 miles away. We had good help from a longtime Chinese friend named Hlun Chin. He and his brother Ah Chau, who was the Union of Burma Airways agent at Kalemyo, had trucks and helped greatly, although not Christians themselves. The long timbers for the dormitory roof, measuring 19, 22, and 24 feet long had to be carried on the Canadian-built snub nosed trucks which were only 8 feet long. Some of the drivers were afraid of such loads and refused, but with the addition of some generous "tea money" we persuaded two of Hlun Chin's drivers to go. A further complication was that the temporary wooden bridge over the Manipur River was gone, taken out by a flood. So every stick of lumber or timber had to be carried by men across a narrow swaying suspension bridge and reloaded on trucks on the Falam side of the river.

Well, the story ends well. With the long rafters and the other lumber safely on hand, the carpenters finished the job. When we left on furlough in May, 1959, the school was ready to resume under the direction of David Van Bik. So we left happy.

Chapter 41

THE TWENTY-FIVE INCREDIBLE YEARS AND A TOUR TO KANPETLET

~~~~

The "Twenty-Five Incredible Years" of Mission

Some historians of mission activities have referred to the "incredible twenty-five years" of mission expansion. These were the years from the end of World War II in 1945 to the Moon landing on July 20, 1969, when Neil A. Armstrong and Edwin E. Aldrin emerged from the Apollo 11 lunar capsule and became the first humans to walk on the Moon.

These two events, the end of the War and man's arrival on the Moon, were destined to become landmarks in history.

These approximately 25 years were also a period of great expansion for Christian missions. Thousands of missionaries of many races and colors and of many church denominations went out from America, Britain, Germany, the Netherlands, and other European nations, from Australia and New Zealand, and from Asian countries also, notably South Korea and the Philippines, to bring the Bible and the Christian faith to far corners of the world. It was a time when the Spirit of God moved over lands and seas to establish the Church in heathen and pagan lands.

What Happened in the Chin Hills?

The ministry that Betty Lue and I carried on in Burma was profoundly affected by this mass movement, as it is sometimes called. We found ourselves almost overwhelmed by the needs of the new converts. They needed Bibles, and many needed to know how to read the Bible. They needed songbooks and choir music. They needed to learn the fundamentals of the Christian faith and ethics, how to live Christlike lives. They needed education and books. They needed trained pastors and preachers to guide the churches. As for the church buildings, mostly rustic ones of wood and roofed with thatch or corrugated iron sheets, these the ordinary villagers could do.

The Need for Village Tours

Most of this we could do from our mission station in Haka. But I needed to make tours of the villages, meeting both animistic Chins and Christian Chins right in their homes. So during my first and second terms I devoted much time to such travel in the open season when paths were dry and the weather favorable.

This type of trudging along on foot, preaching in village after village for ten days to three weeks at a time was difficult but rewarding. The Chins could see me as I was, a weary traveler at times, a foreigner trying to speak their language, sharing their village life, and trying to bring the Word of God to them. Even the non-Christians could relate to me.

The maps we had of the Chin Hills showed areas to the south of Haka labeled "Unadministered Territory." The British officers did not try to govern or have much to do with these rather far-off places. But for me, there was an irresistible urge to visit there, preach there, and establish churches among those people. Hence, the burning desire to tour to Kanpetlet.

The Kanpetlet Area

Just a few lines to explain my field. I was responsible for five of the "Subdivisions" of what was called the "Chin Special Division" (now the Chin State). Of these five, Tiddim, Falam, and Haka had thriving churches. Of the two in the south, Matu had a few pastors and some small churches. The other one, Kanpetlet, bordering the plains of Burma, had five evangelists sent down by northern churches, and had 151 Christian believers at the time I made my trip.

The sixth subdivision of the Chins was Paletwa. This was the most remote from Haka and was to the west, toward the Indian Ocean. This was considered a mission field of the Anglican Church and was out of my area.

Plans for a Trip to Kanpetlet

I planned to leave home on December 27, 1956, and spend about a month touring both the Matu and the Kanpetlet subdivisions, taking in a large association meeting at Rezua and another gathering at Lalui, over on the Kanpetlet border. It would take at least a month.

Instead of returning through the Hills to Haka, as I usually did after village touring, I planned this time to go to the east, down to the Burma plains, and fly from the airfield at Kyauktu to Rangoon. Toward the conclusion of my tour, Betty and the three children would go by way of Falam to the airfield at Kalemyo and fly to Rangoon. With our family reunited, we then would attend the annual missionary conference in Rangoon February 2 to 9.

Surprisingly for Burma, everything did work out right this time.

The Start of the Tour

This tour, my first visit to the Kanpetlet area, was made with my cook Ram Hlun, two mule drivers, three pack horses, and one riding horse. We had to carry many food items for such a long trip, and Betty divided supplies into weekly rations—so much sugar, so much tea, so much condensed milk, etc., per week. Ram Hlun had strict instructions to follow the rationing system lest we run out of something halfway through the tour. Meat, eggs, corn, rice, and perhaps some vegetables here and there were all that we could buy en route.

The Zo-Matu Baptist Association at Rezua

We followed the usual village paths toward the Zotung area. At the first village, Sakta, I preached in the Lai (Haka) language. In the next village the women could not understand Lai, so I used an interpreter. And so it went for a month, my sermon in Lai being interpreted so the people could understand the message.

Thus we went, village after village preaching the Good News every night and stopping on Sundays. On the ninth day we reached Rezua where we spent Saturday and Sunday, January 5 and 6, in meetings with the leaders of the Zotung and Matu areas. How pleased I was to find that there were 1,108 people present for their association meeting! God was opening hearts down in this southern area also. I stayed at the government Health Center, with good friends from Haka, Shwe Zan and his family.

At Rezua the people informed me that there were crop failures in the Lungngo, Rezua, and Calthawng circles. They asked relief aid through the mission. I have not yet mentioned this Christian activity, but aid to needy people in case of famine, flood, or fire was a regular feature of the American Baptist work in Burma, as indeed on all of our fields. I promised to bring this matter to the attention of the Relief Committee in Rangoon.

On to Lalui

It took us 5 days to go from Rezua to Lalui, west of Matupi. It was a rough trip for my ankles and legs. I became partly lame due to a wrenched right knee and swollen ankle tendons on both feet. The roads were very steep up and down, and the downgrades caused the leather of my shoes to buckle inward and rub the backs of my feet, laming me. It was too steep to ride the horse, particularly downhill. Walking was painful.

The day before we reached Lalui, Ram Hlun, traveling alone and ahead of the party, shot a leopard. He was using my .30-06 rifle with a heavy 220 grain bullet. The animal fled, wounded, but Ram Hlun did not dare chase after it, knowing full well that a wounded leopard is a cunning beast, fully capable of ambushing and killing the hunter.

We spent the weekend of January 12 and 13 at Lalui, plagued with bad weather for the large Christian gathering. Thankfully the rain stopped on Sunday.

To Matupi

Another three days on the trail brought us to Matupi. I was still lame and using a cane, but improving. The usual welcoming group of Christians came out along the road to greet us and this time I was bedecked with two leis of marigolds. The two evangelists sent down by the churches of the Haka area, Pastors Pa Hrek and That Dun, had done good work and the Christian witness was reaching out to the little villages, and at Matupi, the central village, a nice church building had been constructed. I have already noted that four new converts from this area came to Haka seeking entrance to the Bible School, and we had to give them instruction as special students for two years.

We Enter the Kanpetlet Subdivision

Somewhere in the Zotung area, I cannot remember just where it was or who was speaking, people warned me of the dangers of travel in the Kanpetlet area. I really think these men were sincere in what they said.

"They are like tigers!" said one man.

"Be careful, they are quick-tempered and murderous," said another.

"They aren't like other Chins. They are more animal than man." said a third.

We were talking in the open, sitting around a campfire, and I looked up at the brilliant stars in the unclouded sky. Nights in the Chin Hills in the dry season are so beautiful. There are no distracting lights to dim the stars. And I thought that someday soon the light of the Star of Bethlehem would shine upon the Kanpetlet people. I knew that there were only five evangelists in that subdivision and so far only 151 persons had confessed faith in Christ. There was so much to do. I did not really believe my informers and felt no undue anxiety as we prepared to enter what was to me a new district. As it turned out, I never felt in danger. In fact, the Kanpetlet Chins were friendly to me. Perhaps strange Chins crossing the area might find animosity, but our party ran into no hardships at all.

Touring villages in the unevangelized Kanpetlet area.
Sometimes the trails are too narrow for pack mules, so villagers are
employed to carry bedding, food, and other baggage.

We left Matupi after a few days of fellowship there and forded
the Lemro River eastward to the first Kanpetlet village, Thlangpang.
At this point we changed plans.

Dangerous Road; a Change of Plans

My original plan was to go north from Thlangpang to a village
where Pastor Khoh Thung had a few converts, the very first Kanpetlet
Christians, and a tiny church building. The road, just a footpath,
went over steep mountains over 8,000 feet high. From there our plan
was to move in a circle south to the village of Mindat where Pastor
Lung Tum had a little church.

We could not carry out this plan because the roads were too dangerous for the pack horses. The side-trip up to Tawinam was absolutely impossible for horses. If we used coolies, we could not carry enough food for this long extra trip. We had to give up on that idea.

However, we still had road problems. Coming from Matupi to Thlangpang we nearly lost one horse over a cliff on the narrow road. We learned that the path to Ro village was also too poor to use horses. So there was nothing to do but to send all the horses back to Matupi and thence on home to Haka. At Thlangpang we hired coolies for the rest of the journey, 7 days in all. On this long journey I had used a riding horse at times to save my strength, but now we sent the riding horse also back to Haka.

On to Ro Village

My trip by foot to Ro, two days, was notable for climbing two mountain ranges, one 7,500 feet high and the other 8,000 feet. It was January and cold. I recall wearing everything I owned to keep warm at night and wishing I had gloves. This in "tropical Burma"! Companions on this trip, at various stages, were our evangelists Khoh Thung, Kai Dawi, To Uk, Lung Tum, and Ceih Kio. When we reached the large village of Ro, where To Uk lived, I had an unusual greeting. In addition to the usual welcome arch with its flowers and decorations, the older men of the village were out with their flint-lock muskets and let go three volleys of shots. It was a picturesque sight, some men with bows and arrows, some with muskets, and the clouds of black powder smoke in the air. There were hundreds of people—men, women, and children. Some had eggs, stalks of sugarcane, and fruit. Thankfully, To Uk had told the townspeople that I did not drink *zu* (Chin beer), so I was spared the embarrassment of refusing that kind of hospitality.

Only a handful of these Ro villagers were Christians. Why, then, the fine welcome? It was because these people under our evangelist's teaching had come to desire education for their children. They wished a mission school. As it turned out, the mission was able to do something later, since they were willing to work for the school themselves and did not want it just as a handout. The little private elementary school that they started became one of the 45 mission-aided schools.

From Ro to Mindat and Rangoon

Up to this point we had been traveling without any undue sense of hurry. But after leaving Ro, we reached the next village of Khreum, and learned from a visiting Burmese official that we had been misinformed about the day on which the weekly airplane flew out of Kyauktu. Flights were on Fridays. I decided that I would have to get the plane on January 25 in order to reach Rangoon on time, for I had to be present for the executive committee meeting.

We therefore pressed on to Bong and stayed the night. On the next day we hiked 23 miles to Mindat, climbing a range of mountains 8,700 feet high. Farther south lay Mount Victoria, 10,018 feet high, the highest peak in the Chin Hills, and if I had had time, I would have liked to climb it to see the Indian Ocean in the far west.

At Mindat I was pleasantly surprised to see a beautiful little sawn wood church, the Mindat Baptist Church, nicely painted and decorated. Rev. Lung Tum was doing a fine job here. It was too bad that we were so pressed for time, but on the next day we went twenty more miles, mostly downhill, to the airfield at Kyauktu. I arrived on Thursday in time to make arrangements for Ram Hlun's return home and then caught the Friday plane to Rangoon.

The whole tour had taken 30 days, most of it in rough, tough mountain travel. All in the party kept in good health; we were able to purchase local food items such as rice, eggs, and chickens; and we made many friends. The Kanpetlet people came to realize that a Christian mission was interested in them, and I was able to talk with those few who knew the Haka (Lai) language. I considered it a successful month of effort.

It was definitely in my mind to make more tours to this far southern region, and Betty and I even seriously considered moving down there at some future date when the Haka Bible translation was completed. This was never possible due to political realities in later years and because our work was cut short at the end of our third term in 1966.

Chapter 42

PRINTING PRESSES AND MISSION-AIDED SCHOOLS

Our second term of service saw the beginnings of two projects that worked together for the education of the Chin people. These were the establishment of three printing presses in the Hills and the start of some 67 mission-aided schools.

Reasons for Printing Presses

When Betty and I went home on furlough in 1951, there was no question in my mind but that we should get a printing press for Haka and for other areas, too, if they wished them.

It was a logical move, for the Chins were asking for literature, new songs, and books of all kinds. It was too costly to make them on a duplicating machine, such as the mimeograph which required stencils for each page. Stencils were expensive and hard to get and, furthermore, cheap paper could not be used. Hence, the books made on the mimeograph were too expensive. A printing press, on the other hand, using lead type over and over again, needed only ink and cheap paper, such as newsprint.

Of course, a press required a lot of labor to set the type letter by letter. But labor costs in the Chin Hills were low. Furthermore, many schoolboys needed to earn money, and a press would give employment to some. Therefore, I determined to get a printing press.

The Kelsey Hand Press

It seemed unreasonable to start off with a large press due to the isolation of Haka and the difficulties of moving in heavy machinery. Furthermore, I had but little money for it. So I purchased a Kelsey hand press that could print up to 6 by 10 inches. Of course I also purchased type, type cases, spacers, and leads, extra rollers, the wooden fillers, and other needed equipment. The press itself was not too heavy; it could be lifted by one man. This came out with our freight and was received in 1953. Unfortunately, during shipment the press broke from its moorings in the box and several important castings were broken. It was unusable until finally, after much difficulty with import licenses, we were able to get replacements for the broken parts.

By July, 1955, Betty and I were ready to start. I made a special table in front of a window in the upstairs of our house; we bolted the press down and set out to learn how to print. Neither of us had ever used a press before. The directions were satisfactory, and so we became self-taught printers. Dick wished to learn also. We taught him how to set type and eventually he earned some money toward the purchase of a guitar.

We soon hired a young lady to set type for us. Girls seemed much more adept at setting type than boys. Later some of the men from the Bible School helped us in the printing. Among them was a graduate of the Bible School who became the full-time printer. This man, Hrat Ling, worked for many years at this job. We also had one helper, a monkey, who thankfully worked only five minutes.

Chico, Our Typesetter

Our pet monkey, Chico, generally was kept firmly in his place by a nylon leash. On occasions he escaped and headed for the cookhouse where he threw flour around. But one day he escaped into the house and went up the stairs in a flash.

"The monkey, the monkey, he's gone upstairs!" our son shouted.

"Go after him, Dick," I replied urgently. "He may get into the press stuff!"

We all hurried up but we were too late. Chico was on top of the type cases, his little fingers stirring up the lead bits and throwing them around. It would be a long job to restore all the types back to the correct boxes. We caught Chico and gave him a strong reproach, which did no good. He remained a mischievous but lovable animal.

The Deirel Press at Haka

After we produced a few small booklets on the press, it became clear that we needed a special building for this project. The Chins contributed gladly and we were able to build an 18 by 30 foot wooden building a few yards from the gate of our front yard. The Chins have a nice word for the morning star. They call it *deirel arfi*. It seemed a perfect name for our press, so the Deirel Press was named and has continued for many years. A special feature of the press building was the north wall, entirely glassed in above the waistline. The north exposure gave beautiful light for setting type and for running the little hand press. Hrat Ling produced booklet after booklet on many subjects. We did not have a paper cutter, so we had to trim each book by hand using a sharp knife — a tedious and laborious job.

As time went on, we were able to secure a Chandler and Price platen press able to print 9 by 12 inch papers. It was run by a foot treadle turning a heavy iron flywheel. This was a gift from a man in Pennsylvania and arrived in June, 1958. We were also given a guillotine paper cutter, which made it easy to trim the books to size. To give a mark of distinction to our Deirel Press building, I constructed a large star using teak wood painted white and erected on the roof.

The Laksawng Press at Falam

Dr. Richard Cummings, the man who was hospitalized with me at Falam after the jeep accident, was able to raise money in America to purchase and send out a Chandler and Price platen press and necessary types and equipment for the Zomi Baptist Convention. This came out to Burma with our similar big press. Falam also received a fine paper cutter. A press building was constructed on the ZBC compound where also the Bible School buildings were built, and operations began in late 1957. Ral Lian Kap, a graduate of our Bible School, became the printer.

Soon it seemed well for the Convention to turn over the press, the building, and the equipment to the Falam Baptist Association. The FBA named this the "Laksawng Press" meaning "Gift Press."

Among books and booklets printed at Falam, a little Chin news magazine was established. The "Zomi Christian" continued for many years under the editorship of James Sang Awi, the man who helped teach one year with us at Haka.

Why Have Three Presses in the Hills?

Somewhat to the consternation of our mission officials in Rangoon, the Chins established yet another press in the Hills. This one at Tiddim. The downcountry folks thought that the Chins should print all of their stuff in Rangoon, where there were presses run by electricity and which would perhaps be cheaper. We upcountry folks agreed that big projects, such as printing of Bibles and songbooks, could best be done in Rangoon, but we argued that non-Chin type-setters downcountry would make too many errors and the delays for corrections would be costly and time consuming. Also, local Chin typesetters could work from a handwritten manuscript, impossible for a non-Chin.

At any rate, the Chins went ahead with the vision of three presses in the Hills.

The Cope Memorial Press at Tiddim

A church in Dearborn, Michigan, contributed the press for Tiddim. Like the others, it was a used Chandler and Price platen press. Along with this machine came the types, type boxes, wood fillers, borders, extra rollers, etc. A fine press building was constructed on the mission compound and was named the Cope Memorial Press in honor of the pioneer missionary to the Tiddim Chins, Dr. J. Herbert Cope. Having a press in Tiddim town, it was no longer necessary to have Kamhau literature printed in Falam. So the presence of three well-equipped presses made it possible to print cheaply and efficiently.

I consider the establishment of these three presses in Tiddim, Falam, and Haka a major accomplishment of the Baptist Christians toward the evangelization and the discipling of the people and the progress of literacy among the Chins in general.

The Chins Hunger for Education

It was immediately apparent when we arrived in the Chin Hills in 1946 that the Chin people were hungry for education. They were asking, pleading, for schools. During the war, life had been disrupted and schools emptied. Now, with the war over, the Burma government established schools as fast as possible with the limited funds available. But it was impossible to give each village a school. The larger villages were chosen for elementary schools. Smaller or more isolated villages determined to start their own little private schools, hoping for the day when the government would take them over and pay the teachers.

Thus many little elementary schools were started. The villagers usually started by constructing a thatched roof schoolroom, and paid the teacher with rice and whatever money they could give. The mission was able to come to the aid of some of these, thankfully.

The Desperate Situation of the Private Schools

During our first term, Franklin Nelson and I made plans for a mission high school. It never came to pass. However, plans were laid for help to the private elementary schools. Early in our second term a survey was made of both government and private schools to determine the need, and the mission began to help 36 primary schools at 120 kyats each per year. A few years later, in 1956, we were able to increase the number to 45 primary schools at K.120 and 22 private middle schools at K. 650 each per year. It seems like a paltry sum to give to each school, but the blessing was that even this small amount of money, added to the rice and other foods given to the teachers by the villagers, made all the difference. With the mission aid the schools continued until the government was finally able to take over their support. Without our mission aid they may have withered and died.

Student Hostels

A further aid to Chin education was the construction of two student hostels, one at Tiddim and one at Haka, to house boys from surrounding villages who came to attend the government high schools. Of course, many boys were able to stay in the homes of relatives and friends, but numerous students had no such luck. For them, the hostels provided shelter and a cookhouse in which they were able to cook their own food, usually in groups of eight or ten. In Haka we had 90 such students living on our compound. A great help to the students was the custom of bringing offerings of foodstuffs to the church, which after the service could be given free to the needy young men. Vegetables, eggs, fruits, chickens, and occasionally cuts of beef or pork were distributed in this way. With these many high school students on our compound we had a ready source of choirs. It was a delight to get to know these young men who became leaders in their own communities and churches.

A Note on Chin Progress

I have noted the burning desire of the Chins for education. In the time of the early missionaries and in pre-World War II days, very few girls were allowed to study. This changed radically as the people began to realize the value of education as a means of escaping poverty. Through the mission efforts described in this chapter and through the increasing efforts of the Burma government, the rate of literacy is rising and both boys and girls are finishing high schools and going on into college and university, and even into postgraduate studies, some men even reaching Ph.D. and other doctoral degrees. From the time of the first missionaries at the beginning of the 1900s to the centennial year 1999, the short space of a hundred years has seen a transformation of Chin society for the good, a transformation of almost unbelievable proportions.

Chapter 43

ELIZABETH JOHNSON'S WORK IN BURMA

~~~~~

Betty's Introduction to Women's Meetings in Haka

One of the features of Christian work in Haka was the Wednesday women's meeting every week. Rather than gathering in the little church or in the homes of Christians, the women sought to meet in non-Christian homes whenever possible, and especially when there was illness in the home. They prayed for healing and for the needs of the home. As the years went by, the number of women who went here and there in the village for these meetings rose to almost thirty.

I believe that it was these women's meetings, almost more than any other activity of the church, that resulted in the spread of the gospel in Haka and the surrounding area.

Betty was included in these women's meetings, of course. After she had been in Haka less than a month, she attended one such meeting in the home of a former village headman. The man, clad only in a loincloth and the sort of turban the men wear on their heads, sat cross-legged on a stool paring his toenails with a foot-long knife just outside the circle of women. He thus occupied himself during the whole meeting, interrupting at times to call out to passing chicken sellers. He seemed not inclined to keep quiet even during prayer time.

During all our years in Haka, Betty Lue went with the women on Wednesdays, often taking Ruth and later Martha along when they were small. The women took great delight in holding our babies. It was a way to their hearts.

A Tribute from Her Husband

Without doubt, the work done by missionary women, particularly missionary wives, is often neglected and frequently quite overlooked in reports made to mission headquarters and to the Boards, unless the wife happens to be a doctor or to have unusual prominence in some mission institution. Even though in our American Baptist Foreign Mission Society both husband and wife are appointed and commissioned as missionaries, so that the wife is fully as much a missionary as her husband, quite often in popular thought the husband is "the missionary" and the wife just his spouse. It should not be so. Certainly, in my own thinking, Betty Lue was just as much a missionary as I, and in many respects a more effective missionary than I. Nevertheless, in our particular case, living in the patriarchal Chin society, I was always given the public prominence. I served on mission and local committees, and I wrote up the official reports.

I feel that Betty's work deserves this special chapter to outline the variety and scope that has only been hinted at in former chapters. Without her love, her support, her capable handling of things when I was away, and her unusual ability to make everyone her friend, my ministry in the Chin Hills would have been greatly lessened, of that I am sure.

Varied Work During Two Terms

In regard to teaching in the Bible School, Betty taught for three years in the first term and for five years in the second term. The teaching of our children depended on their ages, of course, but by 1959 when we returned to the States on our second furlough, Richard was ready for 10th grade, Ruth for 7th, and Martha for 2nd.

In order to have time to do our distinctively Christian mission, we had a cook, a houseman, a gardener, and a woman to cut and carry in firewood. A girl was employed to sell books and medicines at the dispensary which we ran in our home. Betty made up the menus and saw that the meals were done right and the baking and cleaning done. Over the years she translated recipes for Ram Hlun and Chia Ling, so they were both excellent cooks. Quite often, though, Betty made cakes, cookies, or pies. She also always made our Sunday evening meals as our workers were free after the noon dinner.

Incidentally, our usual meal hours were breakfast at 6:45, lunch at 11:30, tea at 3 p.m., and dinner at 6. We ate dinner early so that our cooks could go home early, unlike the custom of the British in the Orient who usually ate much later.

Betty always worked on the laundry. We usually did this on Saturday because she did not teach that day. During the rainy season when it was impossible to dry clothes outside, they were hung in the attic, where they took three days to dry.

We considered family togetherness a very important part of missionary life and the rule was that only English was to be spoken at the table (this was sometimes difficult when the children were small). After all, we had to prepare our children for the day when they would return to their own country.

The Women's Association in April, 1958

The Haka area Women's Association meeting held at Haka for three days in April was the first attempt of Chin women to plan, organize, and run a major set of meetings all on their own. It brought together over a thousand women. Betty Lue had much to do with the planning for it, and she also gave one of the major sermons. The newly arrived public address system made it possible and practical to have women speak at large public meetings.

Extra Teaching Hours During My Absence

Mission money was allocated by committees and the Executive Committee of the mission at four sessions during the year. As the person representing the interests of the Chins, I had to show up for at least three of these meetings in Rangoon. Thus I had to be away from Haka during part of the Bible School year. When this happened, Betty Lue took over my classes. As she always taught the children in the mornings, this meant taking on the additional teaching loads in the afternoons. This extra teaching was not easy, but she never complained.

Teaching Teachers

The concept of a graded Sunday School, dividing children into classes according to age, was something new to the Chins of the Haka area when we first arrived. Gradually over the years the Sunday School grew into an important function of the church. But the problem in the Hills was the lack of books and other helps for the young people who were the teachers of the children. For this reason Betty organized classes each week for the teachers of the Children's Department. An average of 14 girls came every Friday afternoon to learn how to teach their Sunday morning classes. These girls also formed one of the many choirs in the church. Betty prepared songs and anthems, transposing the staff notation into the tonic solfa system used by the Chins. She also tried to change the English words into Chin, but that was too hard. Chin poetry is best done by Chins, so she usually got someone else to translate the words of the songs.

The Laura Carson Guild

In American Baptist churches in the United States, the "Guild Girls" is an organization for young girls, meeting usually on week-days for fun, fellowship, and service. Betty Lue started a group in Haka named the Laura Carson Guild, after the first missionary.

About 45 or 50 girls met in our home once a month. They had their own officers, conducted a short worship service, and did some form of handwork. Betty taught them how to make quilts, and in 1958 they made five as gifts for pastors in distant places. The girls also learned to crochet and knit and make sweaters, baby caps, and booties to give to the poor. These monthly Guild meetings were immensely popular and resulted in many girls learning skills unknown to their mothers.

The Dispensary and Sales

I have described how dozens of people came every day to purchase simple medicines at the dispensary we ran in our front office. Sui Hniar, the seller, was on duty daily but often was not able to determine what remedies were needed, so my wife would be asked. I suppose that on an average, Betty spent 1 or 2 hours daily listening to the needs of people for medicines, or advice on any and all subjects, and talking to those who just wanted to visit. Her faithfulness in doing this relieved me to do other needed mission work. Those long talks with women helped Betty to learn many of the idioms used commonly by them, helping greatly in her comprehension of the finer points of the language.

One time a man ventured to accuse us, or suspect us, of profiting personally from the sales of medicines and books. We showed him the detailed ledger of purchases and sales, page after page of figures, and asked him to add them up himself. He declined. This was before the age of electronic calculators, but we had a device called an "Add-O-Meter" which enabled us to add without error. So we showed him our books and he agreed that we did not take money for ourselves.

Actually, in fact, we sometimes lost personally on sales. When we felt sorry for some poor but needy person, we gave the medicine without charge.

Betty's Literary Work

Another of her time-consuming and challenging tasks was that of preparing the Sunday School lessons in Haka Chin. Early each year she selected material for children's lessons and asked Anthony Ngun Uk and Mabel Zo Kai, Van Bik's wife, to translate them. She checked them over and saw to their printing on the Deirel Press. She did a whole year's lessons. She also translated some adult Sunday School lessons, printing them on the mimeograph machine.

All through our second term, in fact, Betty was involved in literary work of one kind or another. We made excellent use of our two typewriters and the fine new Gestetner mimeograph machine that we purchased in Rangoon. For those not familiar with the Gestetner, an English-made duplicator, it uses two drums over which a silk screen passes ink to the stencil. A heavy consistency ink is used and hence it is easier to print both sides of a sheet of paper without the ink bleeding through. We thank God for all this equipment to make it easier to communicate the gospel of our Lord Jesus Christ.

What More Shall I Say?

I have tried to give an idea of the many activities that kept my wife busy from dawn until dark. I am sure that even our co-workers downcountry did not know the varied nature of her work or how much she contributed to the Johnson team. She took much of the burden on herself. Her gracious ways, her warm hospitality to all callers, and the fine way she exemplified the best in Christian womanhood endeared her to all people and left a rich heritage of goodwill toward the mission and the Christ we came to serve.

Chapter 44

SECOND FURLOUGH AND RETURN TO BURMA

Plans for Departure

Our mission secretary in Rangoon informed us that our family would sail sometime in May, 1959. This suited us, for then Richard was able to finish 9th grade in India and return to travel with us. Ruth would complete 6th grade and Martha 1st grade at home and all would be able to enter American schools in September.

I drove our Crosley Farm-O-Road down to Kalemyo and sold it, spare parts, and little trailer for 4,000 kyats, about $840. It had served us well in spite of broken springs, a broken steering rod, a transmission that sometimes went out of gear, and a broken fan. The money went to the mission, the owner of the vehicle. I determined to bring back to Burma a Jeep, as the advent of wider bridges and truckable roads now made the wider vehicle possible.

We told Chia Ling, who lived just behind our house, that he could be the caretaker during our absence. We told Ram Hlun that he could have our cookstove, as we planned to bring back a new one. We planned to leave the house with furniture, dishes, cutlery, tools, bedding, etc., all intact, unused until we returned after a year's absence.

Final Days in Haka

Eight years previously, when we went on our first furlough, we were so afraid that a Communist army might take the town over that we hid the platen (roller) of our typewriter in the attic rafters lest these intruders steal the machine. This time when we left, it was with light hearts. The Chins had voted for our return. We had finished the new buildings of the Bible School in Falam. Bible translation had been slow, but David Van Bik and I had finished the translation of two Old Testament books, Genesis and Exodus, into the Lai language, the first ever of the Old Testament.

Also, the "new church building" made in 1952/53 was so filled with worshipers that to prevent collapse of the floor we had carpenters shore up the floor with posts and wooden beams. I had lived in dread of a floor collapse that would dump hundreds of people ten feet down to the bottom floor, with injuries or deaths. New plans were under way for a new and much larger church!

We Begin Our Journey

We were almost immobilized by the many visitors who came to say goodbye and by some dinners in our honor. But on the last day of April Betty Lue, Ruth, Martha, and I began our long journey. At Kalemyo we took the Union of Burma Airways plane to Rangoon where we met Richard coming by air from India. Our family of five departed from Rangoon on May 24, 1959, on the *M.S. Sangola,* a very pleasant British ship.

The ship touched briefly at Penang, Singapore, and at Hong Kong where I bought a Philips portable radio run by ordinary flashlight batteries. This marvel used transistors instead of the old fashioned vacuum tubes. A great radio, it kept us in touch with the world during our whole last term.

To Japan and the USA

Besides meeting some of the Baptist missionaries in Yokohama and Tokyo, our whole family of five had a lovely trip by train to Kyoto, the ancient capital, where we enjoyed a stay at a real Japanese inn. We also met a Swedish missionary couple who took us to their little church.

Our ship across the Pacific was the *Saga Maru*, a Japanese freighter which carried 12 passengers. We expected that our daily fare would be typical Japanese food, but to our surprise and delight we were served American meals. There were also luscious oranges, apples, and peaches, things we had not seen for years. So we thoroughly enjoyed the eleven days on board, a trip that took us far north and close to the Aleutian Islands.

The Bells of San Francisco

On Sunday, June 28, we sailed under the Golden Gate Bridge with seemingly hundreds of colorful little flags flying from the masts and with a helicopter flying around us a few times. Perhaps it was to welcome a ship on its maiden voyage, we don't know; Martha thought that the noise and fanfare was to welcome us.

What pleased me most was the sound of church bells on the San Francisco hills pealing out the beautiful hymns of the Christian faith. In Burma we enjoyed the singing of the Chins, often in four part harmony, but we had no bells. So bells on Sunday as we arrived were doubly welcomed.

Long Beach, and then Waukegan, Illinois

Betty's sister Grace and her husband Ralph Nees met us at the dock and took us to Long Beach in southern California to their home. Betty's mother was there, and it was a lovely reunion. After about a week we took the train the long distance to Chicago and thence to Waukegan, Illinois, 35 miles north of Chicago, where we made our home for the year of furlough.

Waukegan was a good place for us, just one mile from my sister and husband, 13 miles from my father, and near many uncles, aunts, and cousins living in the Chicago area. After a few weeks Betty's mother came from California and made her home with us until we returned to Burma.

Betty's Illness

Sometime before leaving Burma, Betty picked up an illness which later was diagnosed as amoebic dysentery. On our return journey she felt so ill at Hong Kong that she decided not to go ashore.In Japan she kept on going, though with some difficulty. On the *Saga Maru* she had a daily controversy with our steward who, as a good Japanese, felt that everyone must have a daily bath. He insisted that she take a bath when she could hardly stand up. She solved the problem by entering the bathroom, scattering soapy water around, emptying the tub, and departing, having never taken off her clothing, thus satisfying the steward.

When we got to Waukegan, I bought a used car and took the family up to Minnesota to visit Betty's youngest sister and family. We stopped on our return journey to see our American Baptist Convention assembly grounds at beautiful Green Lake, Wisconsin, but Betty could hardly sit up in the car to enjoy all this riding. She had physical examinations, but these revealed nothing alarming. Yet she always felt tired, run-down, and depressed.

Finally, in September we found a specialist in gastroenterology. He lived in Lake Forest, another of the Chicago suburbs. This man had been an Army doctor in the Philippines during World War II and knew at once what the trouble was. It was, he said, "a classic case of amoebic dysentery," but one that had been missed by other doctors not familiar with tropical diseases. He prescribed certain medicines, and, thankfully, Betty began to make immediate improvement. But it was not until the end of October that she felt really well and strong again.

I remembered again how bad Franklin Nelson felt when he had this insidious disease in 1946, how he was ready to give up and return to America. It acted on my wife the same way. What a marvelous change when she felt well again, and how we thanked God for knowledgeable doctors and for modern medicines—certainly one of God's good gifts!

The Children Enter American Schools

Dick had finished 9th grade in India, so in September when the school year begins in the United States, he entered 10th, which is the sophomore year of high school. He was a diligent student and had no problems at all making the transition to the American high school. He also took R.O.T.C.(Reserve Officers' Training Corps) and seemed to enjoy the training.

Ruth Kristin

Ruth went into 7th grade at the Junior High School. For her, the transition from home teaching to a school of 1,500 students was more traumatic. She had a difficult time for a few weeks until she learned that the shyness expected of a Chin girl was not the way girls acted in America. She had to learn to speak up in class. Ruth tended to think in Chin and then translate the Chin into English, sometimes forgetting that the word order is different. Her teachers were a bit rough on her until they finally realized her linguistic problem.

One example of this happened one day in home economics class. Ruth and another girl were cooking fudge and the pot began to boil over. Ruth saw the girl carelessly letting it boil over and very excitedly warned her, loudly, in Chin, to take the pan off the fire. As she was calling out these warnings in Chin, the rest of the class thought she was babbling insanely. It took some time for Ruth to begin to think in English. She eventually made the transition and completed a very successful school year.

Martha Anne

Martha also had some problems at first. She entered 2nd grade in the local elementary school, walking five blocks every day with a group of neighbor girls. An amusing thing happened on her first day of school. Betty took her to the school and explained to the teacher that Martha had grown up in Burma, spoke Chin as her first language, and would need some special attention at first until she got used to an American school. At about 10:40 that morning Martha arrived home. She had left in the middle of the morning classes. "I'm not going to stay at that school with a teacher who doesn't even know how to write!" she announced.

It turned out that Martha had written her name on the top of her paper in cursive writing as she had learned in the Calvert course, and the teacher had marked it wrong. Second graders were supposed to print their names. Martha could print, too, and was, in fact, ahead of the other children. But she was incensed that the "dumb" teacher had marked her paper incorrect.

My father was visiting that day, and took Martha aside and said to her, "When in Rome, do as the Romans do," and "When these children study longer, they will know as much as you do." Martha finally agreed to return to school, and Betty discreetly reminded the teacher that Martha's writing was not really wrong. The teacher agreed that she had acted hastily, forgetting that Martha came from a tutored school in the hills of Burma.

Martha did very well in 2nd grade and came to like her teacher very much.

Deputation Speaking in Churches

The months of furlough passed quickly for us. The children were in school almost until the day we left. I was traveling most of the time from city to city, speaking in churches, and telling of the Chin work in Burma. I had interesting stories to tell, and evidently the church folk enjoyed my messages, for invitations to speak came in constantly and our New York office had me traveling through ten states from Maine to California.

I enjoyed this deputation speaking, but it was tiring. I carried a big, heavy slide projector and a box of glassed slides each 3 by 4 inches in size, a heavy burden. But the people loved those beautiful color slides of the Chins, and listened with rapt attention.

Baptism of Ruth

Around Christmas time there was a lull in speaking appointments, and I had the joy of baptizing our daughter Ruth Kristin in the baptistry of the First Baptist Church of Waukegan. She made a beautiful confession of faith in Christ as Savior and Lord. She was then 12 years old.

A Jeep Provided

This church raised all the money to purchase a jeep for us and had it shipped out to Rangoon. The jeep was a CJ-6 model which was 20 inches longer than the ordinary jeep, and it also came with a special 4-speed transmission, steel cab, and winch capstan. I asked for the color to be red; so if the car went over the steep hillside and into bushes and trees, it would be more visible!

An Appraisal of the Furlough

Except for the early months of the furlough period when Betty Lue suffered with the undiagnosed amoebic dysentery, we can say that our year was a rich one. We had Betty's mother with us, my father was able to visit frequently, the children enjoyed good schools, my sister and family lived nearby, and Frank and Phileda Nelson were also living in our town, making it easy to get together and talk over our years together in Burma. I looked forward to working with David Van Bik on the translation of the Old Testament, and I anticipated the joy of helping construct a new and much larger church building.

Return: New York, England, Ceylon, Burma, 1960

We crossed the Atlantic on the magnificent *Queen Mary* in five days, a fast trip in misty cold weather. At Liverpool we boarded the *Warwickshire*, a freight/passenger ship, and went through the Suez Canal to Colombo, Ceylon (now Sri Lanka), having school for the children all the time. Then I made a quick side trip to India to take Dick and Ruth to school.

Dick and Ruth to Kodaikanal School

Kodai, as the school is popularly called, is in the Palni Hills of South India at an elevation of 6,800 feet. Because of the cold climate, the school year begins in June and there is a long winter break from mid-October to mid-January. So Dick and Ruth arrived almost six weeks late for school. But because we had taught them on shipboard, they went right into their classes without trouble.

I stayed only one night at Kodai and then rushed back to Ceylon hoping to rejoin Betty Lue and Martha on the ship. Thanks to a dockside strike that delayed departure, the *Warwickshire* was still in port. We made the last lap of the sea journey and arrived safely in Rangoon on August 4, 1960.

257

Back Among the Chins

When mission business was finished in Rangoon, Betty, Martha, and I went by train to Mandalay, then five days on river boats, by truck to Kalemyo, and by rented jeep (interrupted by two days stuck in mud and broken down) to Falam.

It was good to be back among our Chin friends. We were honored with flowers and dinners. At a dinner given by the Falam church, David Van Bik, who was principal of the Bible School, gave a little speech in English. He said:

"We want you, Mr. and Mrs. Johnson and little Martha, to feel at home among us. We know that you are ten thousand miles away from your kith and kin, and there is no denying the fact that you will long for them. Nevertheless, we thank God that you have chosen to be among us and to cast your lot with us, not for love of fame or honor, but for Christ's sake. We cannot promise you comfort and easy life on these rugged hills, but we want you to know that you are very much in our hearts and this little dinner which we give in your honor is but a poor token of that feeling we have for you. May the Lord bless you and prosper your work."

With the memory of the welcome at Falam and elsewhere along our route up from Rangoon fresh within us, we reached Haka on Saturday, September 3, to be greeted by a happy band of Christian folk along the road and at our house. We had been on our journey for two months and twenty-one days. How wonderful to be home again, home at last! We were ready to settle down now for our third term of service. We gave thanks for God's goodness to our family.

Chapter 45

THE CONVERSION OF
MANG KIO; A NEW PASTOR

≈

A New Pastor for Haka Church

I could never have guessed that a young chief whom we met in 1947 upon our arrival in Haka would ever become the pastor of our church. Chin chiefs were usually arrogant, resistant to the Gospel, often drunken and of low morals. But this could change!

Our pastor then was Rev. Sang Ling. Upon his death, Rev. Lal Hnin became the pastor. In 1962, when Lal Hnin left to take a large circle of churches, a man named Edward Mang Kio Thang, but called Ni Ceu Pa (father of Ni Ceu), was elected as pastor. We met him first under unusual circumstances.

The Young Chief

Mang Kio was the young chief in the village when we came to Haka. At that time he was an animist and was, indeed, opposed to the Christian gospel. The first time I ever saw him, as I recall, was when we visited him in the local hospital where he was recovering from a blow to his head. At one of the animistic Chin festivals, where the chief recreation is to get drunk, Mang Kio was sitting in the court-yard talking to some companions when his drunken uncle came up behind him unnoticed and clouted him on the head with a chunk of firewood. Mang Kio was bloody and knocked senseless, taken to the hospital for repairs, and it was there we saw him first.

Mang Kio at that time showed no signs of interest in conversion to the Christian faith. While not actively opposing Christian efforts, he was openly skeptical and uninterested. But something happened to him. He met Jesus. The story deserves telling, I think.

Mang Kio's Wife Becomes a Believer

Mang Kio was an important man in Haka village. He lived in the Innral Quarter, where there were very few Christians. One day the Christian women, making their rounds for prayer on Wednesday, learned that Mang Kio's son was ill. They called at the home and were invited in by the boy's mother, Ui Te. I am not sure if the father was present at that time; if so, he did not protest the prayer meeting that the women held for the little boy.

The loving concern that the Christian women showed for the son sparked an interest in Ui Te and she asked the women to come again. After a while, Ui Te learned more and more of the gospel story and finally decided to accept Jesus Christ as Savior and Lord. It is not easy for an animistic woman to do this, unsupported by husband, relatives, and neighbors—she was alone in that particular part of the village.

Finally Ui Te came to the point of asking for baptism. Between conversion and baptism the Chins usually ask a person to demonstrate during a six months period that the conversion is genuine, and that the convert really intends to live a Christian life and show the fruits of the Spirit of God.

The Fire

It was during this wait for baptism that the real test came. One night as Mang Kio, Ui Te, and the children were sleeping, a strong wind blew some of the coals from the cooking fire up into the thatch. The family awoke to find the roof ablaze. They escaped with their lives, but the house was destroyed and much of their clothing and food lost. Not only that, the wind blew blazing straw onto neighboring homes, and on that tragic night seven homes went up in flames.

To the animistic mind, this was positive proof that the spirits or nats were displeased with Ui Te because she was no longer propitiating in the old way. The neighbors vented their anger on her.

"It's all your fault that our houses burned up," they shouted at her. "It's because you no longer make the proper sacrifices. You are to blame. You will have to give up this foreign religion and become a lawki (animist) again or even worse things will happen to us!" they urged and prodded.

Poor Ui Te was in a quandary. Was what the neighbors were saying true? Had she done wrong? At this critical time the Christian women came often to support her in prayer and to urge her to faithfulness to Christ.

Then Mang Kio, her husband, said, "Ui Te, I have been watching you. If you are able to stand up against all the slanders of the neighbors and still stick to your Christian faith, then I will know that you have something genuine!"

Conversion of Mang Kio

Ui Te did remain true. Mang Kio was impressed enough by her faithfulness that he was, in a real sense, led to salvation by his own wife. He too finally accepted Jesus Christ and appeared at the church. It was a tremendous step for a man who was a chief among the Chins, considered a very important person by all, and who had now, like the Apostle Paul, come to believe in the One whom he had formerly despised.

Mang Kio made a complete turn-around. He became a faithful disciple of the Lord. Eventually he came to me one day and asked if he could enter the Bible School to study for the ministry. Although in his 30s, somewhat older than most of our students, he had studied through the 7th Standard, knew Burmese, and we enrolled him. He studied in Haka under Betty and me in 1957 and 1958, then continued for the next two years in Falam under the teaching of David Van Bik. He finished his studies in early 1961 and came back to Haka to serve a year as an unordained preacher until he was taken on as pastor in 1962. He became a leader and an effective preacher of the Word of God. He also was much involved in the building of the new stone church in Haka.

When I left Haka in 1966, fearing that the Christians in Burma were soon to go through persecution, Edward Mang Kio was the man who said earnestly to me, "Bawipa, do not weep or be cast down too much. We will be true, no matter what happens. We will be true to Christ to death."

Chapter 46

GROWING UP IN HAKA

Mining for Gems

I first noticed our son Richard's interest in rocks when he was yet a little boy in Haka. He was old enough to have heard stories of minerals and gems in Burma, and no doubt he knew about the jade, sapphires, and rubies found at the Mawchi mines in the Shan State.

We found him one day out near the chicken coop. He had enlisted the aid of his sister Ruth, barely two years old. They had a little shovel and a hoe.

"What are you doing, Dicky?" I asked.

Dick pointed to the hole he was digging, maybe 9 inches deep. "Daddy, we are making a mine," he said. "A mine for gold and silver and rubies and diamonds."

"Maybe you can help us dig," he continued. "It's very hard work."

"Can you get all these things in one mine? Rubies and diamonds are hard to find," I said.

"Well, Daddy, if we can find all these things, we will be rich and we can help all the poor people around here," he concluded.

Intrigued by the children's faith, I helped them for a while, getting down another six inches. And that was the end of mining for the day!

Heavy Pants

In 1951 our little family of four returned to the United States on our first furlough. One day we took the train to go two hundred miles up to Chicago to take postgraduate study in a seminary.

When we boarded the train in Decatur, Illinois, I was busy getting the suitcases aboard while Betty boarded the train with Dick and Ruth. She noticed that Dick's pants were sagging, almost falling off.

Their conversation went like this:

"Dick, what have you got in your pants?"

"Just some stones, Mommy."

"Your pants will pull off. Your pockets are too heavy."

"But these are my special rocks."

"Oh, where did you pick them up?"

"I found them. They are very pretty."

"Dick, let's empty your pockets and you can carry them up to Chicago, but not in your pockets."

Betty got the stones out and our son carried them safely to Chicago. Perhaps this early interest in stones and rocks showed later when he became a geologist.

The Crossbow

Like all boys in Haka, Dick made a bow for shooting mudballs. These bows are made of bamboo with even the bowstring made of bamboo. The mudballs are made of clay and about the size of marbles, hardened in the sun. Boys develop real skill in hitting targets.

But soon Dick wanted something more powerful and accurate. So he made a crossbow. He carved a piece of wood to resemble a gun and added a strong bamboo bow. He devised a trigger mechanism. Instead of mudballs, he made some wooden arrows, even tipped with sharp points. We were really scared of this thing he had made.

At last he was ready and I witnessed his first shots. Dick set up a pumpkin at ten feet distance and prepared to shoot. A half dozen of his Chin buddies watched the inaugural spectacle.

Our son aimed and fired. The arrow headed straight for the target. The arrow hit—and bounced right off the pumpkin!

The look on Dick's face was priceless. He was dumbfounded that the arrow did not penetrate and merely bounced off. We all laughed like crazy and a crestfallen boy returned to the workshop to remake his crossbow.

The Homemade Pistol

Around the time Dick made his crossbow, he decided to make a pistol. I would not let him shoot real guns yet, but he had plans for a firecracker pistol.

I found him busy upstairs in the attic one day. I had a worktable up there and hand tools—hammers, planes, pliers, chisels, and so forth. We had no power tools, for we had no electricity.

Dick loved to work upstairs with the tools, and actually I think he began pounding nails into wood at the age of two. Now he was intent on making a pistol.

He was drilling a hole in a $3/4^{th}$ inch thick iron bolt. I had these bolts in the house because we were building a new church, and these were for joining the timbers.

Dick had a bolt vertically in the vise and he had positioned a hand-operated drilling machine over it. The drilling machine was for drilling holes in steel plates and bar iron to strengthen the great wooden trusses for the roof of the church.

Dick had put a $3/8^{th}$ inch bit into the machine and was rotating the hand wheel. Each turn of the wheel drove the bit steadily downward, a small fraction of an inch at a turn.

I was amazed at what this eleven-year old boy was doing. I asked him to explain.

"Dad," he said, "I'm making a pistol. I need to drill a hole right down in the center of this bolt, to be the bore of the pistol barrel. I'm going to drill it as far as possible, and then I'll put little firecrackers in it and light them. It will shoot out fire and smoke just like a real gun."

I held my peace and even helped him for some hours of drilling. Unbelievably, he succeeded in drilling a straight hole two inches into the bolt. Eventually he added a handle and had fun shooting off little Chinese firecrackers he had found on sale in the bazaar.

Camping Out on a Hunting Trip

Richard always had a keen interest in guns. Of course he was not allowed to touch them until he reached a certain age.

I had a single-shot shotgun, one of the old-fashioned kind with an exposed hammer. It was safer, in that Chins borrowing the gun could easily see if the hammer was cocked or not.

I also had a high-powered hunting rifle, a bolt action Husqvarna in the .30-06 caliber, powerful enough to use on tigers, bears, wild boars, and leopards which existed in the Chin Hills. Chins borrowed this gun also, and if the man shot a barking deer, the custom was for the gun owner to receive one rear thigh. Occasionally we got some venison to eat in this way.

Finally the day arrived when Dick was old enough to use a real gun. This was when he returned home one year from high school in India during the long winter recess.

It was in November, the rains were over, and the days were getting cold when we organized a little hunting trip. We were four: my son Richard, our cook Ram Hlun, a Chin named Phu Sa who was wealthy enough to own a rifle, and myself.

We went up on the mountain behind Haka to a remote area several miles away. Here we built a lean-to with branches. We gathered dry grass for our beds and had dinner. Ram Hlun cooked rice and some vegetables and we swapped stories around the campfire. Truly it was a pleasant evening and I noted how grown-up our son had become, a man now.

Next day we hunted in two groups of two. I had the rifle and Dick the shotgun. There was a heavy mist and it was not too clear for good hunting. We saw nothing and did not fire a shot.

However, in the early afternoon we did hear one shot in the distance. "He must have missed," said Dick. "Only one shot."

So we returned empty-handed to camp. We waited for Ram Hlun and Phu Sa to return. We hoped they would have a barking deer or maybe a wild pig. At last they came. Phu Sa carried his trophy— a single jungle cock torn apart by his rifle shot. Half of this wild chicken was gone and hardly a mouthful of meat remained.

My son was awed by the feat of hitting a wild chicken in the jungle with one rifle shot, and awed even more by the power of a 9 mm. rifle bullet heavy enough for shooting tigers. "Wow," he said. "One cartridge, one half a jungle fowl—what a deal!"

The Geologist

Evidently our son's fascination with rocks carried on into adult life. He finished college with a geology major, went on to graduate study for a master's degree, and ended up with a Ph.D. in geology. His doctoral thesis concerned copper deposits on the Gunflint Trail in Minnesota.

At that time the subject of employment came up. "Dad," he said, "I can get a job in oil exploration, but I don't want that. I don't want to work in oil. What I want is to work on <u>hard</u> rocks." And he did so, using his knowledge of geology in the U.S. Army, Corps of Engineers, in which he rose to the rank of Colonel.

Chapter 47

THE STORY OF NU TIN

One dreary monsoon season I became aware of a very ill young mother in Haka. About a year earlier Nu Tin had contracted cancer. Then her husband found her unattractive and divorced her, a simple act in animist Chin culture. Nu Tin was left destitute and an invalid, with two small children. She found refuge in a relative's house in the bazaar line, and there Christian love reached out to her.

Barbara Hrang Zing and Helen Sui Bor, two young lady workers of our church, found her lying there on gunny bags, with her pillow a wooden block and a gunny bag. They went up almost every other day to visit her and help. Under their loving ministry Nu Tin found peace with God and became a believer.

In September she knew she was dying. She was unhappy because she had not yet been baptized. But she was so weak that she could not be moved to the church's open-air baptistry. Betty and I explained to her that baptism was good and desirable, but was not really necessary for salvation, that she could go to heaven without it, and that it might be difficult for her to be baptized, for our practice is immersion in water. But she desired it so strongly that we decided to go ahead, as her illness was so grave.

It happened that when we came out to Burma for our second term of service, we brought along a sewing machine with cabinet and all, and for this I had made a large plywood box. We still had that box. I made it waterproof and some young men carried it to the bazaar, to the kitchen where the young woman lay. It was raining heavily outside, so we prepared the box in a corner of the smoky cookhouse. Women heated water so the baptismal water would be at a comfortable temperature.

I had never done anything like this, immersing a person unable to walk or stand, so I consulted with my wife. Betty said, "We'll change her ragged clothing, put on something new and clean, and we'll put her on a blanket, and you can have persons lift her in the blanket." I said that this would be okay, so Barbara, Helen, and Betty Lue did prepare Nu Tin for the baptism.

So we proceeded, but not everything went according to plan. The cookhouse was so dark and the smoke so dense that I could not see the page of the Bible to read. I had planned to have four men lift the blanket, but she was so wasted away and light that just two were needed.

As the moment of baptism approached, a wave of emotion almost choked me. Usually the ordinance is a joyous occasion, out in the sunshine and light, and for people who look forward to years of service and life. How different this was! We lifted the corners of the blanket and gently lowered Nu Tin into the water. I repeated the customary words and this dying woman affirmed her belief in Jesus as Savior and Lord. Then as I came to the last part, "in the name of the Father, the Son, and the Holy Spirit, Amen," the water closed momentarily over her. Usually choirs sing "O Happy Day" at baptismal services among the Chins. There was a little choir of twelve girls led by Betty, and they began to sing, but weakly. I looked up and saw that all were weeping. Only four girls were composed enough to carry on with the hymn, "Abide with Me":

> "In life, in death, O Lord,
> Abide with me."

Fourteen days later a serene Nu Tin died and we buried her beneath the pine trees on the mountainside, and loving hands planted a cross over her lonely grave.

Chapter 48

THE OKAY YEARS, 1960—1963

❧

Two Great Jobs to Do in the Third Term

When Betty Lue and I returned to Burma in 1960, we knew that we had, in addition to the usual teaching and village touring, two great jobs to accomplish if possible: complete the translation of the Old Testament scriptures, and construct a new and much larger church building in Haka, of stone if possible.

Translating the Scriptures

David Van Bik and I had worked on the translation of Genesis and Exodus and had seen the actual book produced in England by the British and Foreign Bible Society. I wanted to have David, principal of the Bible School in Falam, devote a lot of time to the translation, for we made a team able and willing to undertake this formidable job. Some way had to be found so we could work together as much as possible.

A New Church for Haka

The two-story wooden church in Haka was so overcrowded that the floor had been reinforced to prevent collapse. Twice the church had escaped destruction by forest fire, being located in a grove of pine, and we hoped to build with brick or stone. No decision had been made by the Chins to rebuild, but just in case we could cut and use stone, I brought out the hardware to make a stone-cutting saw, that is, mandrel, pulleys, v-belts, and a 10 inch diameter diamond blade. Upon return to Haka, I found that the building committee wanted to build a structure with inside dimensions of 50 by 96 feet, without any inside posts to hold up the roof, that is, of clear span construction. In another chapter I will try to explain how, finally, after years of work, the Haka Chins did build this magnificent structure able to seat a thousand people.

So these were the two special and important tasks to do.

The Changing Scene

The home-made stone cutting saw cut thousands of stones for the church. Circular saw blades with diamond-studded rims easily cut stones up to five inches thick.

During our absence in America, the name of the Bible School in Falam was changed to Zomi Baptist Theological School; David Van Bik was the principal and he had a nice group of Chin teachers. The school was doing well.

We felt a sense of impending gloom on the mission as a whole. The Prime Minister of Burma, U Nu, a devout Buddhist, was at the forefront of a move to declare Buddhism the state religion of Burma. No one was sure what this would mean. Did a state religion imply that Buddhism must be taught in all schools? Did it mean that only Buddhists would get the best jobs in education, health, and the military? Did it mean that non-Buddhists, including Muslims, Hindus, and Christians, would face discrimination? Would it mean the end of Christian missions such as ours? No one seemed to know. This was a hot issue all through Burma at this time.

There was a strong feeling among Christian believers that Buddhism should not be declared the state religion, and this feeling was shared by the other faiths. This was one factor in accepting gracefully in 1962 the overthrow of the U Nu government by the military dictatorship under General Ne Win.

Soon after we reached Haka after furlough, there was a political meeting in the town to discuss the state religion problem. Betty, Martha, and I completely absented ourselves from town, making a visit to Nabual, four miles distant, as a one-day trip. I recall carrying Martha in my arms fording a mountain stream, slipping on a rock, and dunking my daughter into the cold water. She laughed it off and we had a fine time, away from politics. As foreigners, we avoided taking any part in the politics of the country.

We found a thriving school on our mission compound, meeting in the lower level of the church building. This was the Haka Christian Primary School. More than a hundred children, all shouting their lessons, made us aware of this new phenomenon a few hundred yards from our front door.

Almost immediately Betty was drafted as a teacher of English, a much desired subject. Since only Martha was at home, she could finish classes for our daughter by late morning, after which she went down to the church to give a half-hour lesson to each of three classes. She had 60 wiggling little children in kindergarten, 21 first graders, and 23 second graders. How lucky that she had been a primary school teacher in a one-room school in Illinois!

The New Church in Tiddim

During our absence, the Christians in Tiddim celebrated the 50th anniversary of the founding of the mission station in that town in 1910. They termed it their Jubilee, as they dedicated the new and beautiful brick church named as a memorial to Dr. J. Herbert Cope. We were sorry to miss this event in April, 1960.

The Schedule for Bible Translation

A very important conference took place in November, 1960, near Kalemyo involving a Bible Society official from London and one from the Bible Society of Burma, from Rangoon. The Britishers gave counsel and encouragement to those of us engaged in Scripture translation. The main decision was to limit full Bibles to three languages: Lai, Laizo, and Kamhau (for Haka, Falam, and Tiddim areas) and to fund translations in those languages. Regarding Van Bik and me, they advised a rotation, namely two weeks in Haka, two weeks in Falam, and two weeks working separately. David and I did put this into effect, and funds were found to help hire another teacher for the theological school in Falam so Van Bik could travel to Haka on the rotation schedule.

This became our rainy season program; during the dry season when village touring was possible, we followed a different pattern for scripture translation.

Following this conference, I drew up plans for building a 20 by 20 foot cabin in Falam to use when I was translating with David in that place. It was later built and we called it the Logos Cabin.

Events in 1961—The New Jeep

The red jeep donated by the Waukegan Church arrived in Rangoon, and I asked Van Bik to go with me to get it. It was the CJ-6 model, about 20 inches longer than the standard vehicle, and had a longer wheelbase. It did have the Koenig Half-Cab already attached, wonderful protection from the rain. But the back was open like a pick-up truck. I found a man in Rangoon to weld together steel pipes to make a framework over the rear part, and then with bamboo matting and canvas we made a proper shelter for goods or people riding in the back. The finished production was marvelous: a modern car in front, an ox cart in the back.

This magnificent vehicle was used well in the Hills for all the years of our third term, as we now had a jeepable road from Haka to Falam, to Tiddim, and down to the plains of Burma.

Kingfish, the Horse

For years I had hiked on the long village tours, but finally the time came when I said to myself, "You're getting older, Bob, don't waste your strength hiking." So finally I found a horse big enough to carry me. Most Chin horses are really ponies, but Kingfish was big and strong. I gave him this improbable name after a character in the Amos and Andy comedy team on radio. I made arrangements for a man to care for him and use him whenever he wished, if I did not need the horse.

Church Vote for Construction of a Stone Building

In July 1961 the church members voted to begin construction of a church to replace the old wooden structure. The inside dimensions would be 50 by 98 feet. The people had debated the issue, some being afraid it would be beyond our ability. I warned them that it would take years of effort and great sacrifice on their part. There was almost unanimous agreement to proceed.

Some were unsure we could bridge 50 feet between walls without poles or posts in the middle. I made a model of a Howe Truss, one inch to the foot, and showed them how the truss would work; it would not collapse. This model truss convinced all that we could succeed.

With the vote to proceed, we were now able to buy needed items. The biggest item was a snub-nosed Ford truck. It was moved from Mandalay to Haka by hired drivers. On a trip to Rangoon in November I purchased needed items, such as shovels, pickaxes, hoes, pails, trowels, wheel barrows, and very important, a 4-horse-power kerosene-operated engine. All of this equipment plus paper and supplies for the Deirel Press, and some things for our personal food supply came to Haka safely in December.

The Year 1962, a Year of Progress

Dlck and Ruth, home for the winter holiday, returned to India in January. This was to be Dick's last semester of his senior year of high school.

In the same month, work began on the site for the new church. The location was where the original school/church had stood when we first arrived. The site to be leveled was 137 feet long and 60 feet wide. It actually took us one year and two months of work on the site before the first concrete was poured.

General Ne Win Takes Power in Burma

A very significant date for Burma was March 2, 1962. On that day General Ne Win in a coup d'etat seized power from the elected government of U Nu and began a military dictatorship which has controlled the nation for over 44 years.

General Ne Win and a Revolutionary Council of 17 members inaugurated a new party, the Burma Socialist Programme Party, supplanting the former political parties, such as the Anti-Fascist Peoples' Freedom League (AFPFL). U Nu and the cabinet members were jailed, some to be released rather quickly, others held for years. The 1947 Constitution was abrogated. Parliament was suspended, and Burma became a one-party state. All of this was accomplished in one swift move, without bloodshed, and with surprisingly little opposition.

When news of this reached the Chin Hills, there was little stir. Few people were aware of politics in Burma anyway. I would say that if anything, there was general approval for this coup, for many believed that Ne Win would stamp out lawlessness and rid the country of the incessant bands of thieves who roamed the countryside. Almost no one knew what socialism was, so the name of the party, the Burma Socialist Programme Party, caused little alarm. Before long, the party was known as "The Burmese Way to Socialism Party."

General Ne Win, although a Buddhist, was not known as a zealot like U Nu, and among Christians there was a satisfaction that Buddhism would not be forced upon the populace as an official national religion.

At the time of the coup in early 1962 there was no way to predict the momentous changes that would occur as a result of the new socialist government that came to power, changes that would result in the expulsion of foreigners in a few years and the end of the American Baptist mission in Burma.

A Vacation Trip to India; Richard Graduates

Betty Lue and I took very few vacations because the climate was good and we did not have to flee summer heat. But we did take time to go to India to see Richard graduate from high school. Thus our family of five was together in Kodaikanal, a pleasant stay in one of the Baptist vacation cottages. Rich graduated with good grades and was salutatorian of his class.

I cannot resist telling of new ways to cook and to bake that we learned in India.

We hired a man named Perry to be our cook. We have some fond memories of this Indian gentleman. One is how he baked things in the kitchen stove. The oven did not heat properly from the wood burning in the regular firebox, so Perry built fires under the stove! The little cookhouse filled with choking fumes whenever he baked. One time Perry planned to serve fish for our supper. We were dubious about the freshness of fish up there in the mountains. Perry assured us that there would be no question of freshness. When we returned home that afternoon, we found our tin bathtub out in the yard, and in the tub, swimming around, was a large fish. "From the ocean," Perry said. We then learned that live fish were brought up from the sea to Kodaikanal in tank trucks of salt water. So we enjoyed fresh fish, less than an hour out of the water.

Bible Translation a High Priority

Van Bik and I worked very hard on translations the rest of the year, putting into practice the rotation between Haka and Falam. The Logos Cabin, 20 feet square, was put up and divided into a large porch and a 6 by 10 kitchen, a 5 by 10 bedroom, and a 9 by 10 bedroom. I built double bunks in the smaller bedroom. This became my residence while I was in Falam and translating with Van Bik. The name Logos came from the Greek word meaning "word," for we were working on the Word of God.

Richard Leaves for America

Dick traveled with us to Burma after graduation, and after a few days in Rangoon he traveled by air to Long Beach, California. It was hard to say goodbye, of course. Four years would pass before we would see him again, and he had those four years of college ahead of him. He would have to work to earn his way, as I did before him. We had confidence that he could do it. Dick went to Long Beach, California, to the home of his Uncle Ralph and Aunt Grace Nees for the summer, and then on to Wheaton College in Illinois.

Ruth, whom we had left behind in India at school, rejoined us in late October and went with us to an important missionary conference in Rangoon in early 1963, then returned to India. It was still possible at this time for school children to fly in and out of Burma freely, and even Betty and I had received permission to return to Burma after our vacation trip to India. This freedom was later to change for the worse.

Year 1963

I have called the years 1960 to 1963 the "okay years" to distinguish them from 1964 and 1965 which were for us the "tough years." The year 1963 began as a harbinger of bad things to come. Even so, I still could go on village tours, and I made a 29-day trip with Kingfish, 3 packhorses, and Ram Hlun as cook, to the southern parts of my field, Zotung and Matu. On this trip I had the unusual experience of having no cloudy weather; every night was crystal clear with the stars brilliant in the heavens. I saw the full circuit of the moon, from full to new and back to full again, every night perfectly clear.

While I was on this tour, General Ne Win's military government nationalized 15,000 business firms, and on February 23 nationalized 24 banks and amalgamated them into four "Peoples' Banks." These radical moves by the socialist government caused but little comment among the Chins, as the Chins had no business firms and there were no banks. Our mission accounts had been for years in the Imperial Bank of India located in Rangoon; this became one of the new Peoples' Banks. The take-over of the banks caused me no problem; we did not lose anything. But I did miss the familiar sight of the burly Indian man, armed with a shotgun, guarding the entrance to the Imperial Bank.

We were definitely worried in early April when some Burmese immigration officials came to Haka and made inquiries about us, what we were doing in Haka, where we were traveling, who worked with us, etc. Our stay in the country was contingent upon annual renewal of our Foreigners' Registration and Stay Permits, and denials of stay permits could mean the end of our work in Burma.

Betty's Long Illness

Although I have called 1963 one of the Okay Years, it was certainly not okay for Betty's health. She endured a long siege in the summer.

Betty, Martha, and I left home on May 17 and jeeped to Tiddim for a Pastors' Conference, staying in the Nelson bungalow. The conference was canceled, so we decided to stay a week to study the Kamhau language. Betty came down violently sick. She did not respond to any medicines we had, so after nine days I took her to Falam. On that trip she rode on boxes and baggage in the rear of the jeep. The Civil Surgeon at Falam was unable to cure her illness, and after Betty's fourteen days in bed in the Logos Cabin, suggested that I take her to Rangoon. Again she lay in the back of the jeep, unable to hold up her head, very ill. A cold mist was blowing in on her, and I wondered if she could survive as we went through the rough and rutty road down to the airport at Kalemyo. Here the English Methodist missionaries, Leslie and Margaret Cowell, welcomed us into their home and cared for Betty until the plane came.

To Rangoon and Maymyo

At Rangoon Betty was admitted to the S.D.A. hospital and there she spent 22 days. The doctor diagnosed her illness as acute gastro-enteritis, asthma, and asthenia, and recommended four weeks of complete rest.

Following the doctor's order, we did go then to the hill station of Maymyo, east of Mandalay, for four weeks in the mission Rest House. There Betty recovered enough strength to travel home to Haka, which we reached on August 28. During this long sickness there were times when I felt that I might lose my wife. During this time all our family members in America, and all the Chins who knew of her trouble, prayed mightily for her recovery. She did recover enough to continue to the end of the year on a reduced schedule, teaching Martha, teaching Sunday School, writing letters, etc., but she was not able to tour with me or go down the steep hill to visit in the lower part of the village.

Bob's Work During this Time

During our absence of 3 months and 10 days from home, I was able to type up manuscripts of our Bible translations, write letters, and while in Rangoon buy hardware items for the church, such as nails, screws, hinges, bolts and nuts, electric wire, switches and sockets, and certain tools, all for stockpiling in Haka. It was most fortunate that I did so, hiding all this material in my attic until needed, because later much of this became unobtainable in the market.

During this same period David Van Bik worked regularly on scripture translation and made great progress.

Construction of the new church building went forward also during the year. In March the first cement was poured for the foundation. Work slowed during the rains but on October 1 we hired a foreman and an assistant to work full time, and on October 13 the cornerstone was laid by U Chia Kawm and Isaac Nu (mother of Isaac). The latter was the first woman to be baptized in the Haka area.

At the end of December the walls of cut stone were up 2 feet high in places.

Ruth came home to Haka from school in India in late October and had two months at home with us and Martha, a happy time together.

Chapter 49

THE TOUGH YEAR, 1964

~~~~~

1964, The Grim Year

I remember 1964 as a grim and unpleasant year, in some ways the most difficult of our twenty years on the mission field. Of course the sun shone, and our work in church construction, songbook revision, Bible translation, and evangelism flourished. But it was the year in which it became apparent that our days in Burma were numbered; that the mission would be squeezed out in a few short years, if not sooner; that in all probability I could not get the church roofed over before having to leave; and that there was a good chance that Betty and I might be deported from Burma before Christmas, or that our goods might be confiscated and I imprisoned.

Rumors abounded of dire things to happen in Burma to the Christian community, especially to pastors and other church leaders, and that tough days lay ahead for those who would be faithful to Christ. The example of Communist China, so close to us, was always in mind. China's repression of Christians was well known—could something like that happen in Burma? Some people thought it could indeed happen. Several educated men thought that Burma would go communist faster than China did, with similar dire results for pastors and even ordinary church people.

Betty Has Another Illness in Early 1964

Betty probably had never fully recovered from her summer 1963 illness when she became sick again on January 22. This lasted about three or four weeks, keeping her in bed much of the time. She did continue to teach Martha from her bed, and whenever possible wrote letters and relieved me of much of the heavy burden of correspondence. We thought the illness was amoebic dysentery until we went to Rangoon where our mission doctor, Barbara Winn, diagnosed it as infectious hepatitis. Probably our treatment by the local doctor in Haka was all wrong, but thanks be to God, Betty recovered and by the end of February was feeling much better.

Emergency Plans for Leaving

In mid-February we received a letter of instructions from our mission secretary in Rangoon to make preparations in case we were all ordered to leave the country. The letter asked us to stay as long as possible, delaying furloughs if necessary. Shortly after this, a letter from mission headquarters in Valley Forge, Pennsylvania, asked us to consider going to another field, perhaps Thailand, if we were forced out of Burma.

The message was clear and urgent: Get Ready! Betty and I packed up a small steamer trunk with treasured wedding gifts, linens, and photos and shipped it downcountry for storage. We had also been given directions for taking care of ledger books, the turnover of cars and property to Association Secretaries, and advised to make 13 copies of invoices of all goods in every box that was marked for shipment home to the States. I was treasurer of the Haka Association at that time, so I turned over the books and money to David Van Bik, elected as the new treasurer.

Many years earlier I had devised a simple system on how to keep proper ledgers of money in and money out, which I taught the pastors. I also taught the importance of written records, receipts, etc., and in truth the Chin leaders did well in this matter after our departure.

The "Emergency Consultation" in Rangoon in March

The letter was soon followed by a call for all missionaries to come to an "Emergency Consultation" in Rangoon for the week of March 21-28. Betty Lue, Martha, and I did go and found that our missionary group in the country at that time numbered 46. Joined with about 50 national leaders and numerous children, we all convened at the seminary and theological schools at Insein, a suburb of Rangoon. It was a week of heavy and deep thinking about the future of the churches. We discussed education, medical matters, evangelism, church organization, and of course the future of the foreign missionaries in this socialist state. We slept men and boys in one dormitory, women and girls in another, and we enjoyed Burmese style meals of rice and curry together—a time of rich fellowship. The national Christian leaders expressed their deep faith in God, and said that they would never deny their faith in Christ, no matter how repressive the new government might become.

One must remember in reading this that Communist China lay just to the east, with 1,200 miles of border with Burma. We heard tales of cruel repression of Christians in China, of pressure on pastors and leaders to deny their faith, and the radio broadcasts from Peking seemed to breathe out fire and smoke against so much of what we held dear in life. There was always at that time the nagging question, Could it happen that way in Burma too?

The Nationalization of Businesses and Shops, April 9

While we were still in Rangoon, the General Ne Win Revolutionary Government on March 28 announced that Burma would be a "one party state, marching on to the goal of socialism." This was done by promulgating a law making the Burma Socialist Programme Party the sole permitted party.

Betty, Martha, and I arrived home in Haka on April 7, a Tuesday. Immediately on arrival I was asked to preach on Sunday. In view of what happened I should have declined, but I accepted.

Two days later, on Thursday, the nationalization of shops occurred throughout all Burma. When Chin soldiers, on pain of 2,000 kyats fine and five years imprisonment if they did not obey, moved in on April 9 and seized 16 shops in Haka, the consternation was complete. The Chins did not expect such a move way up in the remote hills. In one sharp blow people saw their shops nationalized, everything taken over by the government with no express promise of compensation, and not only the stocks of goods but houses also, for in every case the family lived in the back of the store and sold goods from the front. As their private food supply was mixed up with the goods for sale, they were not allowed even to take out some rice, salt, and canned fish for their meals. In an instant, at dawn, on that terrible day, they were left destitute.

Probably the government was aiming only at people identified as "rich capitalists." I have a hard time believing that the government was actually intending to seize small village shops such as those in Haka, shops where people were eking out a living by small-time trading. To think of these people as being rich capitalists is ludicrous. But the order came and the soldiers, most of them Christians and good men, had to obey under threat of heavy fines. The government action was interpreted by the Chins as directed not against the rich but against the poor, and probably a typical Communist act.

We learned later that 17 shops in Falam and 38 in Tiddim were seized in similar fashion.

In addition, there was a rumor (erroneous) that the government was going to take all the Chin children away from their parents and send them to Rangoon where they would be indoctrinated in Communism. A stupid rumor, to be sure, but it was widely believed and caused great agitation among the people.

Thus the air was electric that weekend.

On Sunday morning in the church I told the story of the recent consultation in Rangoon and announced that it was very probable that Betty and I might not be able to finish out our term. Then I read some appropriate Scripture and asked two people to pray, remembering those who were in sorrow at the time.

Fortunately or unfortunately, depending on how one looks at these things, some people broke down with sorrow and wept audibly during the prayers, causing more tears among the congregation. Some wept for their own loss, others wept for their friends' loss of home and business. Evidently the spy or spies in the congregation reported the matter to authorities in Falam, and on Wednesday I was summoned to Falam by an armed escort.

Bob Johnson Under Arrest

I had never been arrested before, and I had a hard time thinking of my situation as being under arrest. I had time to get some clothing packed. I arranged for Chia Ling to go with me. The armed soldier who summoned me to Falam had no transportation, so he asked me to drive my own jeep, with Chia Ling and himself as passengers. My escort was a Haka Chin and was friendly, so we chatted as we rolled along the 46-mile dirt road to Falam. He had a rifle, but I never felt threatened. We ended up at the Logos Cabin where Chia Ling was let off, along with our baggage and food. I then drove to the police lines..

In Falam, the A.D.I.G. P.

My interrogator was the Additional Deputy Inspector General of Police (ADIGP), a Burman of quite high rank, in fact, the highest police officer in the Chin Hills. When he asked me why I was agitating the people, I explained that the people were agitated by the events of Thursday when the shops were seized. I said that I was not agitating the people, but rather, I was trying to calm them down. When some are injured, I said, we try to rally round and help them.

This gentleman, who undoubtedly was anti-western and anti-missionary, informed me that willy-nilly the government was on the path of the Burmese Way to Socialism; that in the United States it was "government of the people, by the people, and for the people," but that here in Burma it was "government of the working people, by the working people, and for the working people." I was surprised at his reference to words of Abraham Lincoln and how he had added words to Lincoln's famous Gettysburg Speech.

I then mentioned the parable of Jesus about the man who had a hundred sheep but one was lost out on the mountainside, and how the shepherd went out to find the valuable lost sheep. So Christians are concerned if even one out of a hundred is lost and in trouble. In reply, the ADIGP said that if in a hundred people one rich man was injured, that didn't matter too much, so long as the ninety and nine poor got along better. I did not dare get into an argument with a closed-mind Burman, so I listened politely to his scolding.

The police officer gave me tea and crackers and was not discourteous, but left me with the distinct impression that he felt I was working and teaching in opposition to the government policy, which in his eyes was a crime and a "very serious charge" for which "action" would be taken against me. He had, by the way, a pile of Cadbury chocolate bars on the table, which we working people had not seen in the shops for years, but I did not dare reach out and take one, and he did not expressly offer me one.

The charge against me was ridiculous, of course. It was not I who had taken away the shops and goods from the bazaar people, leaving some with no food for the evening meal. I never took a stand on Burmese politics or policies, for as a foreigner and guest in the country it was not fitting for me to act as a citizen. Unfortunately, however, when people interpret "politics" to mean all of life, and try to reduce religion to mean only prayers in church and thus make religion irrelevant to everyday life, then inevitably there may come some areas of conflict.

At any rate, I was in a very exposed position, being very conspicuous in the small community of Haka. We knew that there were spies watching us, and even the simplest of sentences, taken out of context and twisted, might be used against us. Obviously, I had to take every precaution against being misunderstood. I determined to be very quiet and just do the translation work and try to get the Haka church building finished before the end of our term, if we could stay that long. Betty would continue her important work with women and children. We decided to send Martha to the International School in Rangoon for at least a half year, starting in June. We would not send her to India; it was too risky.

Concern for the Haka Church Building Project

I will not deny that I was frightened at the summons to appear in Falam before the police and being charged with agitating the people. In Falam, the all-powerful Security and Administrative Committee (SAC) influenced by the ADIGP could very well deny me permission to get a renewal of the Stay Permits needed to remain in Burma. In other words, Betty and I could be deported. This was frightening because when all this happened in April, 1964, the walls of the new church were up only 5 feet high in some places, much less in other places. The walls had to go up to 19 feet and then would come the roof, with the huge and heavy timber trusses we were planning. If I were deported and not able to take charge, could the church ever get done?

Perhaps so, but I felt a terrible responsibility to get the roof on before leaving, and I figured it would take at least two more years. Thus I felt an obligation to do nothing that would jeopardize our stay in Burma, so we could finish out our term in 1966.

Quiet and Tedious Work at Home

During the rest of the year we were aware of spies checking up on our activities. Betty has a keen sense of smell, and she could tell when spies came around at night because of the cigarette tobacco smell. We knew that people could misinterpret much of what we said and did, and report this. We soon found that friendly government officers, formerly willing to be our dinner guests, no longer would accept invitations. Some told us frankly that if they joined us for dinner, they were required to write a report of persons attending and what was said. In that way we were cut off from social events. However, it did not bother us too much. We tried to be quiet, out of sight as much as possible, just doing our work with renewed zeal as we saw the end approaching. We did, however, make a trip to Rangoon to enroll Martha in the 7th grade at International School, where she studied one semester. Rosemary and Clifford Gilson were kind enough to take her into their home for those five months.

Meanwhile Betty and I returned home for solid, intense work. David Van Bik, now residing in Haka, joined me daily in literature work and we accomplished much.

Happy Ending of Year 1964; Martha's Baptism

The Grim Year, 1964, ended on a happy note. Ruth and Martha were at home for the winter holiday, and Martha was baptized by Pastor Mang Kio Thang on Christmas Day. Thirty-five others also were baptized that day on profession of their faith in Jesus as Savior and Lord.

Chapter 50

THE FRUITLESS REVOLUTION, 1965

≈≈≈

The Year that Brought Fighting to the Chin Hills

The big event of the first half of the year 1965 was an armed revolt against the Burmese government by Chin young men, a revolt that accomplished very little, and instead brought Burmese army troops into the Hills. However, the first two months were peaceful. Ruth and Martha went to India to school in early January, Martha for the first time, and Ruth for the last semester of her senior year. Betty and I were now restricted by the government to travel only in three areas: the Tiddim, Falam, and Haka subdivisions. It was not possible for us to go down to the plains, to Kalemyo and the airport, without special permission of the local Security and Administrative Committee (SAC), because Kalemyo was in the Magwe District, not in the Chin Hills. If we wished to go to Kalemyo or Rangoon, we first had to get the permission of the Haka SAC and then the Falam SAC. This worried us greatly. If we had a medical emergency, what if the SAC officers were away from their offices?

Long Tour to Hnaring

Since Richard was in college in the States and the two girls in school in India, now seemed to be the time for Betty and me to travel together to some remote villages. We did this first by a quick trip to

Sakta, 20 miles away, by jeep. That was a good trip, so we ventured a much longer tour to attend the Haka Baptist Association meeting at Hnaring in mid-February. This was a large and important village, but very far away at the great bend of the Boinu River at the south end of the Haka subdivision. It was a 13-day tour with horses. I had Kingfish; we rented a riding horse for Betty; and we had 3 pack-horses. We stopped in villages for evangelistic preaching meetings as we went. The association meetings were well attended and useful.

Betty had suffered some from sore knees and ankles caused by the steep roads approaching Hnaring. On the homeward journey we ran into far worse problems. The shortest way back to Haka was 71 miles, but we went 89 miles in order to visit some villages I had never seen before. Two were large, with 250 houses in one and 315 houses in the other, very large for Chin villages. In one there were only a few Christians, and in the other no believers at all. I wanted to preach the gospel to these people who probably had heard little or nothing about Jesus.

The trails proved to be very steep up and down, so steep that Betty could not ride her horse downhill. When I mention steep, I refer to a 45-degree slope of the hills. The trail zigzags down with sharp bends, so it is sometimes hard to keep one's footing. The road proved too hard for Betty's knees, so she became lame. With difficulty she reached the tolerably level motorable road. Our jeep was in Haka and there were no others, so we covered the last 50 miles on foot in three days, sleeping two nights in the forest, with fires going to scare away wild animals. I slept with my rifle, usually carried by Ram Hlun, by my side and we had no scares.

When we reached home, I continued work on the new church and translation with Van Bik. We completed the first draft of the book of Joshua, and Betty continued typing Deuteronomy in preparation for checking by our translation committee.

Rebel Attacks on Haka

We had been home from our tour only about two weeks when the situation in the Chin Hills grew decidedly worse.

On Friday, March 5, 1965, a few minutes after 6 in the morning, we wakened. Just then Betty said, "What's that?"

I listened and said, "Oh, it's just someone chopping wood."

But after a few seconds, as I began to wake up more, I realized that it was not a rhythmical pattern, and then suddenly we began to realize that it was gunfire.

We hurriedly dressed and by that time there was a regular staccato of fire and the whine of bullets overhead. Just then Pente knocked on the door and said that the town was under attack. I looked out the back door and could hear clearly the whing-g-g of shots. People were beginning to run in the old bazaar line, but whether they were soldiers or attackers, or just people fleeing, I could not tell, as they were silhouetted against the morning sky.

Shots continued on for 25 minutes, spasmodically. We saw only one of the attackers. He came through our yard and looked into our bedroom window, frightening Betty. She called me and I came and saw the man walking out front. I went to the porch and saw a young Tiddim Chin carrying an army rifle. He disappeared out the front gate and down the path to the west.

The "National Liberation Army"

The firing ceased and gradually over the course of the day we learned what had happened. A group of 25 or 30 men of the "National Liberation Army," in revolt against the Revolutionary Government of Burma, had come in during the night and mounted an attack against the police lines in the upper part of the village where the jail and treasury are. Unfortunately for the attackers, the police had advance warning and were in prepared positions. The rebel army lost one man, a Tiddim Chin who was cut down by gunfire near the police cookhouse. The attackers did not succeed in getting the wireless station or the police headquarters, so a wireless message went out and reinforcements were rushed from Falam during the day.

There was no secret about the leader of the rebels. He was Hrang Nawl, a former member of Parliament and a leader in the Chin National Organization (CNO) before the present government abolished all rival parties. We knew Hrang Nawl quite well as he was from the Haka subdivision.

Needless to say, the early morning excitement dominated the day. We spent many hours listening to rumors and trying to find out just what had happened. For a while we thought that the attackers had indeed captured the town. Many people thought that this was just the beginning of a major rebellion; so several hundred people living up near the police lines moved out of their houses, lest they be caught in crossfire again.

We Prepare for Siege

Dozens spent the night in the Shia Khaw Hostel (18-inch thick rammed earth walls); others were in the Rock House; and a dozen or so were under our house in the earth-floored cellar.

Betty and I prepared a barricade in the living room where we figured the various walls would stop stray bullets, and there we slept. Later, we piled heavy planks meant for church pews, each 2" x 10" x 10 feet long, three feet high against the outer wall of our bedroom, thus making a most secure barricade, which we kept there for months, and we slept on the floor.

In that first attack, one was killed and one wounded. The defenders lost none.

More Fighting

A second attack was made eight days later, but this time by only 5 or 6 men. No one was shot or injured, and the raiders did not accomplish anything.

On Monday, March 15, just at noon, while Betty and I were eating lunch and preparing to leave by jeep for Tahan for the Zomi Baptist Convention meetings, a Burmese soldier shot down a Chin policeman on the upper soccer field. The victim was Hram Ling from Falam. Shot in the stomach, this poor man died a week later. There seemed to be no real motive for the shooting, but the Chins interpreted it as racial, Burman versus Chin, and the situation grew ugly and tense. For a while, until the officers could calm down the men, there was danger of a fight between police and soldiers, which would have been disastrous.

Nationalization of Schools in Burma

On April 2, following a prior announcement of intention, the Revolutionary Government nationalized all private and missionary schools. Of over 800 in the country, 124 were taken over in the first batch. Among those nationalized were 24 schools of the Burma Baptist Convention. These included large, well-established, and flourishing schools founded by our Baptist mission.

Uncertainty About the Haka School

On April 5 the school committee for the Haka Baptist Middle School met in our home. In view of nationalization, the committee decided to discontinue our school which that year was to open in June with classes up to the 7th standard. The fear was that since the school met in the lower floor of our wooden church building, the government might seize both the building and the land on which it stood, namely the mission compound on which were also the two missionary residences, various hostels, and the new stone church under construction.

Two weeks later the Haka school committee reversed itself, forced into this by two strong members of the committee. The upshot of all this dissension was that 8 of the 12 members voted to continue KG to 4th standard in the Shia Khaw Hostel and the Rock House, and have the 5th, 6th, and 7th standards meet in what we called the Khuachung church, a secondary wooden church building in the lower quarter of Haka for older people who could not climb the steep hill to the mission compound. The Haka Baptist School continued to limp along in spite of nationalization. At least the higher grades were off the compound and we all felt safer.

Ruth's High School Graduation

In the midst of the turmoil in Burma, our daughter Ruth graduated from high school at Kodaikanal, India, on May 11 without our presence. Martha was the only member of our family to be there. Three years earlier we had gone to see Dick's graduation, but times had changed. We knew that if we left Burma, we could not return. So we had to forego the graduation. We sent a 35mm slide photo of Ruth as a child and that was shown at part of a slide show at the graduation. We also managed to send a pair of shoes for her graduation, a pair sent by mistake to Haka. We mailed those two shoes in separate parcels to discourage theft. A carrier mailed them from a post office in India.

Ruth Returns to Haka

Ruth had written to us in April that she was successful in getting entry visas for return to be with us for a few months before going to the U.S.A. We were overjoyed and made the trip to Rangoon to meet her and do mission business.

Ruth's arrival date was June 5. Just two days before her arrival Betty became ill with a bladder infection. She was not even able to go to the airport. Thankfully we were able to get a permit for Ruth to go with us to the Chin Hills—which was off limits to tourists. Our trip back was notable for the fallen trees on the hill roads. Foolishly I had forgotten to bring my axe; so Ruth and I had to cut through a 5-inch tree with a hammer and a pocket knife. By June 16 we reached home.

Betty's Illness

Betty endured the arduous trip by the mountain road through the mud, landslides, and fallen trees, and reached home very tired. She sat up long enough only to read a few letters and went to bed, utterly exhausted. This began nearly three weeks in bed. Her illness definitely was infectious hepatitis, a severe disease affecting the liver. She turned very yellow, which continued for eleven days. She described her condition as "dreadful" and "wretched." Certainly it was a most difficult illness which would affect her health for almost two years. Thankfully, Ruth was with us in Haka during this crisis and became her mother's nurse.

In addition to the care of her mother, Ruth typed up the handwritten manuscript of Judges; she helped Barbara weigh children in the well-baby clinic and did some other tasks in the medical program we had. One time when both Ram Hlun and Chia Ling were sick, she did the cooking for the family. It was a wonderful blessing to have this lovely seventeen-year-old with us for one and a half months. She was going to the States to begin nurses' training in Oak Park, Illinois.

Ruth's Plan for the Trip to the United States

Ruth had purchased tickets on Pan American leaving Rangoon on August 3, to be joined in Calcutta with a school friend, Peggy Heinemann, for the journey via Vienna, Paris, Madrid, to Chicago. It was therefore imperative to catch the July 28th plane from Kalemyo to Rangoon to allow time for getting government permits. There were only two flights per week, and if she missed the one on the 28th, she would miss Peggy in Calcutta.

To Kalemyo Through the Mud

I guessed wrong on the monsoon rain for the trip to the Kalemyo airport. Roads had not been too bad, so I took a chance and decided we could make the trip down in two days. But it rained heavily on Saturday and Sunday preceding our departure and was raining on the Monday morning we left. Ruth, Ram Hlun, and I went; Betty still was not strong enough. It was a good thing she did not go, for the trip was a nightmare.

We managed to reach Bamboo Camp on the first day, but only after cutting our way through three landslides with shovels and mattocks. Some forty miles short of our goal, we were told that the road ahead, between Bamboo Camp and Teingen, was absolutely impassable. We slept the night at the Bamboo Camp dak bungalow, thankful for a dry and warm refuge from the rain and storm outside. On Tuesday we abandoned the jeep, hired five coolies at exorbitant rates (for they did not want to face the storm), and set off through the mud determined to reach the airport for her flight on Wednesday.

Through the Storm

It was, I think, the only time that I have seen it rain <u>upwards.</u> The falling rain on the steep mountainside was swept upwards by the wind, getting us all soaking wet and shivering with cold (July in the tropics!). The mud was deep and sticky. In no time at all Ruth lost both Burmese slippers in the mud (she had no shoes), and from then on she walked barefoot ten miles through mud and stones. We passed around or over at least 30 major landslides, some of them dangerous, with the road still sliding away downhill. We hoped that we would not have to walk the 40 miles; we could not have done it in time. Thankfully, at Teingen, the junction where the road from Tiddim joined our road, a truck coming from Tiddim picked us up. We paid off our coolies and continued by truck, ending up at the Cowells in Tahan, wet, dirty, bedraggled, but victorious over the elements. We had won the battle and arrived on time for the plane.

Ruth Departs

I watched as the plane bore Ruth off. I was acutely aware that now we would have two children in the United States, and only Martha remained at school in India. We could expect her to return to Burma in October for the long winter holiday. Ram Hlun and I then returned to Haka. It was necessary to walk some ten miles of this through mud and landslides until we reached my jeep. With roads better then, we drove the car home. It was early August.

Chapter 51

THE UNFINISHED BIBLE

Time Given to Bible Translation

It is indeed true that I gave much time to the construction of the stone church building during my third term, often one hour a day and sometimes whole days when needed. But the work on the Bible was never ending. There was a period of two years when Van Bik and I had a rotating schedule, but then it seemed wise to relieve Van Bik of his duties as principal of the Zomi Theological School and have him come to Haka as a full-time translator.

It is true that the New Testament is more important than the Old Testament for Christian believers. Yet pastors and other leaders ought to know the fullness of the Christian scriptures. Without that, they do not know the full story of Abraham, Isaac, Jacob and the patriarchs, David and Solomon and the kings of Israel and the prophets, nor the Psalms and other writings. We determined to try to give the full scriptures to the Haka (Lai) people. We estimated that perhaps about 100,000 people could read this language.

Qualifications for a Bible Translator

The four main qualifications for a translator, I think, are first, to be a native speaker of the language, then to have a good knowledge of English, to have a good theological education, and be a devout Christian and one filled with the love of Christ.

In David Van Bik the Chins were extraordinarily blessed. Born in 1926 in Tlangpi village he was a native speaker. He studied three years in India at the Cherrapunji Presbyterian theological college, three years at the Burma Institute of Theology in Insein (our highest Baptist seminary), and two years at the Berkeley Baptist Seminary (now Baptist Seminary of the West). He knew English, Burmese, and Lushai (a neighboring people in India), and some Hebrew and Greek. He was a dedicated Christian and eager to work for the Lord.

Van Bik, whose name could be translated as "highest heaven," and I renewed our translation partnership in 1961, and we worked together until I left in 1966. What we produced was accepted wholeheartedly by the people and is used to this day.

The Translation Process

For this whole busy period of literary work I sat beside David Van Bik, the chief translator. We worked in the upstairs office of my house, looking northward over the compound. During the cold winter months we had a little sheet-iron stove to keep us warm, and we spread our books out over the large pine table. Here David and I looked at a verse or passage; if he had any questions, we discussed them. Then he dictated the Chin translation and I wrote it down in longhand. Verse after verse, chapter after chapter, book after book, we made our way slowly and prayerfully through the Old Testament.

It was in a sense "quiet work," not very spectacular, and not exciting except to those actually doing the work. I suppose that Chins going to work in the fields, or carrying loads on a rainy day, thought of us with envy in our warm, dry, comfortable room—if they thought about us at all. We were deliberately keeping ourselves isolated as much as possible from the hustle and bustle of other work in order to concentrate on the translation.

We, on the other hand, sometimes envied those who could work in the sunshine and open air. Our eyes got tired, our backs sometimes ached, and our brains struggled with the effort of finding the right Chin words, phrases, or idioms to translate God's Word accurately. We usually worked from 9 until 11:30 in the morning and from 1 to 3 in the afternoon. Four and one-half hours of concentrated mental labor on this was about all David and I could do in a day. Before 9 a.m. and after 3 p.m. there was other important work to do, such as typing up what we had done in handwriting.

Then the committees had to look over, criticize, and improve what Van Bik and I had done.

Brief Explanation of the Three Committees

From time to time I have mentioned the existence of committees dealing with the mechanics of Bible translation. We called them the First, the Second, and the Third committees. This brief word may be of help here.

The First Committee really consisted of just two men, Rev. David Van Bik and me. Our task was to do the original translation into the Haka Chin language. Van Bik was definitely the chief translator and I his helper. We discussed and debated, and often I, as a native speaker of English, could clarify the meaning of the text. Our standard text was the Revised Standard Version, and we had many other versions in English, Lushai, and Burmese as supplements.

The Second Committee consisted of Van Bik and me plus three or four other persons. The job of this committee was to look over and correct the translation to see that the meaning was clear and the language understandable.

The Third Committee consisted of all the members of the Second Committee plus 8 or 10 more people, including some women and some uneducated persons who could not read. This group was to check on the flow of language, the beauty and grace of the translation, and to ensure that even illiterate persons could understand.

The process is long but is not really tedious if we remember that the correct translation of the written Word of God is so important to the health and growth of the churches that nothing must be left undone that will help to bring the Book to all people as quickly as possible.

Progress During 1965 and 1966

At the beginning of 1965, Genesis and Exodus were finished and printed; the Psalms and Isaiah were through the 2nd and 3rd Committees and the manuscript of the Psalms was on the way to London; and Leviticus, Numbers, and Deuteronomy, and part of Joshua were completed in first draft by the First Committee.

There was no Chin who could be trusted to do the typing; we had tried several and they were all too careless. We needed a full-time typist but had no money to hire one and there was no one suitable anyway. So Betty Lue became our typist, often giving two hours a day at the work until she had to leave for the U.S.A.

During 1965 and 1966 Van Bik and I worked faithfully at the task, somewhat begrudging the time we had to give to other jobs.

Sometimes the passages were easy to translate and we could do one whole page of the RSV text in a day. Sometimes it was hard to render and we might spend an hour on one verse. We ran into the usual problems that afflict translators—how to render the names of minerals and gems, animals and birds, insects, articles of clothing, etc., that have no exact equivalents. But I believe that David Van Bik solved these problems successfully and I had no fears on leaving Burma that he would be unable to complete the Old Testament and go on to revise the New Testament.

By the end of April 1966 when I left Haka, the Third Committee had finished the checking of Judges and Ruth, thus completing all the books from Genesis to Ruth plus Isaiah and the Psalms. And we had progressed well into the first draft of the book of First Samuel. More than half of the Old Testament was done!

While Van Bik was thus working full time on Scripture translation, his salary was paid one-fourth by the Haka Association, one-fourth by the Burma Baptist Convention through a mission grant, and one-half by the British and Foreign Bible Society. This good cooperation made his work possible.

By the grace of God, I was permitted to work with David to do this much of the Bible translation, and I am eternally grateful.

The Haka Bible Finished, 1978

It is worthy of special note that Van Bik did continue with his translation of the Bible after I left. It was a long task, lengthened no doubt by the many other jobs that he had to do—touring, preaching, counseling, attending meetings of the Zomi and Burma Baptist Conventions, and serving as secretary or treasurer of various organizations.

After completing the Old Testament, he then turned his attention to the revision of Dr. Strait's translation of the New Testament.

An edition of 10,000 copies of the completed Haka Chin Bible was published by the United Bible Societies in 1978. Its title was *Lai Baibal Thiang*, or Holy Bible in Lai Chin.

Van Bik sent Betty and me an autographed copy dated May 30, 1979, and we received it in September of that year, the first copy we had seen. Van Bik's labors of about twenty years on this book were crowned with success.

I am told that the Bible is very readable and has been eagerly accepted by the Christians using the Lai language.

Chapter 52

THE STONE CHURCH

The Dream

The construction of the great cut-stone church building at Haka during our third term was one those solid accomplishments that a man looks back on with gratitude to God for a part in the enterprise. It was that for me. The rumors constantly flying around that the Christian Chins would be subject to persecutions for their faith, and that probably their witness would be crushed, made me determined that in Haka, at least, there would be a strong symbol of our Christian faith, a building made of enduring rock, made to outlast dynasties and political movements. Also, we would build into the wall a rose window that would somehow glorify God and symbolize the Word of God.

The two-story wooden church building we used in the 1950s almost burned twice by forest fires; so the plan for the new church was to use stone. A few miles out of Haka, on the Sakta road, there was a small stream the Chins call "Lungtha va," meaning good stone creek. All along this creek were great quantities of a limestone or flagstone which separated naturally into layers, some thin, some thick. The stone was free, free for taking and hauling away. If I could make a saw to cut these stones into usable sizes, we could build with stone.

We Plan to Build

As soon as Betty and I returned in 1960, plans for a new church were discussed and debated by pastor and deacons. The first question was "what size?" The present church was always overcrowded, and experiments with two identical services never worked; the first crowd refused to go home. So the new church had to be very large. Saya Huat Kham, our preacher at the time, said, "Let's make it 50 feet wide and 100 feet long." We had already agreed that we did not want interior posts; we wanted it clear span. Some of the deacons murmured, "That is too big and we won't have the money for it."

"How long will it take to build this?" some asked. They asked me and I said, "It will be a long and slow job, and it may take some years. Maybe six years."

If the Jews Could Do It, So Can We!

The Chins are used to building a house in a few weeks, and the idea of six or more years floored some. But Huat Kham rallied their spirits. He said, "In the Bible I read that Jesus said that the Jews worked over 46 years to build their temple and it was not finished yet, and if the Jews could work for so many years, we can do it too!"

The Church Votes to Build

When finally the project was brought to the whole church group in late June, 1961, the vote was unanimous to build a church of stone. The people also voted to take upon themselves the task of paying for it by giving an extra month's wages to the church building project in addition to giving their regular tithe. And this was not for just one year; they were willing to do this until the church was finished and paid for. It was a marvelous display of courage and dedication to the Lord. The church asked me to be the architect. In high school I had taken a course in Mechanical Drawing, and I was the only one in the congregation capable of making the design and blueprints. I agreed to do this. The only requirement was to design a building about 50 x 100 feet in size able to seat 1,000 people, and be clear span, no poles in the middle.

The Stone-Cutting Saw

While still in America on furlough, I had anticipated that we would need to cut stone for a church, so I purchased and brought out a saw mandrel or arbor, pulleys, belts, and two 10" diameter circular blades, a diamond and a silicon carbide. I found later that the carbide blade was useless; only the diamond blade could cut the stone.

I knew of no place to buy a stone-cutting saw, but I already had the important hardware parts. So in July and August, with the help of a carpenter, I made our own saw. I reasoned that the stone had to ride on a little platform or trolley on two steel rails and be cut by the diamond blade which was fastened to a movable arm, an arm movable up and down to control the depth of cut. It would need a barrel of water overhead to drop cooling water on the spinning blade. And it would need an engine to power the machine.

A carpenter helped me make this contraption using ordinary pine boards. We tried an electric motor for power but it was inadequate. Furthermore, electricity in the village was only on at night, and often broken down for weeks at a time. We needed a 3 or 4 horsepower kerosene or diesel engine. We did learn, however, that even with inadequate power the diamond blade did cut our flagstone.

Purchase of Truck, Engine, and Tools

In October of 1961 I went to Mandalay for needed tools for the church construction. First of all, we needed a truck to haul hundreds of tons of stone from "Good Stone River." The Methodist mission in Mandalay sold us an old World War II truck at a low price. It was a snub-nosed Chevrolet truck made in Canada, known as a "fifteen hundred weight" (15 cwt.) but capable of carrying perhaps two tons. Old, rusty, and ugly, it served us well!

To run our saw, I bought a Japanese-made Akitu engine of about 4 horsepower. It burned kerosene and had one cylinder and a big flywheel. It chugged along for years, always faithful. I also bought shovels, pickaxes, chisels, hoes, rakes, hammers, auger bits for drilling in wood, and a hand-operated drilling machine for drilling in iron. This used up all the money we had collected so far. We could get all this stuff to Haka at this time, for in the 60s the road was usable for 4-wheel drive- trucks.

305

The Plan of the Church

Chins build houses of hand-hewn boards, thatch for roofs (unless rich enough to buy corrugated iron sheets), and small in size. They have no need for built-up trusses. They have no need for architects. But the church was to be different. So the people made me their architect and general supervisor for the whole building. When I drew up the plans in November, I felt that the Lord was guiding my thinking.

Think of the church as a big rectangle, 50 feet wide and 96 feet long on the inside, 53 feet by 99 feet on the outside dimension. Think of the long south and north walls each 99 feet long, 19 feet high, and 18 inches thick, made of cut stone and cement mortar. Each of these walls would have one door and seven windows, with the window frames 4 feet by 8 feet in size.

Think of the west end as special. It was designed to have a large arched opening to the baptistry, with a large rose window over the baptistry arch, and six little windows, three on each side of the rose window. That west wall rose to 33 feet, 10 inches high, again all of solid stone 18 inches thick, with added buttresses.

Think of the east wall as different. Part was of stone and part was wood with windows and entrance doors. Think then of a large porch or verandah on the entrance end, 50 feet by 24 feet in size, convenient for people to leave shoes and umbrellas or to comfort crying infants.

Lastly, on the east end, a bell tower, 8 feet by 10 feet at the base, sloping gently inward, and 50 feet high. It was meant to be something like the Washington Monument in the U.S.A. The bell tower also was of stone, except for a central core of rubble.

For the roof, a very simple one of two flat surfaces, I designed trusses using great timbers, 6 by 6, 6 by 8, 6 by 10 inches, heavy timbers to be notched and bolted together to make six great Howe trusses. In a Rangoon bookstore I had found a book which gave instructions on making various trusses. I chose the Howe Truss as being best for us. Many Chins did not believe we could span fifty feet without interior poles, but I made a model, one inch to the foot, showing them how the 23 pieces, held together only by pins, not by glue, would indeed not collapse.

Of course, the building of the roof was years distant. First, we needed to prepare the site.

Preparation of the Site

The Chins began the actual work on the church on a Saturday morning, January 12, 1962. Volunteers came out, a total of 130 people, to level and prepare the site. The area to be cleared and leveled measured 140 by 55 feet. Over a period of months they came, old and young, men and women, children also, to carry in rocks and hammer big rocks into small to help fill the cracks. During the rainy season, it settled. Actually, the site preparation took one year and two months. Looking casually at our compound, nothing seemed changed. Looking closely, one could see that the west end was built up almost six feet by rocks and gravel, and the site was almost level. It was not quite level, though, for I designed the church floor to be three feet higher in the rear so the slight incline would give better vision.

The Foundation

Early in 1963 we dug the trench and made the forms for the massive footing for the walls. The footing had to be of concrete fully a yard wide to take the weight of the stone walls. This took over a month. The concrete used up the cement, sand, and gravel we had on hand. Sand was carried by oxen up from a stream a mile away, about one hundred pounds per ox per day. The gravel was made by women and children pounding rocks into small bits by hammers or pieces of iron. What a blessing these women were, working long hours, sometimes full days, making our gravel. Some also helped by pounding and sifting cement which had caked in the sacks, and mixing concrete with hand tools.

Embedded in the foundation at 12-foot intervals were 18 steel tripod towers reaching up 20 feet into the air. They served a dual purpose: they strengthened the walls by helping to form buttresses, and they provided steel anchors to be bolted to the roof trusses. Men drilled 378 holes in the heavy steel for riveting the towers together.

Quarrying and Cutting Stones for the Walls

While the foundation was being made, many people went out to quarry stones at the little river. One time the whole Young People's group from the church went out for a week of hard work. We had our truck now and were hauling in stones.

However, the 1963 rains came and it was also a time of Betty's illness and our absence from Haka. Work on the church began in earnest again in October. We hired U No Huat as the foreman and U Tei Ing as assistant, paid laborers. These two men remained on the job until after I left Burma and became very skillful in cutting and laying the stones.

Of course we built a little shack, set up the home-made machine to cut the stones, and No Huat and Tei Ing soon learned how to operate the engine, keep it oiled properly, and make sure the water poured on the blade as they cut.

It was amazing how rapidly the diamond saw cut, only a minute or two for a shallow cut and quite fast even on deeper cuts. Stones one inch thick could be cut rapidly. Thick stones, three inches or more thick, were cut in two passes, turning the stone over for the second cut. A blow from a hammer broke the stone apart. Incidentally, I tried to chisel stones to size, but the stones shattered. The circular diamond saw was the only way to cut them. My first blade, ten inches in diameter, cost $40 and lasted surprisingly long. Later we got four 12" blades at $147 each, but two of them were a gift from the manufacturer. With these blades our men cut thousands and thousands of stones over a period of four years. The tiny industrial diamonds embedded in the rim of the blade, a rim about $5/16^{th}$ inch wide, were almost invisible, but they cut even the hardest stone.

Building the Walls

U No Huat and U Tei Ing, the two paid workers, were novices at building a stone wall. So was I. I studied a book on how to make concrete, etc., and we started on the walls. It was challenging, but fun. With our saw we could cut stones to fit, with cement mortar to hold all together. The stones were of varied thickness. We made piles of stones one inch thick, one and $1/4^{th}$ inch thick, one and ½ inch thick, etc., going up every quarter inch to about six inches. By careful planning, we could make the wall level as we went up, foot after foot. At every foot level we laid in whatever steel we could find, barbed wire, chicken wire, and occasionally, best of all, rebars. Rebars are iron bars with bumps which hold firmly in concrete. Ever in mind was the possibility of earthquakes and the need for steel in the walls.

Progress on Walls

No Huat, Tei Ing, and I began to lay stones in mid-October of 1963 and by the end of the year the walls were up two feet. In 1964 when I was taken to Falam for questioning by the police, the walls were up only 5 feet in places, and I was worried that the project might collapse if I were sent to America. By mid-November 1964 the long north and south walls were at the 5 foot level and the west wall at the 16 foot level. Progress depended on having cement, and this was coming very irregularly. The government had decreed that cement everywhere would be sold at the Rangoon price. It was a wonderful boon for us in the hills—it probably saved $4,000 by having cheap cement. But we then had to depend on the government, and the supply was always very low. So there were weeks when the laying of stone slowed or stopped. Then the workers spent all their time cutting stones.

Window Frames

At the five foot level the workmen erected 14 window frames 4x8 feet in size made of pyinkado lumber, a hard wood quite immune to termites. Much later the windows of teak wood made in Kalemyo were installed.

The Walls, On and Up

We wanted something better than flat lintels over the windows. So months earlier we cast half-circle concrete "rose windows" with panes of glass radiating out from the center like petals of a flower. These we cast in concrete. At the 13½ foot level we installed the rose windows over the fourteen window frames, then surrounded them with shaped blocks of concrete.

With the arched windows firmly in place, we continued laying the stones to the full 19 feet level. This final height was reached in July 1965. Meanwhile work continued on the high west wall and work began on the bell tower on the east end of the church.

Cutting Wood

While all this was going on in town, sawyers were hired to cut the timbers and boards in a pine forest about seven miles south of Haka on the truckable road. Twelve men went out to do this job, beginning at the end of the 1964 rainy season. It was a tremendous task, for every timber and board had to be cut by pit saws, each operated by two men, one man atop the log, one man under the log in a pit. They cut with long saws, perhaps 5 or 6 feet long with handles on both ends. There were no sawmills in the Chin Hills, and to buy and bring up lumber from the Burma plains would be prohibitively expensive.

So the men cut away, month after month. We brought lumber in to Haka on our truck when possible, but often we used ox carts, and some of the very long timbers had to be carried in by men. We stored and protected the lumber from the elements on the mission compound.

The West Wall and the Rose Window

The west wall went up to 33 feet 10 inches, and was the site of the baptistry and pulpit. We left a very large opening for a baptistry to be built outside the main wall. Just above that, and centered was the rose window cast of concrete, 6 feet in diameter and surrounded by 39 identical cast concrete blocks. The central circle was surrounded by 12 petals. This was designed as a "Bible Window."

The Bible Window, as the Chins call it, as the very focus of worship in the church, was indeed a marvelous achievement of the workers. No Huat, Tei Ing, and I constructed it on the floor of the old church. We cut and rounded out over a hundred pieces of wood three inches thick. We nailed them to the floor to make the form. After waxing and oiling the wood, we poured cement between the wooden forms, inserting chicken wire at the 1½ inch mark to give added strength against breakage. We kept the concrete window wet for a month to cure. At last we had a circular window of concrete six feet in diameter, with a central circle and twelve radiating petals. A gang of men raised the window to its resting place high on the west wall, a dangerous job of balancing that heavy mass of concrete on the 18 inch thick wall, and we gave sighs of relief and we thanked God for safety from accident or dropping and breaking the window. Of course, at this time the glass had not been installed yet.

Christmas in the Unroofed Church, 1965

Christmas came a few days after the rose window was safely up. The pastor and deacons asked me to preach the first sermon in the new church on Christmas Day, which I did. I was impressed by the beauty and strength of the 19 foot high walls and the west wall almost done. The next thing to do, and very soon, was to put on the roof. The rumblings of my deportation from Burma disturbed me, and of course I missed my wife and family, but I promised to stay on until the end of April if possible.

Betty was in America and did not see the church at this point.

The Rose Window, also called the Bible Window, was cast in concrete by Chin workmen. No Huat is installing lead pegs to hold the plate glass panes. The Circular pane symbolizes Christ.

311

The first of five main trusses for the church was raised in early February, 1966. Trusses were raised by manpower alone.

Roofing the Church

I knew that we had to make 6 main Howe trusses, each 55 feet long, 15 feet high, and built with heavy timbers to cross the 53 feet expanse, with one foot over on each side for eaves. The design called for timbers 6x6, 6x8, and 6x10 inches of various lengths, 23 separate pieces for each truss, notched and bolted together and each joint reinforced by heavy straps of quarter-inch iron bars. They would go up 13 feet apart the length of the walls. A smaller truss would go up at the west end, this one with two posts which would form cloakrooms or offices on that end of the church.

Carpenters planed all these timbers, notched them properly, and bolted each joint with the reinforcing iron. The trusses lay heavy on the ground outside the church. Villagers coming by shook their heads sadly and said, "They will never get those things up onto the walls!"

I myself spent many restless nights in bed thinking how we could raise those trusses safely. I finally devised what I thought would be the easiest way, with the help of a tall "mast" to guide the trusses upright.

I gave some hours carefully instructing the chief workers on what to do, especially if the truss began to fall, and when they understood, we began on the first truss, the smaller west end one, on January 11, 1966, and got it safely up.

Next came the first big one, which weighed about 4,000 pounds, I calculated. This was on February 8.

We rang the church bell and 45 men appeared on the scene to help. We raised the truss upright and carried it into the church. I fastened the top with an iron hoop to the "mast" we had erected, so it would slide up, held by the iron hoop. Then we began to lift, one end, then the other end, two feet at a time, pinning the ends to slotted wooden guides. Lifting first one end, then the other, with great difficulty we pushed the truss with bamboo poles and pulled with ropes to the top of the walls. Then we swung the truss to be at 90 degrees to the axis of the building. Here it was bolted to the iron tripods and fastened with temporary purlins so it could not tip over. What a blessing—no accident. I was prepared with a whistle if things went bad, a signal to run for your life.

In similar fashion, with crowds of volunteer workers pushing, we erected all six big trusses and connected them with purlins of 3x5 inch lumber, 160 purlins in all, each 13 feet long.

Our "Planing Factory"

To give strength and muffle the sound of rain on the tin roof, we covered the whole roof with boards 1x6 inches in size. For planing them, we built a shack to hold the Belsaw planing machine we had imported from the U.S.A. Thankfully, the government loaned us a 5 horsepower diesel engine to run the planer. We used the Akitu engine for cutting stones and the diesel for planing the hundreds and hundreds of boards for the roof and eventually for the floor of the church.

I knew that my time was limited, and although Van Bik and I still worked on translations, I spent more and more time on the church. The carpenters nailed on the roof boards and then the iron sheeting, leaving gaps where we installed English-made milky white plastic panels to give light to the interior on dark days.

The Bell Tower Rises to 26 Foot Level

I urged more and more work on the bell tower to get it to the 26 foot level so we could put in the main beam for the large verandah. We reached our goal in mid-April. In the meanwhile, the Burma government issued deportation orders on March 23, 1966, for all foreigners to leave the country. Post-war missionaries such as Betty and I were ordered to leave by April 30; pre-war missionaries were given until May 31. However, by some chance, I was given until May 31. I was thankful, for I had an extra few weeks to finish my work on the church roof.

Building the Verandah

An important part of the church was the verandah, 50 feet across and 24 feet deep. To construct the five long timbers for the roof we tried a new thing: lamination. We planed the straightest 2x4s and glued them together to form beams. The main beam, to connect the bell tower to the church, was 4 inches thick, 22 inches wide, and 23 feet long. Two beams (for rafters) were 4 inches by 15 inches by 33 feet long, and two similar beams were 35 feet long. I did not trust gluing alone, so we drilled the beams and put in long bolts every three feet.

The bell tower was designed to rise 50 feet. When in mid-April we reached the 26 foot level, we put in the main beam, then the four rafters extending out to stone pillars, and finally connecting purlins. When I left Haka on April 28th, the verandah was not roofed, but at least I lasted long enough in the Hills to see the dangerous work finished. I thanked God for the few extra weeks given me, for it enabled me to see, in outline at least, the completed church.

Finances and the Generosity of the Chins

In writing many years ago about the building of the Haka Baptist Church, I wrote, "It is quite possible that the entire church was built for not more than the expenditure of 25,000 dollars (118,750 kyats)." The mission contributed $6,315; friends and churches in America gave $4,160, and the remainder was all given by the Chins themselves. The venture was a thrilling and unifying experience for all. Little children carried and sold sticks and twigs to give coins to the church. Almost all the members gave $1/12^{th}$ of their yearly income plus the regular tithe. The largest gift was given by a son of our old Pastor Sang Ling, a captain in the Burma army, who gave one half of his severance pay, amounting to 3,000 kyats. The low cost of this cut-stone church, large enough to seat a thousand, was due to the dedicated volunteer labor of hundreds of men and women, often giving days at a time to the unskilled labor needed.

A word of thanks is due the national government for making cement available at Rangoon prices, and the local government for the loan of the diesel engine, a heavy jack, and various pulleys, and to the Public Works officials for engineering advice.

Some Years Later, the Dedication

After I left the village, the carpenters finished the east end of the church with its windows and doors, laid the wooden floor, and built the two cloak rooms on the west end. Then the church was usable. Therefore, with the bell tower unfinished, the congregation met in the new church. For lack of cement, it was about 18 months longer before the tower was finished.

With great rejoicing, the church was dedicated to the glory of God on April 13, 1969. From the ground breaking to the dedication was seven years and three months. Through diligent volunteer labor and the generosity of the members, the church was dedicated fully paid for—with no debt.

Chapter 53

MRS. JOHNSON AND MARTHA LEAVE BURMA

❧

Ruth to the U.S.A.

In this chapter I pick up the story of the last five months of 1965. When Ruth and I got through the landslides and mud on our trip to the Kalemyo airport, we arrived in time for Ruth to catch the July 28 bi-weekly flight to Rangoon. She spent a few days in the capital doing paperwork for departure and did get off on the Pan American plane to Calcutta where her friend Peggy Heinemann joined her for the long trip via Vienna, Zurich, Paris, Madrid, and on to Chicago. She went to the home of my sister Alice Jane and Joe Fryman until she began nursing school in Oak Park, Illinois. An interesting side-light is that in Paris U Za Hre Lian, a Chin and a good friend of the family, met the girls. He was the Burmese Ambassador to France at the time.

The Missionary Meeting in Rangoon

It seemed very important to attend the annual meeting of the Burma Baptist Missionary Fellowship (BBMF) in October, also the meetings of the Burma Baptist Convention (BBC); so Betty Lue and I went to Rangoon. I also needed dental work done. In Tahan, adjacent to the airport, we again stayed overnight with Leslie and Margaret Cowell and learned that the English Methodists were down to 10 missionaries and the American Methodists in Lower Burma were down to 10 also.

At our BBMF meeting we learned that our American Baptist missionaries were down to 26, reduced from 46 in 1963, 33 in 1964, and now 26 in 1965. No new persons were permitted to come in, and anyone leaving could not return. Thus the attrition was speeding up.

Betty Ordered to Leave for Health Reasons

When Betty and I left Haka, it was with the firm intention of returning, in spite of her poor health. But when examined by our doctors in Rangoon, it was apparent to them that she ought to go immediately to the United States to recover her health. The doctors judged that she might not survive in Haka until our term ended in April or May.

Martha was due to come back from school in India in the third week of October, so we waited for her return, at the same time making preparations for Betty's departure to the States. Betty was greatly distressed at leaving Burma without saying goodbye to her multitude of friends, without getting her clothing (she had come to Rangoon with Burmese dress only), and leaving me alone for a half year or more.

The doctors warned of delay because of her liver dysfunction and the difficulty of getting a proper diet in Burma. Anything fatty was bad for her. Rice and curry and the available vegetables were not right for her. Sadly, Betty and I made the decision that she go and I stay.

Martha's Return to Burma

We were very worried about the delay in securing entry visas for Martha and two other missionary girls, Judy Schock and Jeanine Currier, to return to Burma for the long vacation from Kodai. Bryant and Sara Jean Currier were missionaries to the Southern Chins at Thayetmyo; Harold and Estelle Schock were missionaries living in Rangoon. Our daughters were all about the same age. So Harold and I were two fathers who visited the government offices day after day to try to expedite the granting of visas for our young daughters. Day after day we were given noncommittal answers:

"Come back tomorrow."

"The officer is out of town on business today."

"There are some meetings about this and the decision will be announced later."

Never had we felt so frustrated and even irritated. We were not quite sure whether the clerks was choosing this method of extracting large bribes from us to ensure that they present the matter to their bosses, or whether the excuses were valid. So we were left wondering what would happen to our daughters when school ended on October 19.

The Girls Go to Jaleswar, India

The three Burma girls finished school on October 19 and started for Calcutta by bus and train. On the way, on October 21, Martha had her 13th birthday, riding on the dusty train across India. They reached Calcutta on October 22 and were met by Dr. and Mrs. Osgood, American Baptist missionaries on the Bengal-Orissa-Bihar field. Harold and I had telegraphed frantically to them to take our girls to their home until we could get the entry visas.

Thank God for these good people! The Osgoods took the three bewildered girls into their home at Jaleswar, Orissa, after a long train journey from Calcutta. There they stayed for about 14 days.

Martha's entry visa was refused and our appeals denied. Visas for Judy and Jeanine were never granted or denied—just lost somewhere in the pile of papers in government offices. It was hopeless. One hope remained—transit visas good for 24 hours in the country. They could get these. So we planned that Betty would take the three girls to Bangkok, leave Judy and Jeanine there with missionaries, and continue on with Martha to the United States

A 23-Hour Visit

On Friday, November 5, Martha, Judy, and Jeanine flew into Mingaladon (Rangoon) Airport on 24-hour transit visas. It was a teary welcome from their three families, to be sure. We never could be sure why girls of such tender ages would be denied the privilege of being united with their parents for two months. But that was the way it was, and indeed we were thankful to greet them for even so short a time. We almost wished that they did not need to sleep! So three families celebrated their return and short stay with a superb Chinese dinner at a Prome Road restaurant.

When it became known in the Chin Hills (by my telegrams) that Betty Lue could not return home, numerous organizations and individuals sent wireless messages to her in Rangoon expressing their deep regret that they could not say farewell in person and in proper Chin fashion. Chins in Rangoon, however, came by the dozens to say goodbye and there were moving tributes to her at the Chin Sunday worship services. We felt humbled and yet pleased that we had been able to live among them for so long and to enter into their lives for good.

Mrs. Johnson and Martha Leave Burma

And so the day of departure came all too soon. At the airport on Saturday, Nov. 6, we experienced a tearful farewell from the many Chins who came out to Mingaladon to see the final departure of Betty Lue and the three girls. The officer put the official departure stamp in their passports; the UBA airplane took off into the afternoon sky; and they were gone. It was a sad, heart-wrenching day for me, to send off the daughter I had seen for only 23 hours, and to say goodbye to my wife who would be away for me for at least 8 months. It would be lonely in the big house in the remote hills, I knew.

I learned later that Betty and Martha had a chance to rest for a day in the Guest House in Bangkok and attend Sunday services at the International Church. Judy and Jeanine were cared for well in Thailand, going for some weeks to the northern city of Chiang Mai, and later were permitted to return to Burma to be with their parents for a few weeks before going back to school in India.

To the U.S.A.

Betty and Martha continued on through Hong Kong and Tokyo to Honolulu where I had arranged a three-day stopover for rest and relaxation. Alas, it didn't work out that way. My wife almost collapsed on arrival in Honolulu due to illness and fatigue, and spent the three days in Queen's Hospital.

Dr. Beddow at the hospital gave his services free and, further-more, took Martha into his own home and cared for her during those three days. These kind people were joined by a Southern Baptist pastor who came to visit Betty at the hospital. When they left Hawaii, Mrs. Beddow took them to the airport and gave them flower leis. So, many people were helping the weary travelers.

Mother and daughter made the final leg of their long flight on November 11 and were welcomed into the Long Beach, California, home of her sister Grace and husband Ralph Nees. Betty's mother was there too. Betty and Martha lived there until early June, 1966.

Bob Johnson Returns Alone to the Chin Hills

Four days after the departure of my wife and daughter, I flew to Kalemyo and again stayed with the Cowells. On November 13 Erville Sowards arrived by plane to help me with teaching at the Haka Bible Conference soon to start. He brought welcome news—a telegram from Betty saying she and Martha had arrived safely in Long Beach. Although I was sad to be alone, without her wonderful presence and help, I was glad that in the United States she could get the medicines, medical care, and food she needed to recover from her long illnesses. During our third term she had suffered from mononucleosis , amoebic dysentery, diarrheas, hepatitis (twice), asthma, and who knows what else during the dreadful time in 1963. Now she could recover. This hope strengthened me during the long, solid, hard months of work ahead.

My Last Christmas in Haka

When the number of Christians was fewer, it was the custom to kill a cow or other animal and have a festive meal together on the mission compound at Christmas. Finally the logistics of feeding 800 or 900 people got so difficult that for a few years we tried having feasts for smaller groups in three or four of the town quarters. In 1965, the deacons declared that no matter how difficult it would be, all would eat together on this, their Siangbawipa's last Christmas in Haka. So it was done. On Christmas Day there was a great feast attended by over 1,500 people, eating in relays and celebrating the occasion of the Savior's birth.

This was preceded by a Christmas Eve service held in the unfinished stone church. It was a choir-and-Scripture program with Van Bik in charge and Thawng Hup Pa the narrator. Thankfully the village electricity stayed on so the loudspeaker worked well and all heard the words and music clearly on the cold, star-lit night.

On Christmas Day I was the preacher, and I delivered the first sermon preached in the unroofed, unfinished church. My topic was: "Wise Men from the East."

The first worship service in the unfinished Haka church
was held on Christmas, 1965

Chapter 54

THE LAST MONTHS

Life Alone in Haka

From the time that I returned to Haka on November 16, 1965, after saying farewell to my wife and daughter in Rangoon as they left Burma for the United States, I lived and worked alone in the Chin Hills until I left Haka in late April 1966 never to return.

Well, I was not really alone, of course. I had the company of Chin friends with whom I had worked closely in church affairs. I really did not get lonesome and downhearted, even though I missed my wife and family, for the work was so pressing that I threw myself into it to the exclusion of almost everything else.

Those five and a half months were spent mainly in Haka town. My only village touring was a weekend visit to a nearby village for the annual meeting of a circle of churches. My jeep proved useful for a number of quick trips here and there. I went to Falam for the November meetings of a number of important committees. In early January I made two trips to Tahan and Kalemyo on the plains for buying building supplies for the church, and in February to Leilum, a few miles from Tiddim, for the annual meeting of the Tiddim Association. But other than these necessary trips for mission business I stayed close to home, working hard and long on my last big projects—the Bible translation, the completion of the Haka songbook, and the construction of the stone church building.

Although I had no time for vacations or outings or play, and work kept me busy from breakfast time until late at night, it was a good time for me in many ways. My health was excellent, I slept soundly, my cooks kept feeding me well, and my mind was at rest because Betty was regaining her health and the children were doing well in school.

On Running a Household

My most heart-wrenching experience upon coming home to the empty house in November was to realize that my wife was 10,000 miles away. I went to the closet and there were her dresses hanging just as she left them. She had expected to return home from Rangoon and had taken very few things with her. So there they were. I had to put them into a drawer or box, out of sight, lest the pain to my spirit be too great.

Then I moved the furniture around, just to make things slightly different. Little by little, I began to pack boxes and trunks, putting in things that Betty had requested I bring back. The rebel attacks of 1965 had failed, and there was no longer a need for the heavy lumber piled up against the outside wall of the bedroom; I sent all that down to the church for pews.

When Betty was managing the home, we always gave our cook and houseboy the afternoon hours free until tea time. But with her gone, I needed someone to be on duty while I was busy on Bible translation or down at the church, so I put Ram Hlun and Chia Ling on staggered hours, so that at least one of the men was on hand all the time from 6:30 a.m. until 6:30 p.m. They took care of the visitors as much as possible, calling me only for emergencies or unusual needs.

Betty had always made the menus for our meals and kept track of the stores of food we had on hand. Now I gave a more or less free hand to Ram Hlun, depending on him to vary the meals. He did very well in response to Betty's letter to him "to see that my husband doesn't go hungry." In fact, I ate unusually well. This was because Betty and I had brought up stores enough for the two of us to eat, and therefore the sardines, tuna fish, pork and beans, sweetened condensed milk, corned beef, and other items were in abundance.

So I was just a bit lavish. I calculated things on hand and made out a ration of so much of each food per week or month until May. Actually, when I left, quite a bit was left over which I gave away to my workers and friends.

Laundry was traditionally my wife's work. I left this now entirely to Chia Ling. I used mostly rough work clothes and these were done up and then ironed by Ngun Thlia, a young girl. I used one white shirt per week, always on Sunday for church. This was washed and ironed on Monday and used over and over. I had only two other good shirts—most of my clothing was tattered by this time—so I put them into a suitcase to wear on the way home.

I felt especially virtuous about making the bed every morning. Betty and I have always hated messy and rumpled bedding; so every morning, immediately, I straightened the blankets and put on a bedspread. Later, during this period alone, I was reading Roland Bainton's book *Here I Stand*, a history of Martin Luther, and learned that Luther, before his marriage to Katharina von Bora, was rather slovenly, never making his bed, just throwing the blankets into a heap until he needed them again at night. Katharina cured him of that, by the way.

"Well," I said to myself, "here is one way at least that I beat old Martin Luther. If I can't write theology or music like Luther, at least I can beat him in bed making."

Cancellation of Missionary Stay Permits

I have mentioned the cancellation of stay permits by the Revolutionary Government on March 23. The news of this reached me on March 31, and a telegram from our mission secretary informed me that I had to leave Burma by May 31. At that time I was planning to return to the USA by ship, on the *Herefordshire* leaving Rangoon in mid-May. I calculated that I should leave Haka on April 28 in order to get down country, go through the long process of departure, and catch this ship.

This news did not upset me too much. I was expecting to leave anyway and already was more than half packed up. I could not have worked any harder during the previous four or five months than I did, and so, although the news was distressing, my heart was at peace.

I had done the best I could; God was in charge; the foundation for the Christian churches had been laid well; we had wonderful pastors working; many promising leaders were coming along in their education; our American Baptist Mission had followed fruitful policies.

The ZBC-EC Meeting at Haka

The Zomi Baptist Convention, at that time uniting 8 Associations and 548 churches into one central body, was functioning well. The Executive Committee of the ZBC, comprising 23 members, met at Haka in early April to conduct business. The Convention itself was scheduled to meet only every third year, but the EC met several times per year. As the resident missionary, I was always on this committee. As we met at Haka in April, with 100% attendance, there was a fine spirit of unity. As I recall, among the 23 members present were men of 9 different languages or dialects. Representing at least 9 tribes of Chins, a few generations earlier they would have been enemies or at least suspicious strangers. Now, in Christ, they were one in heart and mind. "What tremendous power the gospel of Christ has!" I thought.

One important decision was to make Stephen Hre Kio, a son of Pastor Sang Fen, one of the pioneer preachers, the principal of the Zomi Theological School at Falam. He was well educated in Burma, India, and later the United States to the Ph.D. level, and later on he translated the Scriptures into Laizo Chin, and eventually became the representative of the United Bible Societies, based in Guam. There he coordinated Bible translation for the western Pacific islands. It is mind boggling to think that when the first missionaries came to the Chin Hills in 1899, the literacy rate was zero, and now both men and women are college graduates and higher.

When mentioning Stephen who did the Falam Laizo language, I should also mention one of our Executive Committee members, Kam Khaw Thang, who always represented the Tiddim Association. Kam Khaw Thang became the translator of the Bible into Kamhau, the Tiddim language. It also was a magnificent achievement. These three men, David Van Bik, Stephen Hre Kio, and Kam Khaw Thang deserve great credit for their labors for the Kingdom of God.

This was the last time I was privileged to meet with these leaders of the churches. I felt an inexpressible sadness as many of them, those who were not likely to see me again, said goodbye to me on Sunday, our last day together. They all asked Mrs. Johnson and me to return to the Chin Hills if it ever proved possible in the future. "We hoped you could be with us until you retired or until your death," some of them said.

At this time the Haka church people presented two lovely gifts to me. One was for Betty, a beautiful hand-woven red silk longyi (long skirt) from the Haka women in memory of her years of service to them. To me was given a wonderful red silk blanket ("puan sen") woven by Iang Bor Nu. These are articles of museum quality, perhaps the most gorgeous weaving done in Burma. A woman spends 6 to 9 months creating one of them.

My Last Easter in Haka

Easter Sunday, April 10, proved to be a very busy day. I helped start some bonfires down by the church at 4:30 a.m. The Sunrise Service started at 5:15, with about 200 people present, seated on the ground around the warming fires. Later, the regular morning service was crowded, with David Van Bik preaching. Our cook Ram Hlun's daughter, Hlawn Tial, played the organ for her first time. The service ended with a wedding, a common practice among the Chin Christians. Next was a funeral for an old lady, one of the earliest converts.

After dinner and later in the afternoon, I served tea to my cook Ram Hlun and his wife and my houseboy Chia Ling and his wife, and presented them with farewell gifts. To Ram Hlun I gave our kitchen cook stove and extra six months salary. After my departure he established the "O.K. Bakery" and sold cake, bread, and cookies. To Chia Ling I gave our sewing machine and six months extra salary. I also remembered the gardener and the dispensary worker.

Without these dependable and honest workers we would not have been able to carry on an effective mission under the primitive conditions of life in the Chin Hills, and we have always been grateful for them. In later years we have helped these families financially in the education of their numerous children. Even yet, decades later, we keep in communication with them.

Decoration of the Church

During the final week of my work in Haka, I helped No Huat finish the Bible Window, which I sometimes call the Rose Window. We had one circular glass and twelve petal-shaped glass panes to install in the concrete window. We drilled holes in the concrete and then secured the plate glass in place with lead pegs so they would never rust. These panes were not plain glass; they were colorful. In America, Betty had found a company selling sacred decals guaranteed to never fade or peel off. She mailed them to me and in mid-April No Huat glued on the decals. The round central one was the religious symbol, the Lamb, representing Christ the Lamb of God. The twelve decals for the petals were colorful. When finished, the Bible Window symbolized the Old Testament (the 39 blocks for the 39 Old Testament books), and the New Testament (Christ at the center, the 12 apostles surrounding). We also put decals on the six small windows, each one 12 inches by 24 inches, flanking the Bible Window. Each had a religious symbol decal.

The Cross and the Velvet Curtain

I hunted in vain in Rangoon for suitable material to make a curtain to conceal the baptistry. Only green or pink burlap (gunny bag material) was available. I asked Betty to hunt in California, and eventually she bought 27 yards of beautiful cranberry red velveteen. She sewed this into two curtains and mailed them to me. They arrived just three days before my departure, but in time to show to the church.

These two curtains were made to hang on the wall and hide the baptistry, to be pulled back when there are baptisms. To hang them on the wall, I had a fine piece of teak lumber bolted to the wall.

We also needed a Cross. I had one piece of teak lumber left. It had a defect, a knot. One night when I was thinking what to do for a cross, I thought about that piece of teak. When morning came, I rushed down to the church to measure the board. The knot was 68 inches from the end. It dawned on me that we were building the church exactly 67 years after the Carsons brought the Christian gospel to Haka. Here is the answer, I thought. The upright arm would be exactly 67 inches high, and the crosspiece in proportion. That teak board was exactly right. So we made the cross to size.

The Finished Church at Haka

During construction of the walls and tower, plastic tubing was inserted as conduits for electric wire. There are now electric lights and power outlets for a public address system.

Betty Lue and I have never seen the finished church with our own eyes. However, some nice color photos have shown us the completed interior. Thanks to skylights, the interior is light. The ceiling boards are nicely painted. The trusses, slightly bowed upward in a graceful curve, give a sense of lightness. In the west wall, the Bible Window, the six flanking little windows, the cross, the red curtains some 10 feet by 13 feet in size—all make a scene of beauty and reverence.

Although I spent much time on the church construction, many chances came for relaxation and fellowship with the local people and some pastors and leaders from the area. One such was the meeting of pastors just at the end of April.

The 1965 Pastors' Institute

The Pastors' Institute, which was becoming an annual affair, was held in Haka from April 18 to 29. Thirty-five pastors and preachers came for inspiration and instruction in the faith. My last days with these Haka area leaders were happy and pleasant. There was no need to work ceaselessly, for we could not finish the church anyway, and the dedication had been postponed until later, when the church would finally be completed. April 24 was set as a farewell Sunday for me. So I could relax and visit with these pastors, and occasionally take time to supervise the construction during these ten days.

Friday's "Special Programme"

Two days before my last Sunday in Haka, the pastors and preachers invited me to an afternoon "special programme" down at the church. I discovered that the program was entitled (in English) "A program of joy because Northern Seminary will give a D.D. degree to Rev. R. G. Johnson."

I do not know how the people found out about this, for I had not told anyone. The Northern Baptist Theological Seminary, which Betty and I had attended during our first furlough, had honored me with this honorary Doctor of Divinity degree; I knew this by letters. Although I could not make it back in time for their convocation, the seminary agreed to allow our son Richard to accept the degree in my absence. It seemed almost unreal to me. I was almost unknown, immersed in evangelism and church building in a remote and almost unknown part of the world—why me? My Chin friends made laudatory speeches and I felt embarrassed at the praise. Yet I thanked God for giving me a part in the uplift of these wonderful people. We then had tea and cakes, one of the numerous tea parties and dinners to which I was invited during the last week or so.

Farewell Sunday

Sunday, April 24, was my last Lord's Day in Haka. The day was memorable for the many special songs composed and sung in honor of my wife, of me, of the new church, and of the Lord who made all this possible. Again I was struck by the creativity of the Chin Christians. In America, who composes poetry and songs for such farewells? Not many, I think.

The attendance that day was 2,000, which meant that perhaps half of the worshipers had to sit outside on the ground and listen through loud speakers. Our pastor, Rev. Mang Kio, baptized 42 people in the new baptistry, the first time it was thus used. In the afternoon service the preacher was Saya Aung Dwe, the old Karen teacher who had served Christ faithfully for many years in the Chin Hills. In the evening the preacher was Saya Aung Tun, chaplain of the First Chin Rifles, visiting in Haka. So, all in all, Farewell Sunday was a day to remember.

Thursday, April 28, 1966: Farewell to Haka

The Haka Baptist Association would take over the mission compound and buildings; and the Association secretary, Nun Tum, planned to move into my house the day I left. The furniture had been given to the HBA also. I gave my horse to the HBA and when he was later sold, the money went to the association. The Carson Bungalow was gone, demolished in mid-April and the wood taken to build a schoolhouse on the west edge of the compound. I had given away many of my personal possessions and had sold some things, intending to replace them in America.

Concerning my shotgun and hunting rifle, the government would not let me give them away, sell them, or take them back to America. "What shall I do with them?" I asked. The answer: "Leave them here with the government until you come back." And that is what I did. That was forty years ago!

On Wednesday night I slept at Van Bik's house, knowing that if I stayed in my home I could never get ready on time. Next morning I went down to my house at 7:45, picked up a few things and looked around for the last time. At 8 o'clock the church bell rang and people began to come up to the compound. Meanwhile I went down to the stone church to make "last day" photos. How thankful to God I was that we had the roof on the main part of the church and the heavy timbering done for the verandah. There should be no problem in putting in the doors, the floor, and eventually finishing the bell tower to its full height of 50 feet—if they could get the cement.

At 8:45 we had a 15-minute service of song and prayer under the trees in the yard of my house. At 9 a.m., precisely on schedule, we set out to walk up the hill, past Van Bik's house, to the main road, a long procession of hundreds.

As we continued out to Tlang Hrawn, the mountain "level place" west of the town, we were like a river gathering in tributaries until finally several thousand people were in the crowd. The choir sang a bit as we went.

There was a final farewell service on a little knoll. Some farewell songs were sung, and I gave a final short message which ended abruptly when I choked up. Then our pastor, Mang Kio, gave a prayer but he too choked with emotion and it was hard for him to finish. Then the final handshakes. Women wept openly, mostly because of sadness that my wife was not there to be sent off properly with prayer and song. It was heart-wrenching to me to say goodbye forever to so many friends, not knowing what lay before them and other Christians in Burma.

"We Will Be True 'Til Death"

What pleased me most as I left the Chin Hills was the determination of the Christians to stand true to the gospel of Christ, no matter what happened in their country, no matter what lay before them. This was expressed to me many times by pastors and leaders and again by Rev. Mang Kio as he said goodbye.

There was a real intensity to these assurances of faithfulness to their Christian faith which may not be understood by persons reading these words many years later. One must understand that the Revolutionary Government used the symbol of the hammer and sickle, the emblem of Communism. Although the Burmese leaders talked about "the Burmese way to Socialism," many of the Chins believed that this was actually the Burmese way to communism, and that the militant atheism of Russian Communism or the anti-religious bent of Chinese Communism would come to the Chin Hills. Thus there was a real and terrifying fear of Communism and a fear of persecution of the Christian church. I heard it said many times that Burma was "going the same way as China went, but faster." Those were the years of the Red Guard activity in China when churches were closed, Bibles and hymnals burned, pastors sent away for "re-education," and Christian meetings prohibited. Could this happen in Burma? Many Chins thought so.

Thanks be to God, this did not come to pass. Burma did not follow the lead of China, and to my knowledge there has not been persecution of Christians on account of religion. Churches, Christian meetings, Sunday Schools, seminaries and Bible Schools, and evangelism have been permitted. For this I am grateful. But at the time I left, as I explained above, this freedom was not expected, hence the apprehension of what was to come.

"What fires of adversity or suffering lie before these people?" I thought. "Why can't I stay here to share with them whatever may come?" These bleak thoughts almost overcame me as I walked to the jeep.

David Van Bik had driven the jeep out so I could walk with the crowd. I got in and we drove away, Ram Hlun and Chia Ling accompanying us. At the point about 8 miles from Haka where the road leaves the edge of the valley, I looked back for the last time.

No longer could I see my former home, but I could see the mass of green pine trees on the mission compound, and I saw the sunlight glinting from the roof of the new church.

I savored the view for a few minutes, silent. I thought again of the cloth hanging on the wall behind the pulpit where Saya Sang Ling used to preach in that old ramshackle building we used as the church during our first term:

"Be faithful unto death
And I will give you a crown of life."
Revelation 2:10

I turned away and we drove on to Falam. In Falam on Friday I had to wait until mid-afternoon to get my "No Objection to Departure" certificate for which I had applied two months earlier. This indicates that there is no court case pending against the traveler and that he is not wanted by the police.

Goodbye to Falam and the Chin Hills

Having said farewell to the Falam Christians the evening before, we moved on across the Manipur to Lumbang to spend the night and have another gathering of Christian friends.

On Saturday, David, Ram Hlun, Chia Ling, and I continued, being stopped several times en route by various groups of villagers wishing to say goodbye, and for a nice tea prepared by Rev. Mang Kho Pau and church leaders from Khuasak village who came all the way to Teingen (the "goat farm") to meet me. It was heartwarming to have these expressions of good will and love.

Last Days in the Kalemyo Area

Down on the plains we put up for the weekend at the home of Rev. Sein Twe, pastor of the Kalemyo church. It was 110 degrees F. in Sein Twe's house, and we all were dehydrated and exhausted.

Sunday was May 1, 1966, my birthday. I was 51 years old. I thought ruefully that except for the political situation Betty and I might have looked forward to at least another fourteen years with the Chins, and so much could be done. However, it was too hot to worry much about that.

I spoke in the morning at Tahan to a combined worship service of the Tahan, Taungpila, and Kalemyo churches. We then dedicated the new headquarters of the Kale Valley Baptist Association, a very nice brick nogging structure (bricks between wood posts). I cut the ribbon and we had some suitable speeches. They served tea. When I returned to Sein Twe's house, the temperature was 113 degrees.

Also, on that first day of May I turned over my jeep to the Zomi Baptist Convention, together with spare parts and tools. Rev Kip Vum, pastor of the Taungpila church and president of the Zomi Convention, accepted the gift on behalf of the Convention. This was the vehicle donated to me by the First Baptist Church of Waukegan, Illinois.

Later, when the Burma Baptist Convention gave a Land Rover to the Zomi Convention, my jeep was given to the Haka Association and continues to this day, years later, to be used in Christian work.

On the Back Road to Mandalay

On Monday I hired a truck to take us and my baggage, which had been sent down to Kalemyo earlier, to Kalewa on the Chindwin River. I confess that the heat must have addled my brain, for I cannot remember just when Ram Hlun left me. I think he returned home from Kalemyo. Chia Ling went with David and me to Rangoon. We went down through torrid heat, 113 degrees on the Chindwin River on a crowded Burmese motor launch, and 116 degrees in Mandalay — wretched days of exhaustion. There were no longer missionaries in Mandalay to welcome us and give overnight lodging. It was a dusty and very hot city, and we were glad to push on to Rangoon.

To Rangoon

From Mandalay to Rangoon we went by train and had a cooling breeze. Rangoon was better, for there we had cool water to drink and ceiling fans.

But how things had changed! No longer were there missionaries at Monywa and Mandalay or any other place along our travel route. The 23 Baptist missionaries in Burma at the beginning of the year were down to 5: Herman and Ruth Tegenfeldt, Fred and Bertha Dickason, and me. We felt like a remnant, holding on to the last.

In Rangoon

Until the time I actually reached Rangoon, I thought of leaving by ship and even had reservations to England on the *Herefordshire* of the Bibby line. Then I learned that it was due in port "about the middle of May," would be 10 days or more in port, and would then take 35 days to England. I would not be home until July 13 at the earliest and would miss being home for our 25th wedding anniversary. But could I depend on getting my freight out of Burma if I did not take it personally?

After talking to Tegenfeldt and Dickason, who were the field secretary and the field treasurer of our mission, I decided to take a chance on an agency to ship my goods by sea. I would fly home to the United States. I could take out 66 pounds of luggage by air to Bangkok, Thailand, free on my ticket, and could send one foot locker (small trunk) by air freight to Bangkok with the most precious possessions, such as photos and negatives and treasured mementos of our family.

By this time, restrictions on outgoing baggage and freight were easing. I was told that all my things could go except for pillows and quilts (easy hiding place for gems, hence restricted).

By dint of hard work for over a week I was able to get cleared through the income tax, immigration, and foreign exchange offices, take care of my bank accounts, turn in ledgers and accounts from the Chin work, repack, and make 12 copies of lists for each box and trunk going by freight, and then have an inspector come to check over all outgoing baggage and freight, all in time to leave on May 17.

The Golden Shore

A famous book about Adoniram and Ann Judson, first missionaries to Burma, written by Courtney Anderson, is entitled To the Golden Shore. This refers to the land of Burma where a prominent sight is the multitude of gilded pagodas and gold-encrusted Buddhas. The Burmese people have lavished gold in the decoration of their places of worship.

We American Baptist missionaries had worked on the Golden Shore since 1813. Now, 153 years later, our time was drawing to a close. I was scheduled to fly out on a Union of Burma Airways plane to Bangkok on May 17, and the Tegenfeldts and Dickasons a week later. And with our departures the history of the American Baptist Mission (A.B.M.) in Burma would end, and with it the Chin Mission. Of course, our interests and prayers would continue, and so would our money continue as long as the government permitted foreign funds to come in. But there could no longer be a living presence, so important and necessary for true fellowship. It was sad. All of us had to go out unnoticed by the general population. No newspapers carried the news of the departure of missionaries. Quietly, forlornly, we had to leave.

At the Airport

Before leaving for the airport, Van Bik and I had a little private prayer meeting in the room at the Guest House. We had worked together for most of my twenty years in the Hills and he was like a younger brother to me. Though sad, we were glad that God had given us time and strength to get at least half of the Old Testament translated, plus many other literary works.

At the airport there was a busload of Chins, mostly students from the university, plus some Convention leaders and the remaining members of the mission family — Dickasons and Tegenfeldts. There we held a final prayer service. Rev. Kip Vum and Rev. Sein Twe had flown down especially to see me off. Kip Vum prayed, we sang "Blest Be the Tie That Binds," and Sein Twe gave the benediction. I went through the Customs easily, not having to open a single thing, and then had to wait an hour because the plane was late.

But finally, at 2:30 on Thursday afternoon, May 17, I said farewell to the "Golden Shore" and was gone. The American Baptist Chin Mission was over.

Rangoon to Bangkok to the USA

The story of my trip home can be told briefly. I flew to Bangkok and turned over my small trunk to our Thailand missionaries to ship to the USA by sea. Then I reversed direction and flew to Beirut in

Lebanon, then to Jerusalem, then from Tel Aviv to Europe where I delivered the manuscripts of Joshua, Judges, and Ruth to Dr. Moulton of the Bible Society in London.

The last lap of my long journey was on Sunday, June 12. I flew on a Pan American jet nonstop from London directly to Chicago, Illinois, arriving about 5 p.m. at O'Hare Airport.

Betty Lue was there to greet me, looking so much better and stronger, though not fully over her illnesses. Dick, now 21 years old and ready to graduate from college was there, standing a full two inches taller than I. I had not seen him for four years. Ruth Kristin and Martha were there too, both as lovely as ever. The whole family was together at last! It was an overwhelming blessing and my heart overflowed with joy.

Praise God from whom all blessings flow.

EPILOGUE

A HUNDRED YEARS A MARVELOUS TRANSFORMATION

I am writing this Epilogue in my old age, ninety years, to testify to the grace of God upon the Chin people of Burma as they have progressed in the Christian faith.

I was privileged to proclaim the gospel in Burma during my years of greatest strength, from age 31 to 51, and now look back in amazement at what the Chin pastors, teachers, and church leaders have done since then, entirely without foreign missionary aid—how they have started churches in all parts of the Chin State, how they have continued Bible Schools we started and made numerous new ones, and how they have continued Bible translations in many new languages, and how they have flocked to colleges and universities in Burma and abroad.

When Mrs. Johnson and I left Burma in 1966 with some fear and anxiety for the future of the churches, we could little guess what God would do. We prayed much and corresponded by letter with pastors, church leaders, teachers, students, and ordinary villagers wanting usually medicines or money. We have been receiving and writing letters for forty years. The letters now are fewer, but Betty Lue still writes in Chin to our cook's daughter Angeline, who is one of the first Haka Chin women to be ordained to the ministry. Betty has never been back to Burma, but people still remember her with love and affection.

For many years after we left, foreigners were quite unwelcome in the country. For a long period a seven-day tourist visa was the most given, and for a while only three-day visas were granted. Chins in the higher political and religious positions were afraid to be in correspondence with foreigners, so we found it difficult to get facts and figures on the progress of the churches. Personal visits to Burma were the best way to make contacts, and I was able to make three visits. Unfortunately, Betty was not able to go with me, to the great disappointment of the Chins.

My first time was in early 1971, a visit to Rangoon only. Streets were quite empty of cars. A general malaise seemed to have settled, but hundreds of Chins cheered me up.

A second visit was in 1976 and again I was a simple tourist and avoided being conspicuous. I went as far as Mandalay and there in a little hotel on a side street I had two days conferring with two church leaders who came down to meet me. Again I saw hundreds of Chins in those cities.

My third visit coincided with the great Chin celebration of one hundred years of Christianity among them—they called it the Chin Evangel Centenary. It was held in Haka on April 1-4, 1999. All Christians of several denominations and many independent churches joined with the churches of the Zomi Baptist Convention to celebrate together. The government granted permission for five thousand people to attend, but people came as a tidal wave, often walking several days, and the number swelled to 30,000. To the amazement of the Burmese officials and police, there was absolutely no disorder, no fights or quarrels, no drunkenness; so the soldiers guarding the town had no problems.

To attend this significant celebration, our son Richard and his wife and our younger daughter Martha and her husband accompanied me. We were prepared with blankets and bedrolls to go up into the cold Chin Hills, but we got only as far as Kalemyo and Tahan at the foot of the Hills. We could go no farther. We were denied permission to enter the Chin State.

Denied permission to enter, we saw the Hills only with longing eyes. We had hoped to see Hakha (the new spelling), which we knew as a large village and now a town, the capital of the Chin State, and renew friendships. The children longed to see their childhood home. We hoped to see the big stone church building and the many new Association buildings on our old mission compound, and also the Chin Christian College. We could scarcely imagine a degree-granting Bible college started many years after we left, now a school of 266 students and 13 professors. So we missed all of this, but took joy in knowing that thousands and thousands of people were celebrating the hundredth year of mission work.

I should mention that 700 persons were baptized at the Centenary and 65 preachers were ordained to the gospel ministry. A shipment of Bibles in the Haka language was received just in time for the Centenary, and the whole shipment, 4,680 copies, were sold out in one day. The remaining 5,320 copies were received a bit later and also were sold out—so eager were the believers to have the Word of God.

Stephen Hre Kio, who was one of the 373 baptized at the Jubilee in 1949, was one of the main speakers. He was the translator of the Bible into Laizo, and served as the representative of the United Bible Societies in the Western Pacific region, based in Guam. He brought out forcefully the results of the Spirit of God moving among the Chin masses. He said:

"God deserves all of our praises and thanks:
"Because He has delivered us from pitch darkness
to marvelous light,
"He has taken us from the place of fools to the place
of the enlightened,
"He has taken us from half-nakedness to the status
of fully clothed,
"He has led us from a life-style of animals
to the life-style of human beings,
"He has transformed us from being headhunters
to the status of soul –winners,
"He has provided us with Scriptures and thus enabled us
to be counted as a nation among nations of the world,
"He has begun to turn Chinland around from the land of
Satan
to the land of the Lord,

"He has persuaded us to turn from fighting each other
    to loving each other.
"Because of all these, let the Chins celebrate,
    "I repeat, Let all the Chins rejoice
        and celebrate what the Lord has done!
"Let us proclaim today that our Land belongs to the Lord.
    "Only in this way will our Land enjoy peace and
    happiness.
"Just as the Psalmist declared a thousand years ago,
    "Happy is the nation whose God is the LORD,
        Happy are his people he has chosen for his own."
                Psalm 33:12.

At the 1999 Centenary it was said that 75% of the Chin people were Christian. This I can update a bit. In 2005 the population of the Chin Hills is listed as 503,055 and the total of all Christians as 424,271. This means that 84% of the Chin people within the Chin State are counted as believers in the Lord Jesus Christ. There are 1,948 churches and 2,434 ordained pastors.

It all began in 1899 when a motherly-type woman named Laura and a lean hard-working man with the improbable name (to the Chins) of Arthur, a name meaning dirty chicken, arrived in Haka in the western hills of Burma and began to teach and preach Jesus Christ. The Carsons were followed by the Easts, then the Copes, the Woodins, the Straits, the Nelsons, and last by the Johnsons. Then we western foreigners were gone; the Chins took over without a flaw, without a lapse, and God has given the harvest.

Glory to His Name forever!

Betty Lue and Bob Johnson Photo 1984

APPENDIX 1

MEMORIES OF BURMA

by
Martha Anne Johnson Martens

~~~

My memories of Burma are mostly a series of pictures—little vignettes of things I remember.

We lived in a big house built by one of the early missionaries. When my parents arrived in Haka, the house was very dirty and shot up as a result of World War II. However, by the time I arrived, the house was fixed up nicely, and I remember it as the "perfect house." Whenever we returned from a trip, I would walk all around the house, looking at every room, just because I wanted to see the whole house. It made me feel secure that everything was just the same; nothing had changed during our trip.

The house had a big living room and a big dining room, which we used mostly when it was warm. We also had the "winter living room," which served as both living room and dining room during the colder weather. This room had a fireplace and a stove. Dad always got up early, before the rest of us were up, and lit the stove, so that the room was warm when we got up.

Since Haka is a cold place, we needed the heat of the fire. The bedrooms did not have heat, so we used hot water bottles to warm the beds. I would hold the hot water bottle between my feet as I fell asleep. In the morning, I would carefully slide out of bed, and I prided myself on sleeping so neatly that all I had to do was pull up the bedspread to make my bed. When I was older, I felt a little scornful of friends and roommates who messed up their beds!

My best friends were Ma Mai, Tang Tu, and Iang Khun. Although these three were my closest friends, a lot of younger kids tagged along with us wherever we went. My parents used to talk about "Martha and her gang." Our favorite thing was to play dolls. One of my aunts had sent young-lady dolls (not Barbies) and we loved to sew clothes for them, and on Sunday afternoons, we would go upstairs in our house and play with the dolls. We used books and wood blocks to build houses, and we even made furniture for them. Dad's workshop was upstairs, and he didn't seem to mind little girls pounding nails. Four nails driven into the bottom of a small board made an excellent bed or table, and empty matchboxes glued together made little dressers. Mom let us use some of her quilt blocks to sew clothes—two blocks sewed together made a *longyi* (sarong) for a doll, and one block was sufficient to make a blouse or *angki*. Mom even taught us some decorative sewing stitches, so we could make pretty designs on the doll clothes. Little did we know that we were learning skills that we could use later!

I loved my three best friends so much that I wanted them to have everything that I had. When my aunt sent the young-lady dolls for me, she also sent one for each of my friends. One year for Christmas, Mom made me a new dress with a full skirt and a little bodice that laced up with ribbon, like Heidi must have worn. Mom didn't make just one, though. She made four, one for me and one each for Ma Mai, Tang Tu, and Iang Khun. She knew I wouldn't have been happy to get a new dress if my friends didn't get one too. As I look back, I marvel that Mom and Dad didn't get impatient with me and point out that they couldn't afford four of everything!

We also enjoyed playing games. We played Chin games like *tek bu, nap,* and *lung doi.* We also loved Monopoly, and kept a game going for weeks by the simple expedient of allowing ourselves to go into debt. No one ever went bankrupt, and no one was ever out.

Although my parents were very busy with mission work, we always had a special outing when Dick and Ruth came home from boarding school in India for Christmas. This was a fishing trip to the Timit River. Of course, all of our friends came along. Dad drove us all in the jeep, and we had a great day fishing, and having a picnic.

The Chin way of fishing is not with a rod and reel, but with a basket. We would wade into the river, and we would all arrange our baskets around a large rock. The older, stronger members of the group would wiggle the rock, and when the fish swam out, we scooped them up in our baskets. The baskets were woven of palm leaves, so the water drained out, leaving the fish trapped in the basket.. We picked out the fish, and put them into smaller baskets, which we carried tied to our waists. Of course, the fish were very small, probably what we would call minnows in English. They tasted great fried crisp.

As far as I know, Haka did not have a market where they sold fresh vegetables, although there were stores that sold other things. We had a large garden beside the house, and a full time gardener, Dar Mang Pa, whom I called Pu Pu, which means grandpa. What I remember most about Pu Pu is that he carried cloves in the pocket of his coat, and he would give me one whenever I asked. The garden produced all the vegetables we needed. I remember mustard greens, radishes, and peas. I liked to eat peas raw, and often my friends and I would go out to the garden to 'steal' peas. There were also several large beds of strawberries. Once Mom let me plant my own garden, and I was delighted to present Dad with my very best radish—a huge one that I had grown especially for him. Unfortunately for Dad, it was tougher and woodier than the smaller radishes, but he ate it with good grace.

Christmas was a wonderful time. On Christmas Eve we had a pageant put on by the youth and Sunday School students. Since I was quite young at the time (I left Burma at the age of 12), I didn't have speaking parts in the play. I was usually either an angel in the heavenly chorus, or one of the children of different countries bringing a gift to the Christ child. I suspect that this last was a part of the play added by my mother, since I have never seen it in any other Christmas play. She let the Sunday School students dress up as the children of many lands—India, Japan, etc.—and bring gifts to the baby Jesus. I also seem to remember a child dressed up as a rabbit, hopping down the aisle with a carrot.

On Christmas morning, we three Johnson children would take baskets of gifts which my parents had wrapped for the families of all the people who worked for us—Van Awi Pa, Me Me Pa, Dar Mang Pa, and U U, who started as my nanny and later ran the dispensary.

After we delivered the presents we had breakfast. That was followed by a church service, a gift exchange at church, a community meal, and games in the field by the church all afternoon. I suppose we must have opened family gifts at some point, but that doesn't stick in my memory at all. We did have nice Christmas trees cut from the pine forest on the mission compound, and I looked forward to decorating the tree each year. When we came back to the States when I was 13, it took me many years to get used to the American way of celebrating Christmas, as a totally family-centered thing. I kept expecting activities at church, and it seemed really lonely just to stay home.

The Chin Hills seems to me to have been the ideal place to grow up. I have never felt that I missed anything by being there. I had wonderful friends, a lovely home, great parents, and a very secure, happy childhood. I thank God that I was given the privilege of growing up there.

APPENDIX 2

MEMORIES OF A LAND NOT FORGOTTEN
By
Ruth Kristin Johnson Knutson
(Ruti)

I made a needlepoint picture quite a few years ago which has the saying "Dawt Mi Philh Lo Nak" (loved ones are not forgotten). It hangs in my parents' home today as a testament to love for our friends in Burma.

I was born in Mandalay in 1947, more than a year after my parents, Robert and Elizabeth Johnson, started their mission work in the Chin Hills. I have an older brother, Richard (Deki), who was a year old when my parents arrived in Burma. I have a younger brother, Peter, who was born prematurely, died, and is buried in Tiddim. My sister, Martha (TaTah), is 5 years younger than I. The three of us lived our early lives in the wonderful Chin Hills and have memories that will be with us the rest of our lives.

Although I am an American and have lived in the United States 33 years now, I am still very Chin in many ways. The people who I was around and the culture that I lived in molded me to be the person I am today. I have always had a great respect for the Chin culture. The people are gentle, gracious, and optimistic. They have a strength to be admired that carries them through hardships. I believe that their strong faith in God gives them courage and optimism.

I realize that many years have passed since I left the Chin Hills, and I am sure that many of the places of my memories have changed and may not even be recognizable. However, it is fun to think back on those years which have meant so much to me.

I have several friends that I grew up with and shared many fun times. I think back to the games that I played, like *Tek Bu, Nap,* and *Lung Doi.* I plan to teach my 8 year old daughter, Alana, all of these games except for Nap, which I now agree with Mother is too dangerous. I am happy to report that I never got hurt playing Nap and I never injured anyone else either. (Nap is a game played with hitting short pointed sticks.)

My friends and I used to have great adventures. Of course, we never had radio or TV to entertain ourselves with and we were very creative in our play. We had a few dolls that were sent out to me from America, but we had just as much fun making our own dolls from clay and sewing clothes for them. We would baby-sit the younger kids and often each took turns carrying the youngest on our backs as we went about our play business. I still think that carrying young babies on backs in "baby's cloth" is the best way and I carried my own daughter this way when she was young.

I was introduced to the art of chopping wood at an early age. Meri Nu and Iang Men would teach us how to properly load our baskets so that we could carry them a long distance without dumping the load by accident if we stumbled along the way. I knew that I had mastered it when I could carry a full load of wood on my back and a small baby on my front, walking several miles from Caw Buk. Even today, when I go for a walk in the woods in America, I look at the dead branches on the ground and wish that I had my small Chin axe so that I could fill a basket with good wood. I will always be grateful to the women who taught me how to dye thread, spin silk, set up a loom and to weave. I have not woven anything in a long time, but I hope that I can remember how to do it someday when I have time to do that again. Chin weaving is some of the most beautiful in the world and I have a true appreciation for the effort that goes into making the pieces. I really hope that the young girls in the Chin Hills recognize how special this art is and that they take time to learn from their mothers. I still have my porcupine quill to pick in the designs! I frequently wear Chin clothing with pride and I am not seen without my shoulder bag.

My love of nature and my ability to identify plants was cultivated in the Chin Hills. We used to go for long hikes, gather orchids on Run Tlang (Run Mountain) or Tlang Hrawn, look for mushrooms on the mission compound, hunt for *tumatil* on the road to Dawr Thar, pick *dingkok* on the way to Hai Thlan and of course we could find dates and berries at Hai Thlan. I finally have a *mongkalong* (guava) tree from Thailand that is similar to the ones in the Chin Hills! I was so excited when it actually grew fruit, that I sent some to Richard by Federal Express. I have found green mangoes in Hawaii and I love to eat them with salt and chili peppers—so does my daughter! *Ser* is one fruit that I have never eaten since I left Burma. I have spoken with botanists in America and no one seems to know about it. My favorite tree to climb was on the hill behind our home. We could climb to the very top of this very tall tree and see all the way to Hniar Lawn. Coming down the tree was also fun as we slid down from branch to branch. I learned how to split a banana into three sections and have amazed children in America who had no idea that bananas could be split lengthwise. I am still amazed that my parents would allow me to do so many things and go so many places without worry for my safety. It is only really amazing from the American viewpoint, because I would not allow my daughter to even walk two blocks by herself in our town in America. In the Chin Hills, I never worried about any person harming me. Crime was very low and people were good.

Fishing in the Chin fashion was also one of my fond memories. A group of us would get together and usually go to the Timit River. Wearing a coffee can tied around our waist, with a hole punched in the lid, big enough to slide in a small fish, we would walk through the river holding our baskets downstream from rocks which we moved to scare the fish into the baskets. One time, I picked up a snake in the river, thinking it was an old piece of torn skirt. I split my toe open running away from the snake after I threw it down. Meri Pa's dog and several of the boys killed the snake. I remember it being very big, but maybe I was just small. I think that someone called it a python.

Christmas was the most special time in the Chin Hills. The crisp air and the blooming cherry trees always made it a beautiful time of year. Preparations for Christmas started early. I remember doing a lot of sewing of gifts to give away. Sui Kim Nu taught me how to sew well and she patiently gave me hints how to make the blouses properly. Many groups of young people would sing beautiful Christmas carols going from house to house, their way lit by pine torches. Christmas Eve was a very exciting time for everyone, especially for all the children who participated in the Christmas pageant play. I remember having so much fun with my mother figuring out costumes for all the children. Christmas Day was filled with services at the church, having the Christmas feast, and passing out Christmas gifts on the lawn in front of the church. The gifts were small, being things like a box of matches, an orange, a piece of sugar cane or a banana, but they were all from the heart. To this day, I treasure the spirit of the birth of Christ that was celebrated in Haka.

One time, my friends and I were invited to Hniar Lawn to spend the weekend at Sui Pen's house. We had a wonderful time sitting around the fire in the house, telling stories. We slept on the floor around the fire to keep warm. I must admit that even though I had a sleeping bag and was given a cow hide to sleep on, I woke up in the middle of the night so cold that my back hurt. I was embarrassed that I was so cold in spite of having more warm clothing that the others. A pig was killed in my honor and as the guest of honor, I was given the head to carry back home in banana leaves in my basket. Meri Nu's family got the pig's head when we got home.

Although there were so many people that I loved very much, I felt especially close to Meri Pa and Van Awi Pa's families. Meri Nu (Mary's mother) was my nanny and included me in her family just like one of her own children. Meri Pi (Mary's grandmother) was the very best story teller. I wish that I had written down many of the stories she told. It would be wonderful if someone would write down a collection of stories that are passed down from generation to generation. Van Awi Pa always had a great humor. He called himself "Vitamin" because he had so much energy and danced around the cookhouse. Both of these wonderful men have died, but they live on in our hearts.

I dream of someday returning to the Chin Hills. I would love to be in a jeep, going through the teak forests of Kalemyo into the foothills, climbing higher and higher past Stockade #3, on to Fort White. After a visit to Tiddim, heading back south toward Falam with hills of glorious red soil against the bright blue sky I would enjoy the pine trees singing. Sunsets and sunrises were beautiful in this place which rested in the hills above the Manipur River, which ran like a shimmering ribbon in the distance. I would savor every moment as we traveled on to Haka. Turning the bend at the point in the Haka-Falam road where Haka finally becomes visible at the foot of Rung Tlang is something which appears in my dreams.

I have heard that most of the trees are now gone and that the town has grown tremendously. I wonder if I would recognize it. I wonder if I would be sad that things have changed so. I do know that my main fulfillment would be in seeing those people who I grew up with and loved. I do not know if this dream will ever come true, but I must hope that it will. I want to return to the home of my childhood with my husband and daughter, to show them in person all those places and people who have meant so much to me. The world has become a small place and it is amazing to me that I have had conversations in America with Mang Tiak who is the sister of Tum Tlem, one of my childhood friends. Who knows, one of these years, with help from God who makes all things possible, I may be able to celebrate another Christmas in the Chin Hills! In the meantime, my friends in Lai Tlang, my thoughts and prayers are with you. *Mang Tha, cik cek* (Goodbye, pleasant dreams).

Appendix 3

BOYHOOD FUN IN HAKA
Richard G. Johnson

M y friends cheered as I thundered on a homemade cart down the longest single stretch of the switchbacked road behind our house in the Chin Hills. I was in seventh heaven for a carefree boy, already forming images of my upcoming heroic, sweeping, dusty turn around the switchback to continue my ride down the hill. The three-wheeled cart had a wooden axle in back with two hand-cut wooden wheels, two sturdy, round branches forming the frame and tapering up to flank the single wooden wheel in front, the axle for which extended out as footpegs for steering. I was sitting on a board nailed solidly (I had prudently used many nails) to the two side rails of the frame, to which I was holding on for dear life.

The turn came and went, and so did I, but no longer in alignment with the road. I'm pretty sure I was still holding the cart up under myself, but that didn't help much as I sailed, airborne, deeply into the brush off the end of the switchback curve. Being the missionary kid who had the hammer, and access to lots of my Dad's nails, I had turned my friends' native design of a flexing frame, able to turn tightly because there was only one nail at each joint, into a rigid letter "A" that would turn only a few degrees from the straight line on which I had accumulated all that speed. I wasn't hurt, at least not badly, and I had learned yet another lesson about making things—

don't assume just because you have more tools, that you have any idea what is going on or how things really work.

I learned a lot that way, and somehow survived childhood. I don't believe I handled an electric tool until shop class in high school in India, but by that time I was thoroughly at home with handsaws, coping saws, hammers, sledges, planes, chisels, hand drills, wood braces, and a wonderful tool called a drawknife. A drawknife is like a big horizontal knife or extremely wide chisel, with handles at both ends, that lets you pull back with your whole body to shave a smooth curl of wood from whatever stock you are working; it sounds scary, but provides so much power and control that I never hurt myself with one. I learned through experience that countersunk screws are wonderfully strong fasteners. I developed a fascination with planes, which are wonderfully satisfying tools for smoothing wood when adjusted just right. I learned to love the smell of pine, teak, and rhododendron wood. I learned that bamboo splinters fester in the rainy season, refusing to heal. Our cook, Ram Hlun, introduced me to the wonders of using a shard of broken glass to shave and finish a wood project; if you hold it properly, it won't break and acts like a dainty little plane.

One rainy season, I made friends with one of our Bible School students who was making a little income on the side with black-smithing jobs. I started out being the bellows pumper for his char-coal fire, and soon progressed to actually helping him with some of the smithing. We made several leaf springs for the actions of shotguns and percussion-cap muskets, and I learned how to iden-tify carbon steel (look for sparks on a grindstone), shape it on an anvil, cut it with chisels, and then temper the finished spring. That involved quenching it while red hot, and then reheating it slowly until it turned just the right color (sort of a light blue-gray) and made one of the special wood chips just start to smoke. We restocked a shotgun, which involved a lot of careful fitting with lamp-black smudged on the hardware to see where it was hitting the wood. Many years later, I was fascinated to realize that dentists use essen-tially the same technique to mark high spots in fillings to get perfect adjustment of bite.

Whatever I "needed" as a boy, I just went ahead and made. Those three-wheeled carts were great fun, particularly when we discovered that greasing the axles with ripe bananas made everything faster. I hadn't discovered axle grease yet, and probably would have gotten into trouble for using it had I found some; ordinary oil seemed to smoke up from the friction faster than the bananas. My friends and I would each wear through a set of axles and wooden wheels in a few days of hard riding, but that was just an excuse to go find some more branches of the right size in the woods and a good sturdy plank somewhere in the workshop so we could get out the coping saw, brace, and drawknife to rebuild the carts.

One wonderful thing about living in Asia is the ready availability of strings of Chinese lady-finger firecrackers. At least some of the money I made setting type for Deirel Press went into buying packets of firecrackers, which we would use one at a time in little pistols we made by nailing spent cartridge casings, through holes drilled through their primers, onto the front of crude pistol-shaped handles. The casing would hold the firecracker with the fuse dangling out the front, which we would then light with our version of punk—a piece of dried-out horse manure which would hold a glow for ten minutes or so before you had to start up another piece. Our "wars" were characterized by much crawling around through the tall grass and weeds, wild ambushes, and of course the telltale odors and wisps of smoke as we worked to keep our manure lit. Ever the obedient son who had been instructed to never point guns at people, I was the one who always had to point his pistol over the heads of his many victims.

I was appalled at the waste, of course, when I later learned that people commonly light the end of a whole string of firecrackers at once to thrill at the many explosions. For us, a string was good for a whole afternoon of fun.

I carried firecracker gunmaking to its artistic limit not long after getting a long-desired coffee-table book on firearms as a present. In it was a beautifully detailed drawing of a Beretta pistol, a design that I still admire today. Of course, I had to make one. I built a beautiful grip and receiver out of pine, drilling out space for a copper-tubing barrel before cutting away the scrolled notch of the Beretta that reveals the barrel. Because the barrel was much longer than the firecrackers we used, I dropped a large nail down the barrel and tapped it into the receiver to just the right depth to serve as a spacer for the firecracker. I took my prize weapon out on the road where the Deirel

Press building was eventually built, lit a firecracker, and wisely held it out over my head and closed my eyes. We now call this "smoke testing"—plugging in the appliance you just repaired and waiting to see if it self-destructs. The pistol simply disappeared; I was left holding only the grip. I have no idea where the nail went, and would really rather not know. I never tried that again.

Other projects over the years included dozens of slingshots, kites, and snares, a bed for one of my friends, and the crossbow memorialized earlier in this book. I became an expert slingshot maker, using only well-cured rhododendron wood for its strength, leather from shoe tongues, and either strips of tire inner tubes that we could get in the bazaar section of town or surgical tubing when we were fortunate enough to get some through someone traveling down-country to Rangoon or Mandalay. I was a good shot with my slingshot, and kept a steady flow of small critters going into Meri Nu's kitchen, where they were singed down to remove the feathers or fur, gutted, and hung in the smoke over the cooking fire to cure and dry before use in makphek (a pepper condiment). We used air-dried clay pellets in our slingshots; I can still roll six at a time between my palms without getting them stuck to each other, although I could never match the nine to twelve that one of my friends could handle. The clay came from termite mounds. If you quickly roll up the outer soft layer of clay from a mound, you can get quite a bit without getting bitten; the price for going after more, once the termites are stirred up, is a lot of pain that we endured often for the privilege of skulking around the woods and dispatching virtually anything edible.

My friends and I made diamond-shaped kites from bamboo, rice paste, and kite paper that I now know to be Asian fighting kites. We, of course, didn't yet know about putting ground glass on the strings, and would have been mortified about the idea of attacking someone's precious kite and string.

I learned how to make two kinds of snares from bamboo and string; one was a simple hoop snare that, many years later, I found illustrated in a U.S. Army jungle survival manual. I never found that snare design very effective. I really liked another kind, though, that had a hinged bamboo blade that would snap down in a groove. It seemed more humane than the hoop snare, and I brought a number of squirrels, birds, and field rats back to Meri Nu's kitchen through use of such snares. We also made deadfalls that worked well on squirrels and rats, but you could always tell from their new shape how these victims expired. The reference to rats might upset some, but brown field rats were considered clean and quite tasty; a Chin would never eat a black rat. To be perfectly frank, once they've been skinned, smoked, dried out, and then pounded into a pepper base, I couldn't tell rat from squirrel from bird.

I read about an ancient New World throwing stick in a history book, and of course had to go make one for myself and then several for my friends. Called an atlati, it is an apparatus that extends the effective radius of the arm, allowing its user to fling an arrow or spear-like dart a great distance. Ours worked just fine; we used them to launch long reeds and had wonderful contests. This must have had its heyday sometime around 1957, because I remember a remark by the pastor prior to my baptism that perhaps now I would be spending more time in church than with my spears.

My crossbow project, mentioned previously in the book, built on all my blacksmithing and carpentry skills, but still failed through bad design. While away at boarding school in South India, I discovered that one of the maintenance men at the school had some blacksmithing equipment. I designed a release mechanism for a crossbow that used a rocking lever that could be cocked against some springs and held by a simple double-levered trigger. I reasoned, incorrectly, that the spring would be strong enough to pull down the lever and release the cable of the crossbow. When I later put the mechanism into the elaborate crossbow I built in the Chin Hills, I had to slacken the bow so much to get the release to work that, as described before, the arrow I shot simply bounced off a pumpkin, to my great embarrassment, rather than boldly smashing it to the delight of all.

The rather straightforward result of growing up away from store-bought toys, modern stores, electricity, and electronic entertainment is an independent, self-sufficient person who loves the outdoors and junkyards, hates to throw things away even when they are thoroughly broken, and tinkers constantly to keep his grown-up toys working. My love of the outdoors led to an education in geology and a career in the military. I kept a vacuum cleaner going for nearly another decade by milling a replacement part out of Lucite, rebuilt a horn switch contact plate for a car out of a copper kickplate for an entry door, rescued an expensive fuel pump that wasn't supposed to be rebuildable with less than a dollar's worth of keystock, and fabricated a shaft for a boat's water pump from a stainless steel bolt. These successes are, of course, now counterbalanced with a garage-full of project cars waiting for restoration and a workshop full of fix-it projects, some of them very old.

Rainy days, fog in hills, and wind in pines take me back to the Chin Hills in a heartbeat. If I could go back, I would. With my tools. There is so much there still waiting to be built or repaired.

A Message from Foundations of Grace Publishing

W e are so thankful for you, and we hope this book has been a blessing and an encouragement!

We'd love to hear from you if it has.

Would you be willing to leave us a review or sign up to be added to our mailing list?

If so, please go to FoundationsOfGracePub.org and enter your name and email address and a short, or long, note to us, letting us know who you are and how this book spoke to you. If you do, we'll send you something special.

We also print our books ourselves and sell them through our website.

In the coming years, we hope to offer dozens of brand new products on a variety of subjects from biography, theology, children's books, fiction, and more. We'll have hardbound, paperback, audio, and e-book versions of all of our materials as well. We hope to hear from you soon.

To give a gift to our ministry please go to MissionToMyanmar.com.

You can also register to receive our regular ministry updates about the ongoing work.

For the King and His Kingdom,

M. A. Robinette